FEMINISM

A Reference Handbook

Other Titles in ABC-CLIO's
**Contemporary
World Issues**
Series

Books in the Contemporary World Issues series address vital issues in today's society such as terrorism, sexual harassment, homelessness, AIDS, gambling, animal rights, and air pollution. Written by professional writers, scholars, and nonacademic experts, these books are authoritative, clearly written, up-to-date, and objective. They provide a good starting point for research by high school and college students, scholars, and general readers as well as by legislators, businesspeople, activists, and others.

Each book, carefully organized and easy to use, contains an overview of the subject, a detailed chronology, biographical sketches, facts and data and/or documents and other primary-source material, a directory of organizations and agencies, annotated lists of print and nonprint resources, a glossary, and an index.

Readers of books in the Contemporary World Issues series will find the information they need in order to better understand the social, political, environmental, and economic issues facing the world today.

FEMINISM

A Reference Handbook

Judith Harlan

**CONTEMPORARY
WORLD ISSUES**

ABC-CLIO

Santa Barbara, California
Denver, Colorado
Oxford, England

The affirmative action discussion on pp. 130–136 reprinted courtesy of Women Employed Institute, *Rhetoric and Reality: The Debate about Affirmative Action.*

The list of political action committees on pp. 234–243 reprinted courtesy of Center for the American Woman and Politics (CAWP), National Information Bank on Women in Public Office, Eagleton Institute of Politics, Rutgers University, New Brunswick, New Jersey, 1997.

Library of Congress Cataloging-in-Publication Data

Harlan, Judith.
   Feminism : a reference handbook / Judith Harlan.
      p.   cm.—(ABC-CLIO's contemporary world issues series)
   Includes bibliographical references (p.   ) and index.
      1. Feminism—United States—History—Handbooks, manuals, etc.
2. Feminist theory—United States—Handbooks, manuals, etc.
I. Title.   II. Series: Contemporary world issues.
HQ1410.H365   1998
305.42—dc21   98–2970
                                                                                      CIP

ISBN 0-87436-894-4

04   03   02   01   00   99   98   10   9   8   7   6   5   4   3   2   1

Typesetting by Letra Libre

ABC-CLIO, Inc.
130 Cremona Drive, P.O. Box 1911
Santa Barbara, California 93116-1911

This book is printed on acid-free paper ∞.

Manufactured in the United States of America

For Jan,
who shares my history

Contents

Preface

This book is intended to provide a gateway into the study of modern feminism, to give an overview of resources on the subject, and to present the modern feminist vision of women's issues and status. I have focused on what has come to be known as the "second wave" of feminism and on today's third wave of feminism, but even this involves an enormous amount of information. Feminism is a subject that encompasses a wide array of issues. Feminists have focused on women's work lives both outside and within the home, on women's political power, on equality in educational opportunities, on family relations, and on spiritual dogmas. And feminists have disagreed on points about all of these issues. They have approached the issues from theoretical standpoints, from practical and political ones, and from iconoclastic, radical ones as well. Along the way, they have been criticized for their attempts to change society and have been thwarted in those attempts by those who have their own visions of the future of women and men in the modern world. To study feminism is to study a political, sociohistorical movement; it is to study women, their lives, their opportunities, and their hopes.

The introduction of this book presents a broad overview of second-wave feminist history and gives readers a glimpse into the issues and orientations of modern feminist thinking. Chapter 2 outlines the major events of second-wave feminism in the United States. Chapter 3 gives brief biographies of influential second-wave and third-wave feminists. Chapter 4 offers definitions of feminism and focuses on issues such as affirmative action and the feminist stance on these issues. It includes pertinent legislation, histories, and status reports. Chapter 5 also includes legislation, histories, status reports, and a focus on issues of concern to feminists, but the subject turns to economics and politics. The chapter ends with a selection of quotations by feminists, those most irresistible to the author but just a small sprinkling of the bon mots available. Chapter 6 is a directory of feminist organizations, including Web sites when available, and contains information on contacting the organizations. Chapter 7 is an annotated listing of selected print resources that have been influential in the women's movement or that further explain the feminist position or history. Chapter 8 is a listing of selected available nonprint resources, including Web sites, films, and videotapes. A glossary of important terms and an index complete the handbook.

Acknowledgments

During my research for *Feminism*, I discovered a powerful network of women working in organizations and associations across the United States. Without exception, the women have been generous, ready to connect me to others who had the information I sought or to take the time themselves to clarify data and send me materials. Of all the discoveries I made during the writing of this book, I consider this community of women (and men) who are committed to their own vision of the globe the most valuable. While conversing in one afternoon with women in South Dakota, Georgia, New York, Illinois, and Washington, D.C.— women with ties all over the world—I came to my own personal realization of the profound transformations that feminism has wrought. It's been a revolution. And feminism continues to be revolutionary.

I would like to send my thanks out to all the women and men who helped my research, in particular, Kate Kirtz of Women Make Movies, Inc.; Kelly Jenkins at the National Committee on Pay Equity; Gilda Morales and her staff at the Center for the American Woman and Politics, not only for their excellent data but for their generosity; Danielle McLeod and the staff at Catalyst; Jeanne Nader at Equal Rights Advocates; Carla Eckhardt at the National Abortion Federation; and Robin Hardman at the Family and Work Institute. Also, for her generosity of time and valuable advice, my heartfelt thanks go to professor and author Susan K. Hahn.

Last, I wish to thank the friends who have hashed out their ideas of feminism with me, especially Robin Constable Hanson and Connie Mah; and I thank my husband, Terry Tintorri, who has lent his support in a hundred domestic ways.

Introduction

A Brief History of Feminism in the United States

Women throughout the ages have protested the limitations imposed on their lives by social, political, and religious institutions. In the fifth century, Hypatia, an influential Roman scholar, sought a reawakening of female dignity and power; in the fifteenth century Christine de Pisan chronicled the achievements of women and instigated a debate across Europe on women's equality; two centuries later Anna van Schuman, a Dutch woman, wrote books in support of women's education. In the American colonies, Abigail Adams lobbied her husband, John, to "remember the ladies" as the American Revolution raged on in the name of equality for all men. Soon after, in England in 1792, Mary Wollstonecraft was writing the feminist tract *A Vindication of the Rights of Woman.* But the first wave of modern feminism is usually declared to have begun in 1848, with 100 women and men at the Seneca Falls Convention. There, Elizabeth Cady Stanton and Lucretia Mott threw down the gauntlet for women's suffrage; afterward, feminist Susan B. Anthony joined Stanton to lead the movement. Neither woman ever voted, and both were long dead when women won the right to vote in the United States in 1920.

New Zealand women had been the first to gain the right to vote—in 1893—followed by the women of Finland. In some countries, women began voting when men did, as colonies became independent after World War II, but in others, such as Greece and Switzerland (and the United States), a wide gap of time stretched between men's and women's enfranchisement.

When women first won the vote in the United States, many people harbored great expectations of a continuing, monumental political battle between the sexes. And some feminists did continue to struggle for women's rights. Suffragists who had fought for the vote founded the National Woman's Party and in 1923 proposed an Equal Rights Amendment (ERA) to the Constitution. Yet, the years following enfranchisement became a quiet time for feminists. The majority of women, having the vote, slipped back into their daily lives, leaving politics to the (male) politicians.

Between 1920 and 1960, therefore, much was quiet on the feminist front. Only a small number of women stayed with the political fight, pushing for the Equal Rights Amendment and for loosening of work restrictions. And so it wasn't until the merging of a few new forces and ideas in the 1950s and early 1960s that the impetus for a second wave of feminism and a renewed feminist activism arrived.

In 1953, Simone de Beauvoir's book *The Second Sex* was published in the United States. Women, explained Beauvoir, exist as "the other," and men as the absolute, or the norm, in Western society. This creates deep inequities and is the root of women's unequal status. Many feminists claim that *The Second Sex* was their awakening. But the second wave of feminism didn't begin for another ten years, and it seemed to hit the shores of the United States with a crash upon the publication of Betty Friedan's book *The Feminine Mystique* in 1963. Friedan identified a "problem with no name" that was plaguing American women—a quiet desperation. American women from shore to shore could be heard saying "aha" as they read Friedan's book and saw a reflection of their own dissatisfaction in it.

While women were reading these books, great questions were being asked about American society. The civil rights movement was marching across the country, the Cold War was in full season, and the war in Vietnam was heating up into a battle that would be protested with burning flags. So, while women were reading the new feminist books and beginning to discuss their position in society, many were working alongside men in the civil rights movement and becoming politicized as they marched. One woman, Rosa Parks, sparked a boycott of buses in 1955 when she refused to leave her seat in the front of a bus (reserved for whites) in Montgomery, Alabama. Other women came to the South to participate in the Freedom Summer of 1964, to run freedom schools, and to canvass voters. Women were also joining other political movements that called for change. They were active members of the Students for a Democratic Society (SDS), a new left organization, as well as the civil rights activist group Student Non-Violent Coordinating Committee (SNCC). The second wave for these newly politicized women began as a quiet clearing of throats amidst a roar of political and civil rights protests. They were growing tired of the sexism they saw in these movements and were ready to work for themselves; they created the modern women's liberation movement.

This second wave of feminism has often been characterized as a middle-class white women's movement, and, indeed, this is essentially how it began. It was the product of young, educated, white urban women. Typically, they were women who had a college education, could support themselves, and had few family responsibilities. Some were lesbians; others were heterosexual. These early politicized feminists who caught the second wave when it was still building were soon joined by the women that Betty Friedan wrote about, those struggling against the "feminine mystique." These women were generally also white, middle class, and educated, but they were from suburbs and small cities as well as urban areas, and most had families. They saw the limitations of the roles that society allowed them, and they resented their lack of opportunities for advancement into the high-paying levels of the job market.

For many working women who toiled at unrewarding jobs not out of choice but out of necessity, the feminists' early complaints had the ring of privilege. Friedan's "problem with no name," the dissatisfaction of suburban life, was not a problem for working-class women. They didn't have the free time to experience ennui. And for women of color especially, the early feminist movement held suspicious undertones. Whether they were African American or Asian, Native American or Hispanic, women of color experienced life in the United States differently than white women did; they came to feminism from a different heritage and carried a different cultural package.

For the most part, women of color were skeptical of the feminist movement in the early days. Many argued that the overwhelming problem they faced was not sexism but racism. Many African American women saw more relevance for themselves in the civil rights movement than in the women's movement. They continued their work there and remained unreceptive to the idea that white women could experience any significant discrimination. Other women of color saw few faces in the crowd of feminists that they could identify with, and they hesitated to cross cultural and racial boundaries to join white women—who, for them, too, had always represented the privileged, oppressive class.

In addition, white feminists in the movement, trying to reach out to women of color and to speak for all women, often insulted nonwhite women, who believed that they could speak perfectly well for themselves and did not need a white big sister to lead the discussion. Though a few women of color were influential and important figures in the feminist movement from the beginning (Eleanor Holmes Norton and Aileen Hernandez, for example), most responded to white feminist advances with distrust.

As the 1960s unfolded, feminists formed consciousness-raising groups, and these became the mode for women's meetings. In them, women talked freely about the frustrations and restrictions they faced in their daily lives; they discussed society's underpinnings of sexism; and they experienced a "click" as they suddenly understood the connection between society's sexism and the frustrations of their own individual lives. Women who may not have identified themselves as feminists when they went through the doors into these groups were feminists when they exited. One by one, two by two, and finally by the thousands, women raised their consciousnesses and left the meetings ready to seek change. "The personal is political" became a watchword of what was becoming clearly identifiable as a women's movement.

Things happened fast during this surge of the second wave of feminism. The President's Commission on the Status of Women was established, the Equal Pay Act was passed, and the Civil Rights Act of 1964 Title VII amendment banning sex discrimination in the workplace was voted into law. The Equal Employment Opportunity Commission (EEOC) was established to enforce the law, and feminists mobilized forces even more strongly when it was discovered that the EEOC was not doing its job. Meanwhile, changes continued. In the courts, for example, laws excluding women from jury duty were overturned.

As the feminist movement grew, factions broke off. Out of leftist politics grew Women's Liberation, a radical arm of feminism that sought complete equality and the end of any hierarchy in their organizations. Women's Liberation condemned the patriarchal (male-based) system as being the source of other bigotry in the nation. The faction organized its groups by not organizing them—by having participatory meetings and consensus decisions. Often, members sought to surprise and jolt the nation into recognizing the discrimination that to them was so evident. Women also held "speakouts" on rape, going public with their personal stories on this taboo subject.

The Equal Rights Amendment won Congressional approval in 1972, though it was never ratified by enough states to become law. Also, Congress passed Title IX of the Education Act in 1972, prohibiting sex discrimination in any federally assisted educational program or activity. Feminists formed groups to lobby for the legalization of abortion, and they cheered for states that loosened abortion laws; but meanwhile, opposition to feminist goals was growing within the Catholic Church and the community.

A backlash against women's advances was well underway by the 1970s. Feminist author Germaine Greer called the backlash "a preemptive strike." Feminists had not gained full equality, she pointed out, but the possibility that they might was making people nervous. The backlash came from many sides. The Catholic Church forbade the use of artificial birth control and, after organizing the National Right to Life Committee, supported local demonstrations against Planned Parenthood clinics in an attempt to stop the legalization of abortion. Protestant evangelist Billy Graham declared that the appropriate role for woman was wife and mother. In a cover story, *Time* magazine asked the question, "Who's Come a Long Way, Baby?"—and it was clear that the editors believed the women's movement had not taken women very far. More than one book came out purporting to tell females how to be real women. *Fascinating Womanhood* (Andelin 1974) gave women directions on pleasing men and developing the feminine traits of delicacy and appeal. And Phyllis Schlafly mounted a prodigious and eventually successful effort to prevent the passage of the Equal Rights Amendment.

The mood of the country was changing, growing more "macho." Some theorists place the blame for the swing on President Jimmy Carter's inability to get American hostages out of Iran. (In November 1979, Iranians stormed the U.S. embassy in Tehran and took 90 hostages, holding them captive until Ronald Reagan's inauguration in 1981.) Americans seemed to believe that it was time to toughen up.

Feminist author Robin Morgan published a chronicle of her feminist awakening and activities; she called it *Going Too Far,* an accusation that feminists had heard with every change they achieved. Gaining the vote was going too far, as was working outside the home, seeking equal pay for equal work, and working to become surgeons, astronauts, architects, or president of the United States. As the 1970s lurched into the 1980s, feminists were hearing that once again they had gone too far.

The feminist movement had lost its momentum. In 1980, for the first time since 1940, the Republican Party, with Ronald Reagan as its presidential candidate, opposed the Equal Rights Amendment. It also opposed abortion rights. What's more, to the dismay of feminists, Ronald Reagan was elected president. After the election, though, feminists found that they had scored something of a victory: Voting patterns revealed a significant difference in the way women and men had voted—a gender gap. Women had separated from men, showing a reluctance to go along with Reagan's paternal guidance.

Despite the evidence of an unspoken feminism, women began to lose ground politically. The backlash, feminists pointed out, reached into every phase of women's lives. Women's clinics and Planned Parenthood clinics came under increasingly violent attack. Women in business were advised to dress for success by wearing a female version of the male gray suit. At the same time, a stereotype of feminists as masculine, ugly, and man-hating took hold in the United States. And women in corporate America were held to a double standard of beauty. Women, but not men, at all professional levels—wrote feminist Naomi Wolf—were expected to look good and to look young. And at the same time, fashions for women became not more womanly but more boyish, with extreme thinness the preferred body type. Everything womanly was unacceptable and inappropriate in the workplace.

Meanwhile, much of society blamed feminists for everything from changes in divorce laws to fathers refusing to pay child support to rude men letting doors slam in women's faces. If a woman didn't think a "dumb blonde" joke was funny, she was a humorless feminist. If she complained because she had to work overtime, she should blame it on the feminists because back in the old days before feminists came along there were laws protecting women from such things.

In 1981, Betty Friedan's book *The Second Stage* alerted feminists to a new problem. Women, she wrote, were finding that diving into business and adapting to the rules of the workplace as identified by men was not enough—even if women were enormously successful at it. Feminists were lamenting their disconnection from family and home life. In short, women would not be able to settle for simply succeeding in business. They wanted more. And women were going to need men's help and cooperation if they were going to achieve the social transformation necessary for women's true equality. Friedan's book aroused controversy within the feminist leadership. Many leaders saw her statements as a retreat from her earlier activism. Many also took offense at the implication that they had not valued marriage and family as a part of their feminist politics. They pointed to the many changes they were seeking for married women: child care, an end to domestic violence, equal division of property and finances within marriage and upon divorce, and federal budgetary expansion for families on welfare. Beyond the controversy within the movement, though, Friedan's book signaled an expansion of feminist rhetoric. Many laws had been passed; many doors into the "male domain" had been opened. Women would now move on to working on the "domain" itself, and feminists would not always agree on the best methods of creating change.

The 1980s came to be seen by feminists as the "backlash decade," one in which feminists fought to hold on to the laws and judicial decisions that they had earlier won. Feminist Susan Faludi wrote in her best-selling 1991 book, *Backlash*, that such a backlash is not unusual in women's history and should have been expected in the 1980s. Throughout modern history, women have fought periodic backlashes against their progress. But the question this time was, How effective had women been in fighting this one? Faludi's analysis: Women didn't succumb or give up, but they didn't gain any ground, either.

Despite the losses, many changes did come about. One was the emergence of a men's movement. Though women feminists have had allies and supporters among men from the beginning, they had been simply friends marching alongside women in demonstrations, colleagues supporting women in their business ventures, and fellow politicians on Capitol Hill. A few stood out, such as actor Alan Alda, who has been a vocal supporter of the women's movement since the 1970s. But in the 1980s and 1990s, a distinct men's movement was launched. Feminists reacted with skepticism to many of the organizations that call themselves part of a men's movement, and rightly so. Some are more accurately a part of a mythopoetic movement. Robert Bly, author of *Iron John* and a leader of men's conferences, espouses a need to throw off the soft, feminine nature that has encompassed modern men and urges them to get in touch with their inner warriors. Though Bly's rhetoric often includes a call for a renewed relationship with women, feminists see it as a repackaging of old ideas of chest-beating men and appreciative maidens. Other factions of the men's movement—usually emerging from a religious origin, such as the Christian Promise Keepers—are also not in tune with feminist ideals. Though these groups urge men to act responsibly in marriage and parenthood, they also urge a return to "family values," which means a patriarchal family structure with a man at the head of the household and a wife/mother in the house.

Hidden amidst all the commotion of these men's groups was the beginning of a true male feminist movement. Books that espouse male feminist ideals include John Stoltenberg's *Refusing to Be a Man* (1990); Mark Gerson's *A Choice of Heroes: The Changing Face of American Manhood* (1982, 1992); James Dittes's *The Male Predicament* (1984); and Harry Brod's *The Making of Masculinities: The New Men's Studies* (1987). These authors and those involved in the feminist men's movement call for a deconstruction of masculinity and a "humanizing" of the male. They seek increased personal satisfaction in men's lives, partly through more involvement in parenting and family life but also through a redefinition of true male success (Eisler 1992). They seek access for men to what women want: success and deep happiness in relationships as well as in one's professional or commercial work of choice. Feminists have supported this men's movement. And the men themselves have organized further, with groups such as Men Against Rape, Men Against Domestic Violence, and the National Organization of Men Against Sexism.

In the 1990s, feminism also has a new generation of adherents, a third wave of activists to join the women and men in the movement. This third wave—the second generation of liberated women, daughters of the women of the politically active 1960s as well as long-term active feminists themselves—is bringing an ever-broadening perspective to the bargaining table of women's rights. These women have been delving into some of the early feminist thoughts on the patriarchal structure underlying all modern political, social, and cultural constructs, and they include the problems of racism and classism in their analyses. This generation too, accustomed to contemplating systems (such as ecosystems) and not just the individual factor, is looking at the entire system, from home to work to voting booth to religious institution.

Many are questioning why women are expected to adapt to a world created by men. Many are lobbying for an adaptation that goes both ways. And many are rejecting society's old definitions of what it means to be a woman and replacing them with their own definitions, remembering feminist Mary Daly's admonition that the right to define is power.

In this generation, women are studying at West Point and winning Rhodes scholarships, and they expect to earn equal pay for equal work. This is the Title IX generation, women who grew up with the opportunity to join Little League teams, to play in soccer leagues, and who had access to school basketball and volleyball courts and to softball diamonds. This generation looks out at a world of women surfing alongside men, a powerful third wave.

Challenging Old Paradigms

Mary Wollstonecraft on her deathbed in 1797 declared that "it is time to restore women to their lost dignity and to make them part of the human species" (Chicago 1996, 118). At the 1848 Seneca Falls Women's Rights Convention, attendees pointed to a "history of repeated injuries and usurpations on the part of men toward woman, having in direct object the establishment of an absolute tyranny over her" (Rossi 1973, 416). Fifty years later, feminist intellectual Charlotte Perkins Gilman critiqued women's economic position and found, once again, that men were forcing women into gilded cages and subordinate, childish positions.

Women came forward in the second wave of feminism to point out that the same unacceptable patterns were continuing in modern society. After Simone de Beauvoir established the modern feminist position (and questioning) of women as the "other" and men as the absolute, Kate Millett traced the politics of gender-based oppression, Robin Morgan explored male dominance in cultural and social contexts, and Mary Daly took a close look at religion and its history of misogyny. They and other feminists stated, in many different ways, that male dominance was an imposed and unnatural state of being.

Underlying the criticisms is the feminist understanding that the existing paradigm of modern society is based on a patriarchal and hierarchical foundation. It is a paradigm invented by men and advantageous to men. Patriarchy depends on the assumed dominance of men over women in social, economic, and political systems. Hierarchy stems naturally from patriarchy, which by definition begins with two tiers of power and then easily expands into an entire system delineating who is above whom. Women have long occupied the lower, less valued spheres. Feminists identified this patriarchal foundation of society and have set out to change it. They have bumped into many obstacles along the way.

Early in the second wave, feminists kept running into the same response to their questioning of patriarchy: It is just the way it has always been, so it must be the way it must be—patriarchy as biological destiny. Though a few whispers challenged these assumptions, no loud challenge was heard until Marija Gimbutas, a Lithuanian American archaeologist, came forward in 1974 with her study of old European civilizations and pointed out the male bias of previous interpretations of Old World relics. Her interpretations revealed some prepatriarchal societies that were based on female gods and nonpatriarchal political organizations. "The pantheon reflects a society dominated by the mother," Gimbutas wrote. "The role of woman was not subject to that of a man" (Gimbutas 1974, 237). The societies that developed then allowed both women and men to develop to their fullest. Following her lead others took a new look at old relics and were also astonished at the clues that had been missed by heavily male-biased anthropologists.

In 1987 Riane Eisler brought the studies of Gimbutas and others to the best-seller list in *The Chalice and the Blade,* which includes her views on some of the world's prehistoric societies—societies that worshiped female gods and that were both matrilineal (property was inherited through the female line) and matrilocal (upon marriage, men moved into their wives' homes). As she described them, the societies were not the mirror image of patriarchy but in fact were of less hierarchical design. The power women had was equated more with responsibility and love than with oppression, fear, and privileges, says Eisler. The idea that patriarchy is "just the way it is," therefore, has been officially and scientifically challenged. "Almost everything we have been taught about antiquity is based on conjecture," Eisler wrote. What we "think of as our cultural evolution has in fact been interpretation" (Eisler 1988, 16). Scientists draw conclusions from fragmentary data and bring with them their own cultural biases. In response to Eisler and now to other anthropologists as well, some historians have argued that it is impossible to prove that a woman-centered era existed; yet, the new interpretations continue to challenge the male-centered interpretations of the past.

Meanwhile, books like the best-selling *Women Who Run with the Wolves,* by Clarissa Pinkola Estés, have continued the discussion of gender destiny in more levels of society. Psychology and myth interpretations have also been heavily male biased, Estés and other authors assert. Through female eyes, the world is, or can be, quite a different place than the one that has been described by historians so far.

Feminists also have begun to focus ever more closely on the question of why one gender is valued over the other. Scholars point out that almost all of society is based on the male as the norm. Inherent in all of the feminist discussions about women's status as "other" is the thought "It's time for a change." But this change that feminists seek would not simply be a change in day-care availability or in job access; it would be a fundamental change in what is perceived as male, what is perceived to be female, and what is valued in both.

Feminists, followed by scholars and others, have begun to focus on gender differences and similarities. Differences between males and females have been the most entertaining to discuss and became of the focus of lighthearted and pseudo-serious books that purported to explain the exasperation that women often feel with men's behavior, and vice versa. But serious scholars also lent their attention to the issue, producing works such as Dale Spender's *Man Made Language* (1980), a study of gender in communication styles. The gender differences in communication were popularized by linguist Deborah Tannen; she explained them as chiefly taught, or culturally imposed, styles. The learned communication styles of males and females in American society, she pointed out, almost creates two separate cultures. Psychologist Carol Gilligan explored and described a new model to explain some of the differences between males and females, finding the roots of difference in early childhood. She concluded that women are more relationship-oriented in their judgments; men use cooler, more abstract reasoning. Both approaches are successful, she wrote, and equal in value; but what the public heard, in summaries and quick news bites, was simply that men and women were different, with women labeled the emotional ones.

Meanwhile, popular culture embraced the idea of right- and left-brain activities and of feminine and masculine attributes of all personalities (a model now called essentialism). Some feminists expressed concern that the traits were being identified as feminine (female) and masculine (male). They argued that this approach used an ancient dichotomy harking back to the Greeks, when popular thought was that men have reason, women have feelings; and to the Victorians, who created different spheres for men and women, with logic and business being men's domain, and emotion and home being women's. Feminist author Charlene Spretnak explained feminists' objection to the dichotomy: Masculine traits were the ones seen as "essential, positive, admirable"; the feminine ones were the ones that were "peripheral, weak, often contemptible" (Spretnak 1982, xx).

Cynthia Fuchs Epstein added her frustration at the burgeoning of feminine and masculine stereotypes, writing that "the same social scientists who pride themselves on appreciating the fine distinctions between wines of neighboring vineyards in France . . . feel comfortable in describing the entire female sex in terms of such undifferentiated qualities as 'caring' or 'nurturing' or 'good at detail'" (Epstein 1988, 44–45).

Some feminists worry that the discussion of gender differences, though clothed in new-millennium verbiage of self-discovery and personal growth, harks back to a difference of opinion that has threaded through the feminist movement from its very beginning—whether women and men are equal and should seek equal treatment and opportunities, or whether there are great differences between the sexes and women should seek separate but equal status and protection. Feminists who agree with the former stance are sometimes called "equality feminists"; those in support of the latter are referred to at times as "difference feminists."

Naomi Weisstein, an equality feminist, is blunt about her objections to separate but equal status. "It is no use to talk about women being different but equal; all of the tests I can think of," she says, "have a 'good' outcome and a 'bad' outcome" (Weisstein 1968, 228). Feminists who have sought absolute legal and social equality for women have argued that women are underestimated by society and that the laws that protect them also limit them. As evidence, they point to a history of career opportunities closed to women under the guise of protecting them.

On the side of difference feminism, analysts point to the particular needs of women in the workplace, including flexible time, day care, and child-care leave. They argue that women, through the biology of pregnancy and the cultural expectations of child-care responsibility, simply have different work requirements than men. Pregnant women also may need protection from certain dangerous toxins and from heavy equipment. And, these feminists add, whether the differences are culturally imposed or biological imperatives, women think and act differently from men.

Both schools of feminism seek equality for women. But equality between the sexes, though conceivable by most feminists, is not an idea easily grasped by those immersed in the hierarchy of today's patriarchal system. "Men seem unable to feel equal to women: they must be superior or they are inferior," writes Marilyn French in her 1992 book *The War Against Women* (French 1992, 200). Weisstein earlier wrote that we do not know what the real differences are, "but it is clear that until social expectations for men and women are equal, until we provide equal respect for both men and women, our answers to this question will simply reflect our prejudices" (Weisstein 1968, 228).

Feminists today have also gone beyond simply questioning the differences and similarities between the sexes. They have come to question the very legitimacy of hierarchies, which have in the past been accepted as necessary modern constructs (French 1992). Men have demonstrated that they are willing to fight to preserve these hierarchies, as evidenced by their battles against changes in sports departments resulting from Title IX of the Education Act, their struggles to keep women out of military academies and fraternal organizations, and their attempts to keep political "old boy" networks intact.

Despite the evidence of extreme male reluctance to give up patriarchal privilege, though, the core of feminism seems to envision a world of acceptance and respect for all. This vision includes opportunities for girls and boys to develop into whatever personalities they authentically are, void of the influences of a patriarchal society. Feminists envision a world where status is accorded to those females and males who offer something to the world rather than being based on a rigid hierarchy of gender, race, religion, or class. Feminists see a future where human beings are individuals, with less role playing by women trying to exhibit the ultra-feminine ideal or by men trying to assume the masculine ideal. Feminists today search for *and* instead of *either/or.*

Can there be such a world? Within the business sector, a more cooperative, less competitively based corporate structure is being tested. Corporate consultant and author Nina Boyd Krebs writes of "participative management" in business. This management style involves a paradigm shift from competitive to cooperative management, a collaborative method that many organizations today are finding more effective in the modern complex business environment (Krebs 1993).

In politics, in addition to focusing on developing the world, feminists also bring the focus back to developing people, including women, and to sustainable development. Ecofeminists see their political role as one of replacing the male paradigm of control over nature with one of working in cooperation with nature, acknowledging that people are a part of nature, not above it.

In the home, feminists question the traditional role of the man as chief breadwinner and final authority. Feminists acknowledge that children need structure in their lives, but they would replace the traditional hierarchy of the family with one of partnership parenting. Men would step into more nurturing roles and share the daily chores as well as the close bonding of parent with child that females now have.

But some feminists take the challenge a step further. Some suggest that women be perceived as the norm and men "the other." Feminist Beryl Benderly explains that selection of the norm is more than a matter of semantics: Which sex—if either—we take as the ground plan of humanity has important implications for theories about why we grew the way we did. Generations of scientific habit have made the male body the human standard, she says, despite the fact that males develop from a process "extra" to the one producing females. Recently, a few scientists and many feminists have begun to suggest that a female standard makes more sense (Benderly 1987).

In religion, that fundamental expression of human constructs, women might also make major changes if they were taken out of second place. Feminist author Naomi Wolf suggests that "women might recast human sexuality as proof of the sacredness of the body rather than of its sinfulness, and the old serviceable belief that equates femaleness with pollution might become obsolete" (Wolf 1991, 90).

The world seen without the filter of patriarchy and its male orientation might look entirely different. Feminists have studied and analyzed this filter and learned, too, that other filters are in effect as well—filters of racism and classism. An examination of how these filters work in conjunction with sexism is ongoing.

Multicultural and Global Wisdom

From the beginning of the second wave, feminists knew there was a division within women's activism between those who saw the world filtered by patriarchy and those who saw it filtered by racism or by class. Thus, whereas white feminists typically defined their oppression and society's restrictions on women in terms of patriarchy, women of color typically defined their oppression in terms of racism, combined with sexism and the caste system of class. It took years of heated discussion and philosophical exploration before women began to find a common ground, a process that is still under way today.

"On the road to equality there is no better place for blacks to detour around American values than in forgoing its example in the treatment of its women and the organization of its family life," Eleanor Holmes Norton, an African American feminist, once declared (Morgan 1970, 356). Norton, who was elected to her fourth term as District of Columbia delegate to the U.S. Congress in 1996, is a lifelong champion of civil rights as well as of women's rights. She has also said that women of color "have a chance for something better" than the white culture brought over from Europe. They have that chance because they were never truly integrated into the majority culture that created a happy homemaker myth for women in the 1950s and 1960s and a protected class for middle- and upper-class women in previous eras. Typically, African American women since the Civil War have been working women who financially supported or helped to support their families.

The rift that developed between white feminists and feminist women of color was based partially on this unprivileged versus privileged status in American society. But much has changed in the past three decades. According to feminist authors and analysts Midge Wilson and Kathy Russell,

> the political relationship between White and Black women has much improved since the beginning of the modern women's movement in the 1960s. African American women activists are beginning to accept that it is not necessary for them to agree with White female activists to appreciate the new terrain they helped open up for all women. White feminists are finally starting to listen when African American feminists state that women's rights are not always going to be their top priority. (Wilson and Russell 1996, 216)

A few watershed moments and events have led to the current third-wave understanding and mutual cooperation of the country's varied women. The 1981 publication of the book *Ain't I a Woman,* by bell hooks, was such a moment of awakening. The author took white feminists to task for not including class and race in their analyses of society. In 1981, Cherríe Moraga and Gloria Anzaldúa published an anthology of feminist writers, *This Bridge Called My Back: Writings by Radical Women of Color.* It brought diversity to the table, with discussions of racism, classism, and feminist self-knowledge by Native Americans, Chicanas, Puerto Ricans, African Americans, and Asian Americans— providing a forum for a new understanding amongst all feminists and giving voice to a growing coalition of power. In 1982, the first African American women's studies book was published, titled *All the Women Are White, All the Blacks Are Men, But Some of Us Are Brave* (edited by Gloria T. Hall, Patricia B. Scott, and Barbara Smith). Meanwhile, works by Audre Lorde and June Jordan were challenging feminists to reach out and expand their consciousness. These contributions and others broadened the discussion, sometimes with angry words, frustrations, and accusations, at other times with advice and reconciliations. The road to today's multicultural, multiracial feminism has not always been smooth, and perfect integration and cooperation has not been achieved. But feminists are moving more and more in that direction. They are communicating.

At national women's conventions and conferences, women of all ethnic and racial heritage are coming together and bringing with them a great wealth and diversity of cultural experience.

Women are listening to each others' stories about relationships and cultural training. And together, women are forging new paths for all feminists. The third wave of feminism, which includes today's young generation, includes, too, women of every background in America.

Feminists are showing up in surprising places, too. In 1996, Muslim women scholars in the United States were making the news because they were examining the Koran and were questioning many of the rigid rules that regulate Muslim women's conduct. "For 1,400 years men have been using the Koran to tell women how to act," said one scholar. "But now there are many women who are making the point that it has been men's interpretation of our religion that has limited women's progress, not our religion itself. This is a new and important development in Islam"(Ribadeneira 1997).

American feminists often perceive themselves as global leaders and as more advanced on feminist issues than the rest of the world. But in many ways, this is not true. Women in many other countries have come further and done more. For example, women in Finland, Sweden, Norway, and Denmark have achieved the passage of legislation comparable to the Equal Rights Amendment and have obtained abortion rights, inexpensive institutional child care, and generous parental leave policies—all issues that are still hotly debated in the United States. Politically, women are better represented in these countries than in the United States as well, with 33 to 39 percent of parliament seats held by women. Women in the United States, by contrast, celebrated in 1996 when their representation on Capitol Hill reached the 11.7 percent mark.

Females also have been elected heads of state in other countries; recent well-known examples include Ireland, Great Britain, Turkey, Nicaragua, and Pakistan. As political leaders and a political force in their own country, then, American women are not as successful as women in some other parts of the world.

Nevertheless, American feminists do play a leading role in global feminism and are perceived as leaders in effecting social change. But hope for real change for women globally rests not just with feminist leaders but with the efforts of feminists at all levels of organization working together across both cultural and national borders. This cohesive and wide-ranging effort is in the works. It began in earnest when feminists met for the 1975 United Nations first World Conference on Women, held in Mexico City;

it continued through succeeding conferences and today progresses toward future conferences and goals.

The women's conferences have made a difference worldwide. "What is developing, world-wide," explains one analyst, "is an intangible but critical factor that is less measurable in numerical terms. It is an awareness and acceptance of the fact that women's equality is a human right. The periodic coming together of tens of thousands of women has helped to bring all women out of the shadows" (Sivard 1995, 5). On the tangible side, most United Nations countries have signed on to the Convention to End All Forms of Discrimination Against Women (CEDAW). And in 1995, the United States joined many nations in announcing they would take actions to implement the Beijing Platform for Action, the document produced by the fourth World Conference on Women. In 1997, the White House reaffirmed its commitment to pursue U.S. ratification of CEDAW.

While American women are taking a leading role in global feminism, they are carefully maintaining an awareness of a historical Western bias in previous international decisions. That awareness of differences, and the decision not to impose Western methods on women worldwide, has led American feminists to a more careful and open analysis of what changes will benefit women. Women are taking the lead in questioning policies of the World Bank and structural adjustment programs, pointing to the Western bias and disastrous outcomes of some of the programs.

Women have also established women's rights as human rights, and they are in the beginning stages of inclusion in international decision making. Feminists see these changes as part of a chain that will affect women and men positively. International feminist activists Rhonda Copelon and Rosalind Petchesky explain: "As women develop a consciousness of having rights, define them from their own needs and experience, and feel empowered to demand them, women's human rights become . . . a powerful vehicle for social transformation." They add that "the androcentrism of the traditional human rights paradigm" is eroding as women enter the discussion (1996, 343).

Feminists are united in their goal of improving conditions for all women and, by extension, to children and men. To make those improvements, women turn to their major goals—the inclusion of women in policymaking bodies of all countries and of the United Nations, economic independence and self-sufficiency for women, and social equality. Politically, if women are to change their world in any fundamental way, they must be partners with men in policymaking, not recipients of policy as they are now. Economically, they must have access to well-paying work. Socially, they must have the freedom to rule their own lives. Through a network of organizations, including United Nations commissions, nongovernmental organizations, and internationally focused organizations, feminists are working toward these goals. They believe that their success will be good for all. As Hillary Rodham Clinton expresses it: "An important lesson of the last several decades is that where women prosper, countries prosper" (Sivard 1995, 3).

References

Andelin, Helen B. 1974. *Fascinating Womanhood.* Santa Barbara: Pacific Press Santa Barbara.

Benderly, Beryl L. 1987. *The Myth of Two Minds: What Gender Means and Doesn't Mean.* New York: Doubleday.

Chicago, Judy. 1996. *The Dinner Party.* New York: Penguin.

Copelon, Rhonda, and Rosalind Petchesky. 1995. "Toward an Interdependent Approach to Reproductive and Sexual Rights as Human Rights: Reflections on the ICPD and Beyond." In Margaret A. Schuler, ed., *From Basic Needs to Basic Rights: Women's Claim to Human Rights.* Washington, D.C.: Women, Law & Development International.

Eisler, Riane. 1988. *The Chalice and the Blade: Our History, Our Future.* New York: HarperCollins.

———. 1992. "What Do Men Really Want? The Men's Movement, Partnership, and Domination." In Kay Leigh Hagen, ed., *Women Respond to the Men's Movement: A Feminist Collection.* San Francisco: Pandora/Harper.

Epstein, Cynthia Fuchs. 1988. *Deceptive Distinctions: Sex, Gender and the Social Order.* New Haven, Conn.: Yale University Press.

Faludi, Susan. 1991. *Backlash: The Undeclared War against American Women.* New York: Crown.

French, Marilyn. 1992. *The War against Women.* New York: Ballantine Books.

Gimbutas, Marija. 1982. *The Goddesses and Gods of Old Europe: Myths and Cult Images.* Berkeley: University of California Press. (Originally published as *The Goddesses and Gods of Old Europe: 7000–3500 B.C.* Berkeley: University of California Press, 1974.)

Krebs, Nina Boyd, ed. 1993. *Changing Woman Changing Work.* Aspen, Colo.: MacMurray & Beck.

Morgan, Robin, ed. 1970. *Sisterhood Is Powerful: An Anthology of Writings from the Women's Liberation Movement.* New York: Random House.

Ribadeneira, Diego. 1997. "Women Take a Fresh Look at Koran." *Boston Globe.* January 25.

Rossi, Alice, ed. 1973. *The Feminist Papers: From Adams to de Beauvoir.* New York: Columbia University Press.

Sivard, Ruth Leger, with Arlette Brauer and Rebecca Cook. 1995. *WOMEN . . . A World Survey.* Washington, D.C.: World Priorities, Inc.

Spretnak, Charlene, ed. 1982. *The Politics of Women's Spirituality: Essays on the Rise of Spiritual Power within the Feminist Movement.* New York: Doubleday Anchor Books.

Weisstein, Naomi. 1968. "Kinder, Küche, Kirche as Scientific Law" [excerpt]. In Miriam Schneir, ed., *Feminism in Our Time: The Essential Writings, World War II to the Present.* New York: Random House, 1994.

Wilson, Midge, and Kathy Russell. 1996. *Divided Sisters: Bridging the Gap Between Black Women and White Women.* New York: Anchor Books, Doubleday.

Wolf, Naomi. 1991. *The Beauty Myth: How Images of Beauty Are Used against Women.* New York: William Morrow and Company.

Chronology 2

The focus of this chronology is on recent feminist events, chiefly those taking place since the early 1960s, when the second wave of feminism began. In the years leading up to the feminist activism that began with the second wave, a few advances (and some retreats) were made by feminists; an overview of these is provided.

1920s   The Nineteenth Amendment to the Constitution is ratified by the Sixty-sixth Congress, extending voting rights to women on August 18, 1920. It says, "The right of citizens of the United States to vote shall not be denied or abridged by the United States or by any State on account of sex."

The League of Women Voters is founded, and so is the Miss America beauty pageant. Also, in 1923, the National Woman's Party first proposes an Equal Rights Amendment for women to the U.S. Constitution. It is opposed by organized labor and some women's groups on the grounds that it threatens protective laws for women. It is written by Alice Paul and presented to the U.S. Congress; it is

1920s *(cont.)*	thereafter reintroduced yearly but seldom even comes to a vote.

1930s   This is the decade of the Great Depression. Though the Equal Rights Amendment gains some support among male politicians, the feminist movement is stalled as the country struggles with unemployment and poverty. More married women are forced by family need into the job market, but the national view maintains that jobs should go to male bread-winners. In 1933, new First Lady Eleanor Roosevelt brings high-profile leadership to social causes such as prohibition of child labor, welfare benefits for mothers and children, and minimum wages. In an atmosphere that celebrates women's place in the home, white women establish themselves in the lower rungs of women's professions in positions such as store clerk and secretary. Women of color lose ground, however, as they have been concentrated in domestic labor, jobs that are cut during the Depression; in addition, they are denied access to white-collar jobs allowed white women.

1940s   The United States enters World War II. Across the country, protective labor laws that have prohibited women from lifting heavy weights, working night shifts, and operating heavy equipment are lifted. Women become the emergency workforce, the "Rosie the riveters" of World War II. Women of color also find jobs in manufacturing but are still virtually barred from white-collar fields. Then, with demobilization in 1945, women are laid off and men reclaim the nation's job market.

In Washington, D.C., the Equal Rights Amendment is endorsed by the Republican Party in 1940. The Democratic Party endorses the amendment beginning in 1944. But a coalition of powerful organizations, including the League of Women Voters, the American Association of University Women, and numerous trade union groups, unites to defeat the amendment. Women are divided over simple equality versus separate-but-equal status issues. And though in 1946 a majority of the U.S. Senate approves the amendment, the necessary two-thirds majority vote cannot be raised.

On the international front, the United Nations is founded in 1945, providing women a possible global platform for change. In 1948, the United Nations adopts *The Universal Declaration of Human Rights,* which condemns discrimination based on sex.

The final year of the decade, 1949, is "the year the feminine mystique really hit us," according to Betty Friedan.

1950s   After World War II demobilization, a record number of marriages and births are recorded, resulting in what comes to be known as the Baby Boom. The patriarchal view of husband as breadwinner and woman as homemaker prevails, as does the vision of a "true woman" as one who happily accepts a domestic role and obtains fulfillment as mother and financially dependent wife. Though the national view is one of prosperity and satisfaction, many women are not at all satisfied with the limitations placed on their lives. Studies of the 1950s report a rise in depression among women.

In 1953, *The Second Sex* by Simone de Beauvoir is published in the United States. Many second-wave feminists credit *The Second Sex* with awakening them to feminism.

1960s   The beginning of the second wave of feminism. As women begin to mobilize, women's rights become a topic of conversation and political debate. The birth control pill is approved for sale in the United States, giving women reliable control over their fertility for the first time in history. The civil rights movement and the anti-Vietnam war movement take the spotlight. Marches and demonstrations dominate the news as political activists demand change. Many

1960s
(cont.)

women in these movements object to the sexism in the leadership and to the way work and speaking duties are assigned. They experience the feminist "click" (i.e., a deeper understanding suddenly "clicks" into place). Their consciousness is raised, and they break out to form their own women's liberation movement.

1961

President John F. Kennedy establishes the President's Commission on the Status of Women at the urging of Eleanor Roosevelt, who dies while the commission's work is underway (November 1962). The commission is chaired by Esther Peterson, who is adamantly against the Equal Rights Amendment but seeks equal pay legislation and protective laws for women in the workforce.

1963

The President's Commission on the Status of Women report reveals sex discrimination permeating American society from elementary classrooms to corporate boardrooms. It recommends equality in employment and educational opportunities as well as in wages. It advocates government-assisted day care and mandated maternity leave. Kennedy establishes an Annual Conference of Commissions on the Status of Women to work on overcoming discrimination. This annual conference brings together women from throughout the country. They share experiences, strategies, and phone numbers; a national network of activist women is begun.

Betty Friedan's book *The Feminine Mystique* hits the stores and is a vital part of the consciousness-raising of a generation of mainstream American women. Friedan puts into words the dissatisfaction that white middle-class housewives feel, and she points to "a problem that has no name." Women of color, who are in the labor force in larger proportions than white women, do not identify as readily with *The Feminine Mystique*. They feel oppression from racial discrimination as well as from gender discrimination.

The United States Congress passes the Equal Pay Act, the first federal law against sex discrimination. It prohibits unequal pay for equal or "substantially equal" work. It was first introduced in Congress in 1943.

On November 22, while on a trip to Dallas, Texas, President John F. Kennedy is assassinated.

1964   The Civil Rights Act of 1964 passes with an amendment, Title VII. The Civil Rights Act prohibits discrimination in employment on the basis of race, color, religion, or national origin; Title VII prohibits discrimination in employment on the basis of sex. Title VII is akin to an "accidental" amendment. Congressman Howard Smith of Virginia, a Southern Conservative who opposes the Civil Rights Act, proposes the sex discrimination amendment. His action goes down in history as an attempt to kill the bill by attaching what he believes to be an unpassable amendment to it. But he is a long-time ally of National Woman's Party leader Alice Paul, so his true motives remain unclear. His proposal of Title VII, though, creates hilarity and havoc on the Congressional floor. Smith has the Assembly laughing wholeheartedly at his clever jokes about women and henpecked husbands. Then Congresswoman Martha Griffiths of Michigan, in a preorchestrated tactical move, takes the floor and quiets the laughter. Her arguments play on the men's prejudices about both African Americans and women. President Lyndon Johnson, eager for passage of the Civil Rights Act, throws his political weight behind Griffiths and mobilizes support for Title VII. Opposing the amendment are liberal groups that do not want to endanger passage of the Civil Rights Act by adding sex discrimination to it, and traditionalists who fear that the amendment will endanger traditional family relationships. Griffiths wins the day (Woloch 1994). Sex discrimination is placed beside racial discrimination and voted illegal.

The Equal Employment Opportunity Commission (EEOC) is created to enforce the new law, but

1964
(cont.)

Howard Edelsberg, director of the commission, opposes Title VII and promises to ignore all sex discrimination complaints brought before him. His antifeminist stance is partly responsible for the founding of the National Organization for Women two years later.

As part of an event called Freedom Summer 1964, student volunteers—female and male—from Northern college campuses are bused into the South to help with voter registration drives targeting African Americans. The drives, organized by the Student Nonviolent Coordinating Committee (SNCC), bring together thousands of black and white activist women and men. African American women express displeasure at the preferential treatment they see white women receiving both in the movement and in media attention. White and African American women in the SNCC begin to question the built-in male supremacy of the organization. Ruby Doris Smith Robinson, a young, prominent member of the SNCC and a woman of color, presents a paper questioning the position of women within the organization. Stokely Carmichael, an SNCC leader, reacts with his infamous joke: "The only position for women in SNCC is prone!"

1965

Mary King and Casey Hayden, white members of the SNCC, publish a position paper on women's subordinate position in the civil rights movement. The paper is greeted with derision by men and some African American women in the SNCC. Most of the women of color see racism as the reason for their oppression. King and Hayden pursue their line of reasoning, and some of the women break away from the increasingly male-dominated SNCC to form their own committees on women's issues. The early groups chiefly attract white women (Wilson and Russell 1996).

Dolores Huerta, working with activist César Chávez, leads the United Farm Workers' strike against California grape growers. The workers are striking for better wages and working conditions. Huerta is part of the leadership and of the workers' negotiation team.

The term "affirmative action" is coined by President Lyndon Johnson in an executive order.

1966   Women are booed out of a Students for a Democratic Society (SDS) conference for demanding equal rights. Men in SDS, like the male leaders in the SNCC, expect women to do all the cleaning, cooking, and typing. The women within these organizations increasingly question their subordinate role while the men continue to issue statements on the "equality" of people.

In October, as feminist leaders gather at the Third Annual Conference of Commissions on the Status of Women, they discuss their disappointment in the EEOC: It is not enforcing Title VII of the Civil Rights Act. Betty Friedan and 27 other attending women take action. They create what is to become the largest feminist political organization in the United States, the National Organization for Women (NOW). NOW immediately petitions the EEOC for action and embarks on its still-ongoing crusade for an end to discrimination. Betty Friedan is NOW's first president.

1967   At its second annual conference, NOW argues heatedly over whether to support the Equal Rights Amendment and abortion rights. Members vote to support both. Several members leave over the controversy and later form the Women's Equity Action League (WEAL) in 1968.

The Chicago Westside Group, the nation's earliest radical women's liberation collective, is formed, with Shulamith Firestone as one of its founders.

Women, led by NOW, picket outside the *New York Times*, demonstrating against sex-segregated want

1967
(cont.)

ads, whereby newspapers list jobs as male or female. Women point out that the high-paying jobs are under the male classification, and when women ignore the classification and apply, they are in turn ignored, ridiculed, or simply sent away.

1968

Women protest outside the Miss America pageant. They march, they sing, they drop tokens of exploitation (such as bras, girdles, and high heels) into a "freedom trash can." A journalist stages a photo of a burning bra, and the myth of bra-burners at the pageant is born. The protesters carry signs such as "Welcome to the Miss American Cattle Auction," and they protest the absence of African American women in the pageant with "Miss America Is Alive and Angry—in Harlem." Then, at the moment of Miss America's crowning, women seated in the balcony inside the auditorium unfurl a banner that boldly says, "WOMEN'S LIBERATION." Television cameras turn to the balcony, and the excitement of a new, iconoclastic political movement reaches out through television screens into the living rooms of American society.

On Halloween, an event is staged by WITCH (Women's International Terrorist Conspiracy from Hell, or sometimes Women Inspired to Commit Herstory, or at other times, other names—the group creatively uses whatever is appropriate to their event). WITCH is an offshoot of the New York Radical Women. Members make a dramatic appearance in Up Against the Wall Street, an all-day guerrilla theater procession on New York's famed financial avenue. They put a hex on the stock exchange and then continue into the night, hexing all-male bars and burlesque houses.

The EEOC rules, in a three-to-two vote, that sex-segregated want ads in newspapers violate Title VII guarantees against sex discrimination in the workplace.

1969

The first "speakout" is organized by the New York radical feminist group Redstockings. Twelve women speak out, describing their abortions to an audience of 300. Other speakouts follow on subjects such as rape, sexual harassment, and incest.

WITCH demonstrates in protest of a New York bridal fair held in Madison Square Garden. The women appear in black veils, carrying signs with sayings such as "Confront the Whoremakers," "Always a Bride, Never a Person," and "Here Comes the Bribe." WITCH's point is that in patriarchal marriages women are selling their female selves for goods and that society's consumerism is part of the system's bribe (Morgan 1977).

Over a four-year period ending with the legalization of abortion in 1973, the Jane Collective, a Chicago-based group of women, provides "safe, effective and supportive illegal abortions" (Boston Women's Health Book Collective 1992). The Jane Collective, often simply called Jane, at first referred women to abortion clinics but then began providing them themselves. They are part of the movement to "demystify" women's health issues and are credited with helping over 11,000 women obtain first- and second-trimester abortions. Other anonymous health collectives also exist during this time.

The modern lesbian and gay rights movement begins when patrons at the Stonewall Inn fight back against New York City police who come to harass them.

1970s   This is a decade of great hopes and major battles won by feminists. New ground is broken, and many "firsts" are achieved by American women—Anne Armstrong cochairs the Republican National Committee (1971–1973); Shirley Chisholm is a candidate for the Democratic presidential nomination (1972); Ella Grasso is elected Connecticut governor (the first woman governor not to succeed or be a surrogate for her husband, 1974); Barbara Walters coanchors on the network evening news (1976); Eleanor Holmes Norton chairs the EEOC (1977); Janet Guthrie drives

1970s
(cont.)
in the Indianapolis 500 (1977); Sally Ride and five others are NASA's first women astronaut trainees (1978).

1970
Susan Brownmiller leads a sit-in at the *Ladies' Home Journal*. Seventy-five women meet in front of the magazine's Manhattan building one morning and take the elevators to the office of editor John Mack Carter. He has been tipped off by a reporter but expects a delegation of ladies whom he can charm into going away. The women burst into his office, taking over the floor, windowsills, chairs, and desk, and spilling out into the hall. They present their demands: Carter's resignation; child-care centers for employees; a ban on degrading, exploitative ads; elimination of the magazine's focus on marriage as the best or only option for women; an end to articles tied to products; an end to romance fiction; and a contract for one issue of the *Journal* to be edited by members of the women's liberation movement. Carter says very little as the women present their demands. About 200 more women arrive by mid-morning. Carter still says little except that he is not turning his magazine over to the women. Some of the demonstrators want to overturn file cabinets, but Brownmiller stops them. Carter is sitting on the edge of his desk. Someone yells to get him off the desk. Shulamith Firestone lunges at him. Another woman does a karate chop with her arm, catching Firestone, who then flies over the head of Carter, landing on the other side. No one is hurt, but chaos and shouting results. A few of the women want to throw Carter out the window. Brownmiller regains order. The women stay for eleven hours, talking to *Journal* staff members and holding press conferences and meetings. Finally, Carter agrees to a feminism supplement, with a $10,000 fee to the writers. It appears in the August 1970 edition (Cohen 1988).

In August, the Women's Strike for Equality is held. Women across the country take to the streets to march for equality. Conceived and organized by Betty Friedan, and held for the fiftieth anniversary of women's suffrage, the strike is hailed as an over-whelming success by feminist leaders. In New York City, an estimated twenty to fifty thousand women join arms and walk jubilantly down the middle of Fifth Avenue. Participants include Bella Abzug, Shirley Chisholm, Betty Friedan, Flo Kennedy, Beulah Sanders (of the National Welfare Rights Organization), and Gloria Steinem. The day is a turning point for the women's movement, for the sheer numbers of marchers impress the media, and reporters begin to take the women seriously.

Hawaii and New York become the first states to legalize abortion. The Catholic Church forms the National Right to Life Committee to oppose abortion.

Lesbian issues surface in the women's movement, as lesbians demand public support for their rights. A "purge" of lesbians from the leadership of the National Organization for Women is led by Betty Friedan, an action she later regrets (see Chapter 4).

1971   Three hundred people attend a Manhattan speakout on rape. Forty women speak out on rapes they experienced. Their stories reveal not only women's vulnerability to attack but also the justice system's indifference and disbelief as well as police officers' attitude that women cause rape by their sexy appearance.

A group of women in London opens a shelter for battered women, inspiring other women, including those in the United States, to open shelters.

Ms. magazine publishes its first edition as a 40-page insert in *New York* magazine. The feminist magazine's first full issue is to be published a few months later in 1972 with editor Gloria Steinem at its helm. The editors derive the title, *Ms.*, from a 1930s secretarial handbook for proper address if a woman's marriage status is unknown. It has since become the accepted manner to address any woman, unless she requests her marriage status be included in her name.

1971
(cont.)

Toni Morrison writes an essay for the *New York Times Magazine* voicing some of the criticism of the "White women's movement" coming from African American women. For example, she writes: "It is a source of amusement even now to black women to listen to feminists talk of liberation while somebody's nice black grandmother shoulders the daily responsibility of childrearing and floor mopping" (Morrison 1988, 314).

In Washington, the Senate Rules Committee allows girls to become pages. The National Women's Political Caucus is formed to help women get elected to office; this group appeals more to women of color than NOW does, and African American feminists join along with white feminists.

In a reversal of its earlier stance (see 1970), NOW passes a resolution declaring lesbian rights to be part of its agenda.

1972

On March 22, Congress passes the Equal Rights Amendment. Hawaii ratifies it one-half hour later. Within one week, five more states ratify it; a total of 28 states ratify it by the end of the year. Phyllis Schlafly launches STOP-ERA, an offshoot of the Eagle Forum, Schlafly's conservative organization. STOP-ERA is dedicated to halting all equal rights progress.

Title IX of the Education Act passes, prohibiting sex discrimination in any federally assisted educational program or activity. The law has far-ranging effects on girls' education. Girls' sports programs in schools grow tremendously, and policies that set quotas for women or differentiated financial aid requirements are dropped.

At the Democratic National Convention in Miami, Florida, women make up 40 percent of the delegates, up from 13 percent in 1968. Shirley Chisholm runs for the Democratic nomination for president, the first

American of color to do so. She loses in the Democratic primary to George McGovern; Republican Richard Nixon wins the election.

The National Black Feminist Organization is formed, with Eleanor Holmes Norton as one of the founding members. Its goal is to address both racism and sexism in the lives of African American women, and it grows rapidly but is short-lived, going into decline by 1974.

1973   The U.S. Supreme Court decision on *Roe v. Wade* makes abortion legal in all states. (Abortion had been illegal in almost every state from 1900 until just before the 1970s, and states were in charge of deciding to regulate or outlaw it.) The decision comes in the wake of feminist efforts throughout the country to make abortion legal, and it strikes down a Texas law that allows abortion only to save a woman's life. The Court declares that any restrictions on a woman's right to abortion in the first trimester are illegal. For a while, abortion is both legal and available in the United States (see Chapter 4, "Reproductive Freedom," for further discussion).

AT&T pays more than $38 million in higher wages and back pay for a class-action suit brought by 13,000 women and 2,000 men of color who sue for discrimination in the workplace. A landmark case, it sets new standards for employment policies.

The New Jersey Division of Civil Rights rules that Little League baseball must allow girls to join.

The first shelter for battered women in the United States opens in St. Paul, Minnesota.

Helen Reddy wins a Grammy Award for her hit song, "I Am Woman," a feminist celebration of women's power and strength and the unofficial anthem of the feminist movement.

1974   The Equal Credit Opportunity Act (ECOA) passes. It prohibits discrimination against women on the basis of sex or marital status. Before the ECOA, women reported numerous forms of financial discrimination.

     The Women's Educational Equity Act (WEEA) funds research, materials, and training to help schools eliminate sex bias. WEEA includes a broad range of projects, from helping schools comply with Title IX to encouraging girls to enter math and science programs.

     The term "sexual harassment" is first coined by an attorney for a Cornell University employee who files a claim with the Equal Employment Opportunity Commission.

     The first March for Life, an antiabortion rally, is held in Washington, D.C., on the January 22 anniversary of passage of *Roe v. Wade*. Six thousand participants turn out for the march, which will become an annual event drawing 25,000 protesters in 1975 and up to 70,000 in special event years.

1975   The United Nations declares this International Women's Year and holds the first World Conference on Women in Mexico City. The modern global women's movement begins as women from throughout the world meet and find common ground.

     The U.S. Supreme Court rules that women may not be excluded from jury duty on account of sex.

1976   Feminists support and lobby for the Day Care Services Act, which would have provided financial aid to child-care centers and hired welfare mothers to staff the centers. Feminists win Congressional approval, but the act is vetoed by President Gerald Ford.

     The Republican National Convention includes the Human Life Amendment, an antiabortion statement, in its political platform. Feminists attending the Democratic National Convention convince party leaders to promise equal representation for women. President Ford, a Republican, loses to Democratic candidate Jimmy Carter.

The prestigious Rhodes scholarship is opened to female applicants.

1977   Oregon drops its marital exemption from rape, one of the first states to do so.

Dade County, Florida, led by celebrity Anita Bryant, overturns an ordinance protecting homosexuals from discrimination.

Planned Parenthood offices are set on fire in St. Paul, Minnesota, one of the first violent acts of the anti-abortion movement. After this, vandalism, arson, bombings, assaults, and death threats become a common form of attack on women's clinics from pro-life extremists.

The Hyde Amendment to the Health, Education, and Welfare Labor appropriations bill prohibits the use of federal funds to pay for some abortions.

A National Women's Conference is held in Houston, Texas, and 20,000 women attend. More than one-third of the delegates to the conference are women of color, and these voices and their concerns are included in the debate. For example, Wilmette Brown, of the Black Women for Wages for Housework Campaign, states, "Our fight for money of our own is not so we can join the *man* sitting on top of the world. Our victory is an open invitation to share the wealth" (Boston Women's Health Book Collective 1992, 720). However, some states send anti-ERA, antiabortion fundamentalists as representatives to the conference. Feminists realize a serious backlash is forming. They hustle to hold the line on issues.

1977
(*cont.*)

After 1977, no more states ratify the Equal Rights Amendment.

1978

The Pregnancy Discrimination Act is passed. An amendment to Title VII, it states that pregnancy discrimination is sex discrimination.

An extension of the deadline for ratification of the Equal Rights Amendment wins House approval, and soon wins Senate approval too, giving ERA supporters until June 30, 1982, to win state ratification of the amendment.

1979

The annual March for Life in Washington, D.C., draws an estimated 60,000 people. Proabortion activists establish a fund for low-income women unable to get Medicaid funding for abortions.

The first National March for Lesbian and Gay Rights is held in Washington, D.C. Over 100,000 people take part.

Domestic violence is under scrutiny. President Jimmy Carter establishes the Office of Domestic Violence, a clearinghouse for information. The Conference on Violence Against Women is held in Denver, Colorado. Another conference, Confronting Woman Abuse, is held in Chicago. The first congressional hearings on domestic violence are held.

Judy Chicago's work of art *The Dinner Party* opens its ten-year tour. A monumental piece exploring women throughout history, *The Dinner Party* is a huge, triangular table upon which are laid 39 oversized place settings, each representing a woman of achievement from prehistory to the twentieth century. The place settings are multimedia, collaborative works combining various forms of needlework, porcelain sculpture, and paint. The placemats describe and symbolize the individual woman's work; the plates illustrate, chiefly through vulval symbolism, the women's position, their growing discontent, and feminist identity. *The Dinner Party* is controversial, bringing accolades from some in the art community and sneers from others. And when it was reconstructed in 1996 and shown again, it was still controversial. Chicago says her goal for *The Dinner Party* "was and is twofold: to teach women's history through a work of art that can convey the long struggle for freedom and justice that women have waged since the advent of male-dominated societies, and to break the cycle of history that *The Dinner Party* describes" (Chicago 1996, 3).

1980s   A decade of backlash and loss. A gender gap begins to appear in presidential voting, with women favoring Democratic Party policies on social and economic issues. The changes that feminists had been celebrating—pay equity, day care, equal access to sports facilities and other school programs, an increase in women in business and government, a new self-reliance fostered in women—changes that seem to feminists to be gains for women, are seen by others as threats to the fabric of society. Reaction to these changes fuels a backlash through the late 1980s and into the 1990s. Antifeminists speak of "family values" and a desire to get back to the "traditional family," code words meaning a return to patriarchal ruling of families, with a lessening of a woman's influence outside the family as well as a reduction of her independence within it. Feminists and feminist ideas suffer virulent attacks from the political right wing. During this decade of conservative leadership, federal courts are packed with conservative judges, and reproductive rights slip. Nevertheless, the women's movement continues to expand. Ecofeminism (see Chapter 4) grows as an offshoot. A women's spirituality movement, separating itself from patriarchal religions, gains adherents.

1980   The first year of the new decade is declared International Women's Year. Copenhagen is the site of the second World Conference on Women. A parallel con-

1980
(cont.)

ference of nongovernmental organizations grows, with 8,000 participants.

The Democratic National Convention, under pressure from feminists, includes support for both the Equal Rights Amendment and abortion in its political platform. Forty-nine percent of the voting delegates at the convention are women. Candidates are incumbents Jimmy Carter and Walter Mondale.

With presidential nominee Ronald Reagan at its helm, the Republican National Convention continues its antiabortion stance and strengthens it by endorsing a Constitutional amendment to ban abortions; the party platform also sets forth that only abortion opponents would be considered as federal judges. Twenty-nine percent of the delegates at the convention are women. George Bush switches his position to antiabortion when picked as Reagan's running mate. Reagan easily wins the presidency.

1981

Sandra Day O'Connor becomes the first woman to serve on the U.S. Supreme Court.

Rallies are held in cities across the country as feminists scramble for a last-minute ratification of the Equal Rights Amendment. The Last Walk for ERA is held in Los Angeles; 10,000 participants march down the Avenue of the Stars to publicize and raise money for the National Organization for Women ERA Countdown Campaign.

The Family Protection Act, supported by President Reagan, is introduced in Congress. It would eliminate federal laws supporting equal education, forbid "intermingling of the sexes in any sport or other school-related activities," require marriage and motherhood to be taught as the proper career for girls, deny federal funding to any school using textbooks portraying women in nontraditional roles, repeal all federal laws protecting battered wives from their husbands, and ban federally funded legal aid for any woman seeking abortion counseling or divorce (McCue 1995). Congress defeats the legislation. President Reagan also endorses the Human Life Bill, which would define an embryo as a "person" from the moment of conception, and the Human Life [Constitutional] Amendment, which would ban abortion as well as intrauterine devices and some other forms of birth control.

1982   The June 30 deadline for the Equal Rights Amendment arrives. The ERA is defeated after coming up just three states short of ratification.

1984   Democrats nominate Geraldine Ferraro for vice president on a ticket alongside Walter Mondale. They lose to Republican incumbent team Ronald Reagan and George Bush. The gender gap seems to have decreased, and Reagan, despite feminist efforts, wins by a landslide.

The U.S. Supreme Court rules in *Grove City College v. Bell* that Title IX applies only to *programs* receiving federal funds, not to the entire institutions, thus weakening Title IX.

The U.S. Attorney General establishes the Task Force on Family Violence and holds hearings on the problem in six cities. Nearly 300 witnesses testify. The task force recommends that special units be established to process family violence cases, that complaints be automatically charged, that victims not be required to testify, and that a protective order restricting access to the victim be issued when the offender is released.

The Family Violence Protection and Services Act passes, earmarking federal funds for domestic violence programs.

1985   The third World Conference on Women is held in Nairobi, Kenya. Building on the two previous conferences' goals, the third conference recommends pay

1985
(cont.)
equity, child care, and flexible working schedules and calls for wells, dams, and water facilities for rural African women, who spend much of their time fetching and carrying water.

EMILY's (Early Money Is Like Yeast) List is founded. A fundraising instrument for Democratic women candidates, the group is a political action committee (PAC) that successfully raises money and supports feminist candidates. It is the forerunner of many more women's PACs.

The annual March for Life in Washington, D.C., draws 70,000 protesters against legal abortion. President Reagan addresses the group.

1986
The gender gap resurfaces, as women's votes boost Democrats back into a majority of Senate seats.

The March for Life draws 36,000 people, and President Reagan addresses the group for the second year in a row. NOW sponsors a series of Marches for Women's Lives across the country: 125,000 people attend in Washington, D.C.; 30,000 gather in Los Angeles; and eight more marches are held during the year.

The term "glass ceiling" is coined by the *Wall Street Journal* to describe the invisible barriers that stand between women and their rise to corporate executive positions and to top levels of business and political structures.

1987
The U.S. Supreme Court rules that male-only clubs discriminate against women. The Rotary, Lions, and Kiwanis clubs open their doors to women.

The domestic violence case of Joel Steinberg makes headlines. Over a period of nine years, Steinberg beat and tortured his live-in partner, Hedda Nussbaum, and their adopted six-year-old daughter. Nussbaum's abuse included broken bones, burns, blows, and kicks that left permanent eye and ear damage, knocked out teeth, and damaged sexual organs. The child died from Steinberg's abuse; Steinberg is convicted of manslaughter but not murder. Charges against Nussbaum for the child's death are dropped when she cooperates with police in their case against Steinberg. The trial brings to light biases still extant in society: Some jurors blame Nussbaum for driving Steinberg to violence. Debate rages over Nussbaum's guilt and responsibility for protecting the child, regardless of her own injuries.

1988   Republican presidential candidate George Bush wins the election despite a continuing gender gap in voting.

Women from all over the world attend a New York City conference on prostitution. South Korean and Philippine women talk about prostitutes near United States military bases, about the women's poverty, and about sex tours to the areas. A Japanese woman tells stories of Philippine, Taiwanese, and Thai women imported to Japan for prostitution. Also, sex tours to Asia for European and American males are revealed.

Congress passes the Civil Rights Restoration Act in reaction to U.S. Supreme Court decisions that have reduced the effectiveness of Title IX and other laws. The act reaffirms that Title IX applies to all educational programs in an institution, not just those that draw federal funds.

The Reagan administration institutes a "gag rule" barring federally funded clinics from providing abortion information to pregnant women. The programs have a budget of about $200 million per year for low-income women and are overseen by the Secretary of Health and Human Services. Under the gag rule, if women ask about abortion, they are to be told that "this project does not consider abortion an appropriate method of family planning" (Costa 1996, 43).

1989   The annual March for Life rally in Washington, D.C., draws 67,000 participants. In April, a march by reproductive rights activists draws an estimated 300,000. (Feminists estimate the number at 600,000.) A week later, 300,000 Italians march to the Vatican in sympathy with the U.S. protest and in support of reproductive rights. In response, the National Right to Life Committee holds a Rally for Life in Washington, D.C., drawing 350,000. The stakes are higher this year: Both sides of the debate await the outcome of the U.S. Supreme Court decision on *Webster v. Reproductive Health Services.*

The U.S. Supreme Court rules in *Webster v. Reproductive Health Services* to uphold a Missouri statute that prohibits the use of public funds to perform an abortion unless it is to save the woman's life. This opens the door for other states to pass laws curbing women's access to abortions.

In December, 14 female students at the University of Montreal in Canada are executed by a 25-year-old man who enters a classroom, separates the men from the women, and murders the women. His stated reason: "You're all fucking feminists." In a suicide letter he claims that "the feminists have always enraged me" (Sheffield 1995, 5).

1990s   Global thinking and interacting have become a major part of feminism as women stretch across borders and cultures to form coalitions. The backlash continues, as First Lady Hillary Rodham Clinton is held up to a public trouncing unprecedented in U.S. history. Conservative talk show hosts gain fame and enormous audiences while they rant against the First Lady's public work, her image, her mannerisms, and her liberal views. They attack feminists' attempts to fight sexual harassment, to gain entry into all-male military academies, to fly fighter aircraft within the military itself, and to insist on women appointees in the White House. Religion-based men's movements hold mass gatherings in stadiums and convention centers, focusing on how men should reclaim their responsibility in families. Feminists applaud some of these gatherings but question the rhetoric of those that call for patriarchal structures, not partnerships, in marriage and parenting.

1990   After many repeated tries over 20 years, feminists succeed in getting a child-care bill through Congress with the passing of the Act for Better Child Care. The act provides tax credits to low-income working parents for child care and funds to states for use in child-care programs.

1991   During the Senate confirmation hearings of U.S. Supreme Court Justice Clarence Thomas, law professor Anita Hill steps forward to accuse Thomas of sexual harassment. Her testimony, received with skepticism by the all-male hearing committee, galvanizes the women's movement.

Twenty-six female active duty officers of the U.S. Navy are sexually assaulted by at least 70 navy aviators at a Las Vegas convention of the Tailhook Association. Lt. Paula Coughlin reports the incident, resulting in the resignation of the Secretary of the Navy and the early retirement of several senior officers; but Lt. Coughlin's career is sacrificed, as she resigns, citing stress as the reason.

1992   The Civil Rights Act of 1992 provides victims of job discrimination—including sexual harassment—the right to a trial by jury and makes employers liable for damage of up to $300,000 to victims. The act is a victory for feminists. In the post–Anita Hill hearings political climate, President Bush, says Patricia Ireland, president of NOW, was "trapped." He had vetoed the same bill in 1990 (Ireland 1996, 248).

The media proclaim this the Year of the Woman because a record number of women now hold elective office. President Bill Clinton celebrates because he won the election with 45 percent of the women's vote

1992
(cont.)

and 41 percent of the men's. (Republican George Bush lost with 41 percent of women and 38 percent of men.) A record number of female U.S. representatives and senators hold seats, bringing the total to 47 women in the House—plus delegate Eleanor Holmes Norton of the District of Columbia—and six in the Senate.

In January, an estimated 70,000 people gather in Washington, D.C., for the March for Life, sponsored by the National Right to Life Committee. Outgoing president Bush sends a message to those gathered: "I'm out there with you in spirit," he says. In April, the March for Women's Lives, sponsored by NOW, is held in Washington, D.C., to protest the erosion of women's abortion rights and access to abortion. Estimates number the participants between 500,000 and 750,000.

1993

The Family Leave and Medical Act is passed. It mandates unpaid time off for pregnancy, adoption, or family illness. The same legislation was vetoed by President Bush during his term; now it is signed into law by President Clinton.

Clinton lifts the ban on importing RU-486, a drug already in use in China, France, and England that induces miscarriage by preventing an egg's implantation in the uterine wall. He also revokes the administrative gag rule that Reagan and Bush administrations had imposed to ban abortion counseling or referral by federally funded clinics. And he reverses previous administrative policies on denying foreign aid to international family-planning agencies that support abortion rights.

As of July 5, marital rape is a crime in all 50 states. Thirty-one states maintain exemptions from prosecution if "only" simple force is used or if the woman is legally unable to consent due to the severity of a disability (temporary or permanent, physical or mental).

The United Nations World Conference on Human Rights reaffirms women's human rights as an "inalienable, integral, and indivisible part of universal human rights" (Fisher 1996, 43). The UN General Assembly adopts the landmark Declaration on the Elimination of Violence Against Women.

1994   Capitol Hill swings to the right with the influx of newly elected conservative representatives and senators.

The Violence Against Women Act (VAWA) passes. The National Organization for Women Legal Defense and Education Fund serves as principal technical adviser to the U.S. Congress on VAWA and also mobilizes and leads a 1,000-member national task force in support of the bill.

In June, Nicole Brown Simpson and a friend, Ronald Goldman, are viciously murdered in front of her house in a Los Angeles suburb. Simpson's former husband, football star and sports broadcaster O.J. Simpson, is arrested for the murders, then acquitted by a jury. The case sparks national debate over racism and domestic violence. (O.J. Simpson is African American; Nicole Brown Simpson was white.) The country's racial tensions come to the surface as the population splits its belief in the innocence or guilt of Simpson down racial lines. For feminists, the murder points out the intertwined problems of racism and sexism. A few feminists step forward to use the momentum created by the trial's attention on violence. The victim's sister, Denise Brown, joins with Los Angeles feminist Tammy Bruce to establish a foundation to educate the public about domestic violence. New York passes a bill mandating arrest for anyone committing domestic assault. California increases funding to domestic violence programs. Colorado enacts tough anti–domestic violence laws.

The new Freedom of Access to Clinic Entrances Act (FACE) makes blocking access to abortion clinics a

1994
(cont.)
federal crime and provides criminal penalties for using force or threat of force to injure, intimidate, or block anyone entering an abortion clinic. It also includes a budget for a National Domestic Violence Hotline, shelters, interstate enforcement of protective orders, training for state and federal judges, and funding for school rape education programs. It also identifies gender-based crimes as violations of a woman's civil rights; thus, it allows her to sue the perpetrator of a gender-motivated crime in federal court.

1995
The seventy-fifth anniversary of women's suffrage is celebrated nationally.

Shannon Faulkner becomes the first female cadet at the Citadel military college in South Carolina. Her battle to win acceptance to the Citadel began in 1993, when she gained admittance as a student by omitting her gender from the school's application; since then she has sued the college to win admittance. She matriculates in August but drops out after only six days, and the Citadel men send up a cheer of victory.

The fourth World Conference on Women is held in Beijing, China. More than 4,000 delegates attend, and an estimated 30,000 participate in the parallel nongovernmental organization forum. Human rights is the theme, and women call for decision-making roles in national governments and international forums.

1996
This is declared the Year of the Woman at the Olympic Summer Games. Women win 38 of the 101 U.S. medals, including 19 of the nation's 44 gold medals.

Affirmative action is voted down in California by a landslide proposition vote. Conservatives celebrate, and liberals mourn the threat to California's programs. The proposition is taken to court and is upheld in early proceedings. Political pundits are calling this the death knell of affirmative action.

President Clinton vetoes legislation that would out-law dilation-and-extraction abortions. Abortion op-ponents had renamed the procedure the "partial birth abortion" and gained support to outlaw it in the Re-publican-dominated Congress. Supporters of the ban promise to bring it up again in future sessions.

The Welfare Reform Act is passed by Congress. Fem-inist leaders oppose the act, arguing that it penalizes poor women without giving them any needed aid for child care and health care. NOW president Patri-cia Ireland begins a hunger strike and leads an ex-tended protest against the act. Ireland subsists on water and vitamins for ten days and also holds a nightly protest in front of the White House, where she is joined by other NOW staff members, the Rev-erend Jesse Jackson, and human rights activist Dick Gregory.

Despite this pressure, Clinton signs the Welfare Re-form Act. Feminists in this election year are left choosing between Clinton and Republican Bob Dole, who opposes reproductive rights and affirmative ac-tion. Feminists support Clinton as their best option. The gender gap in voting is the largest ever, with women declared the reason for Clinton's reelection. Also, after significant victories, a record number of women will sit in the 105th Congress.

The U.S. Supreme Court rules that public military schools cannot discriminate against women. Though the Supreme Court case concerns the Virginia Mili-tary Institute (VMI), the Citadel in South Carolina re-sponds by opening its doors to women. Four women matriculate into the Citadel. Two quit the college after one semester, accusing several men of sexual harassment and abuse that goes beyond the school's accepted hazing. Citadel officials respond with re-newed promises of an equitable and safe education for female students. Two of the women stay in the college, and additional women sign up for the 1997–1998 school year.

1997   By a 6-3 vote, the U.S. Supreme Court in *Schenck v. Pro-Choice Network* upholds part of the New York injunction that keeps protesters 15 feet from the entrances to clinics and from their driveways, but the buffer zones around patients entering clinics is done away with.

A federal law outlawing female genital mutilation (FGM) in the United States takes effect April 1, 1997, as part of the Illegal Immigration Reform and Immigrant Responsibility Act of 1996. Immigration officials will now provide information on the harmful physical effects of FGM and information about the law to all who enter from countries where FGM is widely practiced.

Madeleine Albright becomes the nation's first female secretary of state. She promises a proactive stance on international women's rights and pledges to urge U.S. ratification of the Convention on the Elimination of All Forms of Discrimination Against Women (CEDAW).

Title IX is strengthened when the U.S. Supreme Court allows a lower court ruling, *Brown v. Cohen*, to stand. The case is a suit brought by female students against Brown University in Rhode Island. They charge that Brown has fewer women than men overall in sports and was in violation of Title IX when it dropped women's programs. In the lower court ruling, the value of Title IX is affirmed: "One need look no further than the impressive performances of our country's women athletes in the 1996 Olympic Summer Games to see that Title IX has had a dramatic and positive impact. . . . What stimulated this remarkable change in the quality of women's athletic competition was . . . the enforcement of Title IX's mandate of gender equity in sports" (National Women's Law Center 1996, 2).

Capitalizing on the momentum of the 1996 Olympic gold medal won by the women's basketball team, the

Women's National Basketball Association (WNBA) is inaugurated. It is supported by the men's National Basketball Association, and league sponsors promise three national game telecasts each week during the season. The first game is played to larger crowds than anticipated, with parents bringing both daughters and sons to experience the groundbreaking event.

References

Boston Women's Health Book Collective. 1992. *The New Our Bodies, Ourselves: A Book by and for Women.* New York: Simon & Schuster Touchstone.

Chicago, Judy. 1996. *The Dinner Party.* New York: Penguin.

Cohen, Marcia. 1988. *The Sisterhood: The True Story of the Women Who Changed the World.* New York: Simon & Schuster.

Costa, Marie. 1996. *Abortion: A Reference Handbook, Second Edition.* Santa Barbara, Calif.: ABC-CLIO.

French, Marilyn. 1992. *The War against Women.* New York: Ballantine Books.

Friedan, Betty. 1963. *The Feminine Mystique.* New York: W. W. Norton.

Ireland, Patricia. 1996. *What Women Want.* New York: Dutton.

McCue, Margi Laird. 1995. *Domestic Violence: A Reference Handbook.* Santa Barbara, Calif.: ABC-CLIO.

Morgan, Robin. 1977. *Going Too Far: The Personal Chronicle of a Feminist.* New York: Random House.

Morrison, Toni. 1988. Article, *New York Times Magazine,* as quoted in Marcia Cohen, *The Sisterhood: The True Story of the Women Who Changed the World.* New York: Simon & Schuster.

National Women's Law Center. 1996. "Appeals Court Sides with Center, Sets Precedent in *Cohen v. Brown Univ.* Decision." *Update* newsletter, vol. 9, issue 2.

Sheffield, Carole J. 1995. "Sexual Terrorism." In Jo Freeman, ed., *Women: A Feminist Perspective, Fifth Edition.* Mountain View, Calif.: Mayfield Publishing.

Vienna Declaration and Program of Action [excerpt from Section One]. 1996. In Elizabeth Fisher and Linda Gray MacKay, *Gender Justice: Women's Rights Are Human Rights.* Cambridge, Mass.: Unitarian Universalist Service Committee.

Wilson, Midge, and Kathy Russell. 1996. *Divided Sisters: Bridging the Gap between Black Women and White Women.* New York: Anchor Books, Doubleday.

Woloch, Nancy. 1994. *Women and the American Experience, Second Edition.* New York: McGraw-Hill.

Biographical Sketches 3

To list all of the feminists who have been instrumental in forwarding the progress of women's issues in the second wave and third wave of the movement is impossible in a single volume. Instead, listed here are some of the women who have devoted their lives and careers to the feminist cause. Those included have all been influential, but it is important to remember that many other women have worked tirelessly to reform the workplace, win family-friendly policies such as pregnancy leave and day-care facilities, reform laws to remove biases against women, and encourage women into educational achievements.

Bella Abzug (1920–1998)

Born in the Bronx, New York, educated at Hunter College, and then rejected by Harvard Law School because of its men-only policy, Abzug entered Columbia University School of Law (one of six females in her class) and earned an LL.B. in 1947. She specialized in labor law. Very few women attorneys were in the courts, but there were many women working as legal secretaries. In her first year of law practice Abzug was often mistaken for a secretary; therefore, she began to wear hats—which would become her lifelong trademark—as a way to distinguish herself from the hatless secretaries and court clerks. She earned a reputation defending clients during the anti-communist Senate hearings led by Sen. Joseph McCarthy in the 1950s and earned further recognition as a civil rights attorney, defending indigent African American clients. She worked with minority groups to help draft the Civil Rights Act of 1957. In 1961, she helped found Women Strike for Peace, which worked for nuclear disarmament. A vocal supporter of women's rights, Abzug in 1971 was elected to the U.S. Congress from New York partly through the efforts of women who turned out to support her. In 1976 she took the risk of running for the U.S. Senate and lost; the following year, she ran for mayor of New York City and lost. That's when she blossomed into a really effective feminist, as an activist and advocate for global women's rights. She won international recognition at the United Nations World Conferences on Women held in 1975, 1980, and 1985. In 1990 she helped create the Women's Environment and Development Organization (WEDO), a worldwide network of women that analyzes every UN document for its impact on women and monitors government actions. Her work as a global link and as a leader among leaders internationally helped the development of an international sisterhood of feminists.

Gloria Anzaldúa (1942–)

Born and raised in a poor farming and ranching community in South Texas, Anzaldúa is a seventh-generation American of Mexican descent, a Chicana by her own definition. Along with her family, she worked in the fields as she was growing up and continued to do so while going to college. The first in her family to earn a college degree, she received her B.A. from Pan American University in 1969. She then earned an M.A. from the University of Texas, Austin, 1972, in English and education. She gained national notice in 1981 with the publication of the award-winning book *This Bridge Called My Back: Writings by Radical Women of Color,* which she coedited with Cherríe Moraga. The anthology opened discussion and doors between white feminists and feminists of color. Through the years it has remained an indispensable feminist text. Anzaldúa edited another anthology of works by women of color, published in 1990: *Making Face, Making Soul/ Haciendo caras: Creative and Critical Perspectives by Feminists of*

Color. She authored her own book in 1987, *Borderlands/La Frontera: The New Mestiza.* In it she takes an autobiographical approach and combines poetry, prose, and storytelling to critique the U.S., Mexican, and Chicano cultures. Focusing on her own struggles with feminism, lesbianism, and family disapproval, Anzaldúa also takes the unusual step of revealing (to the majority community) the negative side of the Mexican culture. "Culture (read males) professes to protect women," she writes in *Borderlands* (p. 17). "Actually, it keeps women in rigidly defined roles." Anzaldúa finds the rigid roles stifling and absolutely incompatible with her needs and desires; she calls on all three cultures to allow women the freedom to carve out their own identities and roles. She reveals the strength of Chicana women despite their continuing secondary status in their culture, and she describes the depth of her own female heritage and roots. Anzaldúa is also author of *Friends from the Other Side/Amigos del otro lado* (1993).

Charlotte Bunch (1944–)

A feminist author and activist, Bunch was born in North Carolina. She attended the University of California, Berkeley, and earned a bachelor's degree, magna cum laude, from Duke University in 1966. Active in civil rights and student Christian organizations during her college years, Bunch became involved in the women's movement soon afterward. She served as a member of the board of directors of the National Gay and Lesbian Task Force of the National Organization for Women from 1974 to 1981 while maintaining leadership membership in numerous other organizations at the same time. She is an influential leader within feminist circles and has been a key contributor in forming feminist ideology. Bunch is also director of the Center for Women's Global Leadership, an organization whose mission is to coordinate the global campaign for women's human rights. It is a coalition of 900 women's groups and is credited with getting violence against women classified as a human rights abuse at the United Nations International Human Rights Conference. Bunch has written numerous essays, some of which are collected in *Passionate Politics: Feminist Theory in Action* (1987); she has also edited seven anthologies and is author of her own book, *Demanding Accountability: The Global Campaign and Vienna Tribunal for Women's Human Rights* (1994).

Hillary Rodham Clinton (1947–)

Hillary Rodham Clinton grew up in a Chicago suburb and demonstrated her leadership abilities from an early age. She earned a B.A. in political science from Wellesley College in 1969, where she was a leading member of the Young Republicans and president of the student government. She gave a graduation commencement speech that was published in *Life* magazine. She next attended Yale Law School, where she specialized in children's rights and did legal research for the Carnegie Council on Children. While at Yale, Clinton did volunteer work for a congressional lobbying and advocacy group that later became the Children's Defense Fund. Future president Bill Clinton was also a Yale law student, and the two began a romance that led to marriage in 1975. Meanwhile, Hillary Rodham Clinton was forging a name for herself as an attorney and was a member of a team of lawyers working for the House Judiciary Committee on the impeachment of President Richard Nixon. But instead of joining one of the many prestigious law firms that sought her out, she went to Arkansas in 1974 to organize Bill Clinton's (unsuccessful) campaign for Congress. While her husband served as attorney general and then governor of Arkansas, Hillary Rodham Clinton served in responsible posts: President Jimmy Carter appointed her to the board of directors of an organization overseeing federal funding to legal aid bureaus; she chaired committees on health issues and education; and she founded an advocacy group for low-income children. After Bill Clinton was elected president, she drafted a controversial national health insurance reform plan. She has weathered numerous attacks on her personality and is considered "too confident" by her detractors. As an intelligent, well-educated, and professional woman, Hillary Rodham Clinton has been a lightning rod for antifeminists. Ironically, she is a feminist doing exactly what conservatives say they want women to do: supporting her husband's political career and focusing on family and children's rights and issues. She is also author of the 1995 book *It Takes a Village: And Other Lessons Children Teach Us.*

Mary Daly (1928–)

Born in Schenectady, New York, Mary Daly was educated at Catholic schools. She became a scholar in religion, philosophy, and theology, earning a bachelor's degree in 1950 from the College of St. Rose, a Master's degree in 1952 from Catholic University of America, a Ph.D. from St. Mary's College, Notre Dame, and a doctorate in philosophy and one in theology from the University of Fribourg, Switzerland, in 1965. She was teaching at Boston College when she completed and published her book *The Church and the Second Sex* (1968). It examines the Catholic Church's long history of misogyny and patriarchy and criticizes the Church's antifeminist stance. Daly was fired from her teaching post but rehired when students and leading feminists protested. She continued to explore religion's impact on women's lives, writing that established modern religions are patriarchal and are the foundation for patriarchal attitudes in society. Daly broadened her focus in 1978 in her book *Gyn/Ecology: The Metaethics of Radical Feminism*, which tells the story of women's journey through patriarchy, including its Christian origins and the woman-controlling rituals of Indian *suttee*, Chinese footbinding, European witch burnings, female genital mutilation, and American gynecological practices. In the book's new introduction for a 1990 reprint Daly says she "wrote to expose the atrocities perpetrated against women under patriarchy on a planetary scale" (p. xxv). She wrote with a new lexicon, one of her own devising, creating words such as "Be-Speaking" (speaking the words to make them real) and "repossessing" words such as "crone" and "hag." Daly continued her experimental language, writing *Pure Lust: Elemental Feminist Philosophy* in 1984, *Webster's First New Intergalactic Wickedary* in 1987 (with Jane Caputi), and a memoir, *Outercourse: The Be-Dazzling Voyage: Containing Recollections from My Logbook of a Radical Feminist Philosopher* (1992). Through the years, her writing has become more and more complex, with greater and greater experimentation as Daly has striven to relay the full dimensions of her thoughts and concepts. She continues to challenge patriarchal religion and to see the women's revolution as transformative to all of society and religion.

Andrea Dworkin (1946–)

Born in Camden, New Jersey, Dworkin earned a B.A. degree from Bennington College, Vermont, in 1968, then traveled and lived in Europe until the mid-1970s. While in Europe she got married, but she soon discovered that her Dutch husband was physically abusive, and she left him. Meanwhile, she was finding a strong and independent writing voice. She moved back to the United States and saw her first book, *Woman Hating,* published in 1974. In it, she revealed her philosophy on men's subjugation of women, and she argued for sexual equality and for the end to culturally imposed gender roles. Dworkin has been a vocal presence in feminist discussions ever since. One of her major works, *Pornography: Men Possessing Women,* published in 1978, opened a long-lasting, often angry debate among feminists and others about the definition of pornography, the effect of pornography on women's lives, and what should be done about it. Whereas many feminists argue against censorship of pornography on freedom of speech grounds, Dworkin, often working with feminist attorney Catharine MacKinnon, has argued that pornography is a civil rights issue, not a freedom of speech one. She argues for an end to censorship but a beginning to pornographers' civil and legal responsibility for the effects of their images. Along with MacKinnon, she has worked to get laws passed that allow lawsuits against pornographers. (See Chapter 4 for a more detailed discussion of pornography.) In all of her writing, Dworkin has challenged feminists to look deeply and critically at the culture that surrounds them. In a 1994 *Ms.* magazine panel discussion, Dworkin described her writing as "a series of assaults on male culture, and as a way of destabilizing male control over women." In her 1987 book, *Intercourse,* Dworkin draws a connection between misogyny and sexual intercourse. The book generated great controversy, being eagerly embraced by some and soundly rejected by others. Dworkin is a self-described radical thinker. Her ideas have consistently introduced new perspective into feminist discussions. Dworkin's other books include *Our Blood: Prophecies and Discourses on Sexual Politics* (1970); *Right-Wing Women* (1983); *Letters from a War Zone: Writings 1976–1989;* and (with Catharine MacKinnon) *Pornography and Civil Rights* (1988). She also is a writer of fiction, including *The New Woman's Broken Heart: Short Stories* (1980); *Ice and Fire* (1986); and *Mercy* (1990).

Shulamith Firestone (1945–)

Born in Ottawa, Canada, Shulamith Firestone later attended Yavneh of Telshe Yeshiva, a Jewish school, and Washington University, St. Louis. She went on to earn a bachelor's degree in fine arts from the Art Institute in Chicago. She made her name not in art but as a feminist activist and writer. She helped to form some of the women's movement's most radical groups—the New York Radical Women, the Redstockings, and the New York Radical Feminists. Firestone's approach to politics was birthed from the left-wing protest movements of the 1960s and 1970s. Not one to work within the system, Firestone organized and was an activist in several women's liberation events. In the midst of a 1968 anti–Vietnam War peace march, she helped stage a mock burial of traditional womanhood; she was part of the Miss America pageant protest in 1968; her group the Redstockings held the first speakout on abortion in 1969; and she was part of the takeover of the *Ladies Home Journal* offices in 1970. Firestone served as editor and chief writer on publications of several radical feminist groups. But her greatest fame came in 1970 with the publication of *The Dialectic of Sex: The Case for Feminist Revolution.* It was an assault on the tyranny of the biological family. In a Marxist paradigm, she asserted that sex and reproduction are the foundations of a class system. Examining Freudian ideas that still prevailed, she argued that the patriarchal family structure was a fundamental psychological barrier. She sought a radical change. The traditional division of labor between men and women "was continued only at great cultural sacrifice: men and women developed only half of themselves," she wrote (Schneir 1994, 247). To right this imbalance for society and for women especially, she asserted, would require that technology take over childbearing, thus freeing women. Childbearing and child rearing needed to be diffused through society and not left as a woman's burden. She sought a society in which gender, class, and family played no role. Her book became a best-seller, and Firestone is frequently acknowledged as a powerful force in shaping the ideas of second-wave feminists.

Betty Friedan (1921–)

Friedan was born and raised in Peoria, Illinois, by a mother who was early living proof that the feminine mystique was not working. Friedan's mother, a local journalist before she got married and a homemaker afterward, was a discontented woman. Yet, Friedan herself followed in her mother's footsteps. She attended Smith College, earning a B.A. in psychology in 1942, and worked briefly as a journalist before marrying in 1947. She gradually settled into married life and motherhood. She continued to write part-time and in 1957 hit upon the idea of interviewing her cograduates from Smith to disprove a theory about female college graduates that was circulating at the time—that higher education ruined a woman's femininity and lessened her satisfaction in life. (Post–World War II America exhorted women to leave the job market and accept their role as dependent on men.) Instead of discovering that education helped women cope in suburban life, Friedan found that women were dissatisfied. She wrote of this "problem with no name" in *The Feminine Mystique,* published in 1963; the book hit a nerve with American women. Friedan was swept into the beginnings of the second wave of feminism, called by many (against her will) the mother of the second wave. In 1966, she cofounded the National Organization for Women and became its first president. In 1970, she conceived the Women's Strike for Equality on the fiftieth anniversary of women's suffrage. Thousands of women marched that day, which is considered a turning point for the women's movement. She was at the center of NOW's 1970 purge of lesbians, a position that she later regretted (and that in 1971 NOW rejected when it voted that lesbian and gay rights were feminist issues). She has continued to be a leader among mainstream feminists. In 1981, her book *The Second Stage* sparked controversy within the movement. It suggested that women were indeed more home- and family-oriented than men and that the movement had created "male clones." Women were discovering that achieving success in the world of business was not satisfying enough; they wanted children and family, too. Friedan sought both recognition of the differences between the sexes and equality between the sexes. Her recent book *Fountain of Age,* published in 1993, took a critical look at Americans' expectations of and opportunities for the elderly. In 1997 Friedan examined gender roles in the marketplace and the family in her book *Beyond Gender: The New Politics of Work and Family.*

Edith Green (1910–1987)

Edith Green was born in South Dakota but grew up in Oregon. She attended Willamette University in Salem, Oregon, but earned her bachelor of science degree from the University of Oregon in 1939. She taught school and was a radio announcer before entering politics through service activities, working as legislative chairman of the board of the Oregon Congress of Parents and Teachers and also working for the Democratic Party. She was elected to Congress in 1954 and began her work for women almost immediately, introducing a bill in 1955 to require equal pay for equal work for men and women. She worked to end segregation in schools and in 1972 shepherded Title IX of the Education Act through Congress. She served in Congress until 1974 and was one of the most powerful women ever to serve there. She remained throughout her career a champion of women's rights.

Germaine Greer (1939–)

Born and raised in Melbourne, Australia, Greer spent her early years dreaming of ways to get out to see the world. Her view of her mother as flirtatious, superficial, and dependent on men's responses to her fueled Greer's desire to explore what women truly could be if they had the opportunity. She attended the University of Melbourne, then won the Commonwealth scholarship to the University of Cambridge, England, for doctorate study in the early writings of William Shakespeare. Her personal charisma and flair, along with her writings exploring heterosexual feminist vitality and eroticism, quickly made her a media star. She was part of a panel of New York's Town Hall Dialogue on Women's Liberation, arguing with Norman Mailer in 1971 after the U.S. release of her book *The Female Eunuch* (1970). Greer brought her own joy, intelligence, and eroticism to the movement; but even more, her unabashed heterosexuality and her lusty persona attracted thousands of women and men to the movement who had been put off by its more militant leaders, some of whom were lesbians and many of whom were simply less charismatic academics and writers than was Greer. Among her other works are *The Obstacle Race: The Fortunes of Women Painters and Their Works* (1979), *The Madwoman's Underclothes: Essays and Occasional Writings* (1989), *Kissing the Rod: An Anthology of Seventeenth Century Women's Verse* (1989), *Daddy We Hardly Knew You* (1991), and *The Change: Women, Aging and the Menopause* (1992).

bell hooks (1952–)

bell hooks is the pen name of Gloria Jean Watkins, a feminist writer born and raised in Hopkinsville, Kentucky. hooks is the name Watkins took to celebrate her female heritage, the name of her Native American great-grandmother. She uses no capital letters to spell her name so that readers will focus on the contents of her writings, not on her. She earned a bachelor's degree in

English from Stanford University in 1973, a master's in English from the University of Wisconsin in 1976, and a doctorate from the University of California at Santa Cruz in 1983. She has taught literature, composition, and women's studies and served as lecturer in ethnic studies at various institutions, including San Francisco State University, the University of Southern California, Oberlin College (Ohio), and the City College of New York. She has been an instrumental voice in the feminist movement, focusing on the intertwining forces of racism and sexism. An outspoken critic of the stereotype of African American women as strong matriarchs, she argues that the myth has weakened the bonds of women of color; she suggests a closer sisterhood. And she has taken African American men to task for internalizing the white culture's patriarchal structure. What's more, she has analyzed and studied the white feminist movement, delineating where it has failed black women and where it can, and needs to, change. Her writings, insightful and erudite, have jolted many feminists (of all heritages and races) into an understanding of the complexities of the cultural structures that bind them. hooks has written numerous articles and several books. Her first prose book, *Ain't I a Woman: Black Women and Feminism*, published in 1981, opened the discussion. She wrote: "Usually, when people talk about the 'strength' of black women they are referring to the way in which they perceive black women coping with oppression. They ignore the reality that to be strong in the face of oppression is not the same as overcoming oppression, that endurance is not to be confused with transformation" (p. 6). Her other works include *Feminist Theory: From Margin to Center* (1984); *Talking Back: Thinking Feminist, Thinking Black* (1989); *Yearning: Race, Gender, and Cultural Politics* (1990); *Breaking Bread: Insurgent Black Intellectual Life* (1991); *Black Looks: Race and Representation* (1992); *Sisters of the Yam: Black Women and Self-Recovery* (with Cornel West) (1993); *Outlaw Culture: Resisting Representations* (1994); *Teaching to Transgress: Education as the Practice of Freedom* (1994); *Art on My Mind: Visual Politics* (1995); and *Black Is a Woman's Color* (1996).

Patricia Ireland (1945–)

Born and raised in Indiana, Ireland earned a bachelor's degree in German from the University of Tennessee in 1966, then a law degree from the University of Miami in 1975. Between her undergraduate and law student years, Ireland worked as a flight attendant for Pan American World Airways. The press still likes to refer to her as a former flight attendant, but she is also a former high-powered corporate attorney. She spent twelve years working her way up to a partnership in a Miami law firm before moving to Washington, D.C., in 1987 to become vice president of the National Organization for Women. She assumed the presidency of the organization in 1991. A likable public speaker, Ireland excels in getting NOW's message out to audiences. In 1992, she organized the March for Women's Lives, one of the largest-ever marches for women's reproductive rights, in Washington, D.C. She is a grassroots activist at heart and has led many marches, been arrested, and acted as a human shield for women seeking abortions in medical clinics. During the 1996 presidential campaign, when President Clinton announced that he would sign a massive Welfare Reform Act, Ireland led feminists in a ten-day hunger strike in front of the White House. She also has authored an autobiography, *What Women Want* (1996).

Audre Lorde (1934–1992)

A poet, essayist, and feminist, Audre Lorde was born in New York. She earned a bachelor's degree from Hunter College, New York (1959), and a master's degree in library science from Columbia University (1961). She first worked as a librarian, but her true calling was writing, and in 1968 she won a National Endowment for the Arts grant. Throughout her life Lorde resisted categorization, not wanting to be labeled by any one distinction but to be seen in the totality of her being. She expressed her pains and joys as an African American lesbian feminist poet, and she spoke out and against sexual and racial oppression. She is often quoted, having said, "The Master's tools will never dismantle the Master's house" (Lorde 1978, 112). Among her prose works are *I Am Your Sister: Black Women Organizing across Sexualities* (1981), *Sister Outsider: Essays and Speeches* (1984), and *A Burst of Light* (1988). Her poetry books include *Passion: New Poems, 1977–1980, Our Dead behind Us: Poems* (1986), and *Undersong: Chosen Poems Old and New* (1992).

Catharine MacKinnon (1946–)

Born and raised in Minnesota, MacKinnon graduated magna cum laude from Smith College with a bachelor's degree in government in 1969. She earned a law degree from Yale University in 1977 and a doctorate in political science from Yale in 1987. MacKinnon has been both an instrumental voice in the feminist movement and a controversial one. Her thesis was a study of sexual harassment, published in 1979 as *Sexual Harassment of Working Women: A Case of Sex Discrimination*. In her study she redefined sexual harassment as sex discrimination, thus bringing the Civil Rights Act of 1964 into play in protection from sexual harassment. She served as visiting professor at Yale, Harvard University, Stanford University, and others and received a tenured professorship at the University of Michigan Law School in 1989. In 1986, MacKinnon was cocounsel in *Meritor Savings Bank v. Vinson*, a case that refined the definition of sexual harassment even further: Instead of being simply quid pro quo (a "trade" of sexual favors for employment benefits), sexual harassment now legally includes the creation of a hostile environment. Meanwhile, MacKinnon was beginning work against what has so far been her other life's focus: pornography. Working with Andrea Dworkin, MacKinnon has redefined pornography as sex discrimination against women. The two feminists have drafted and lobbied for legislation that gives a person the right to sue producers, distributors, and perpetrators of pornography if the person has been harmed as a result of the pornography. In the United States, Dworkin's and MacKinnon's efforts have met with limited success; their legislation, though passed into law, has been struck down by the courts. MacKinnon has endured tremendous criticism for her work, both from the general public and from feminists who disagree with her. Yet, she has had an impact: She has redefined the terms of the debate surrounding pornography and has forced people to see the impact of pornography on women's lives, regardless of whether they agree with her solution to the problem. MacKinnon is also the author of *Feminism Unmodified: Discourses on Life and Law* (1987) and *Pornography and Civil Rights: A New Day for Women's Equality* (with Andrea Dworkin, 1988).

Kate Millett (1934–)

Born in St. Paul, Minnesota, Millett took part-time jobs to help her mother through the slim years following her parents' divorce when she was fourteen. She graduated magna cum laude and Phi Beta Kappa from the University of Minnesota in 1952 and, with the financial help of a wealthy aunt, studied at Oxford University, England. Her doctoral thesis, completed for her studies at Columbia University, won her a place in feminist history. The thesis explored modern patriarchal oppression of women through analysis of Western literature, including D. H. Lawrence, Henry Miller, and Norman Mailer. Published by Doubleday in 1969 as *Sexual Politics,* Millett's study is one of the central writings of second-wave feminism. Millett was cast into the spotlight, and during a time when feminists were eschewing individual glory and preaching equality among themselves, *Time* magazine splashed a picture of Millett across its cover to illustrate a story on feminism. Radical feminists vilified Millett for her supposed elitism. A few months later, she was challenged at a public forum to publicly admit her bisexuality. Millett did, and then faced the censure of the public as well as her family when her bisexuality was noted in the December 14, 1970, issue of *Time.* Even her work was called into question as it had not been before. Millett continued to lecture and teach, but the ensuing years were rough ones. Her family at one point had her committed to a mental institution. Millett has moved out of the spotlight but remains true to her cause and has written autobiographies, chronicles, and essays on women, including the books *Sita* (1977), *The Basement* (1980), *Going to Iran* (1982), *Looney-Bin Trip* (1991), and *The Politics of Cruelty: An Essay on the Literature of Political Imprisonment* (1994).

Robin Morgan (1941–)

Morgan was born in Florida but grew up in Mount Vernon, New York. A poet and essayist, she is one of the leaders of the early second wave of feminism. Her poems have appeared in both established and underground publications from the *Yale Review* and the *Atlantic* to *Rat.* Morgan had once been active in New Left politics but came to believe that the Leftist movement was a male-only club. Along with other women's liberationists, she staged a takeover of *Rat,* a major underground New Left newspaper, in 1970, and produced an all-woman version in which her essay "Goodbye to All That" appeared. This was a seminal essay that waved a definitive good-bye to male-dominated organizations of all kinds. Morgan is usually labeled a radical feminist and was the primary engineer behind the 1968 Miss America pageant demonstration. She stepped in as editor of *Ms.* magazine in 1990 when it reorganized into a no-advertisement format. She was editor of *Sisterhood Is Powerful: An Anthology of Writings from the Women's Liberation Movement* (1970) and is author of other feminist books including *Going Too Far: The Personal Chron-icle of a Feminist* (1977), *Demon Lover: On the Sexuality of Terrorism* (1990), *The Word of a Woman: Selected Prose* (1992), and *Anatomy of Freedom: Feminism in Four Dimensions* (1994).

Eleanor Holmes Norton (1937–)

Norton grew up in Washington, D.C., graduated from Antioch College, Ohio, in 1960, and earned a master's degree in American studies (1963) and a law degree from Yale University (1964). As an attorney, she was soon working for the American Civil Liberties Union (ACLU) in New York City, representing Vietnam War protesters, civil rights activists, Ku Klux Klansmen, and feminists. She specialized in freedom of speech cases. In 1970 she was appointed to the New York City Commission on Human Rights, where she immediately made clear that she would be zealously defending the principle of nondiscrimination and extending it to women. She worked for maternity benefits for female employees, supported the liberalization of abortion laws, helped to establish child-care centers at the workplace, helped institute affirmative action in New York City, and even opened the doors of a bar in a private men's club to women. In 1973, she helped found the National Black Feminist Organization to address the particular problems of African American feminists. Norton chaired the Equal Employment Opportunity Commission under President Jimmy Carter. She also held a tenured position as professor at the Georgetown University Law Center. In 1990 she was elected to Congress as a nonvoting delegate from the District of Columbia, the first woman elected to the district's seat. She has held her seat through subsequent elections and has served as vice chair of the Congressional Caucus on Women's Issues, on the Government Reform and Oversight Committee, and on the Transportation and Infrastructure Committee, as well as others. In a 1970 speech she expressed her understanding of feminism, saying, "No change in society has ever been seen or envisioned as deep as the prospect of equality of the sexes."

Camille Paglia (1947–)

Born in Endicott, New York, Paglia earned a B.A. in English from Harpur College of the State University of New York and a Ph.D. in English from Yale University (1974). Through the following years she taught at Bennington College, Wesleyan University, Yale University, the University of New Haven, and the University of the Arts in Philadelphia. Paglia gained national attention with her book *Sexual Personae: Art and Decadence from Nefertiti to Emily Dickinson,* a best-seller published in 1990. Paglia herself quickly became a thorn in the side of feminism. While declaring herself a modern feminist in support of reproductive, lesbian, and political rights, Paglia expressed utter contempt for modern feminism and its leaders. In *Sexual Personae* she stressed sexual stereotypes and a biological basis for gender differences. She also placed emphasis on personal responsibility and individualism, angering feminists with her evaluation of date rape: Strong women, she asserted, should take responsibility for judging a social situation and, if they misjudge it and are raped, accept the consequences and not make that mistake again. Her message was described as neoconservative, and Paglia gained attention as the new media darling. Her speaking style is staccato, and her opinions uncompromising. Paglia's ideal women are independent and strong-willed individuals who struggle valiantly against their feminine nature. She has advocated abolishing women's studies programs and has criticized feminist leaders as being victims of mushy thinking. Feminist leader Susan Faludi, in turn, criticized Paglia's work in a 1995 *Ms.* magazine article as being "packed with loopy observations about women, men, and feminism" (Faludi 1996, 33). Paglia's published works include a collection of essays titled *Sex, Art and American Culture* (1992) and *Vamps and Tramps: New Essays* (1994).

Adrienne Rich (1929–)

First and foremost, Rich is a poet and writer, one of the finest in America. She is also a feminist, and so she is claimed as a feminist poet. She was born in Baltimore, Maryland, and graduated cum laude from Radcliffe College in 1951, the same year her first book of poetry, *A Change of World,* was published. Rich was married from 1953 to 1970, when her husband died, and her writing and poetry of the time reflected her beginnings as a typical (extraordinarily talented) American woman of her generation. Her poetry changed with her as she moved through marriage, motherhood, fame, loss, and feminist awakening. By 1971 her poetry, which had been embraced by the literary community as works of beauty and power, was reflecting her political awareness and feminism.

Criticism of her work grew, focusing on its harsh depictions of males and its challenge to poetic conventions. She expanded her resume to books of prose, including *Of Woman Born: Motherhood as Experience and Institution* (1976), *On Lies, Secrets and Silence: Selected Prose, 1966–1978*, and *What Is Found There: Notebooks on Poetry and Politics* (1993). She also wrote a pamphlet, *Compulsory Heterosexuality and Lesbian Existence* (1980). She came out as a lesbian in 1976 and challenged the assumptions of heterosexuality that are part of today's world view. She has won numerous awards, recently including the Robert Frost Silver Medal for Lifetime Achievement in Poetry from the Poetry Society of America (1992) and the Lambda Book Award in Lesbian Poetry (1992). She won the National Book Award for poetry in 1974 and accepted it not as an individual but on behalf of the other two poets nominated, Audre Lorde and Alice Walker, and "in the name of all the women whose voices have gone and still go unheard in a patriarchal world." In her 1986 book, *Blood, Bread and Poetry: Selected Prose, 1979–1986*, she suggests that heterosexuality is a political institution and should be studied as such; she also asserts that heterosexuality is imposed on women as compulsory to their acceptance. It also supports the system of patriarchy that withholds equality from women. In many ways, Rich has been the poet of the feminist movement, opening new lines of communication and voicing the feminist perspective on the hard truths of a woman's place.

Patricia Schroeder (1940–)

Schroeder served as a strong and confident voice for feminist causes throughout her 24 years in Congress as a U.S. representative from Colorado, 1972–1997. She was born in Portland, Oregon, and attended the University of Minnesota, graduating magna cum laude and Phi Beta Kappa in 1961. She earned a law degree from Harvard Law School in 1964, married classmate James Schroeder, and moved to Denver, Colorado. She worked for the National Labor Relations Board and later as legal counsel for Planned Parenthood of Colorado. She also became active in Democratic Party campaigns, working as a precinct committeewoman in 1968 and 1969. Her husband, defeated in a bid for Colorado state legislature in 1970, turned his focus to campaign management. He needed someone to run on the Democratic ticket against an incumbent Republican representative who was considered unbeatable. Pat Schroeder ran, beating the incumbent, and became the first woman sent to the U.S. Congress from Colorado. As a member of the House Armed Services Committee, Schroeder brought a new voice to the discussions of military budgets, one that questioned funding of increasingly volatile nuclear weapons. She also championed legislation to fight child abuse and to provide school lunches and preschool programs; she established her own pro-choice position, fought for many forms of equal rights legislation for women, and authored the Family and Medical Leave Act. She declined to run for reelection in 1996, voluntarily retiring from Congress.

Eleanor Smeal (1939–)

Born in Ashtabula, Ohio, Smeal was educated at Duke University, then earned a master's degree in political science and public administration at the University of Florida in 1963. She became nationally known when she took over the presidency of the National Organization for Women in 1977. She worked her way up in NOW, beginning with the presidency of the NOW chapter in South Hills, a suburb of Pittsburgh, in 1971. In 1972 she was elected president of Pennsylvania NOW. The next year she was elected to the board of directors of NOW, and in 1975 she became its chairperson. She was a vocal proponent of grassroots organization, arguing that NOW would be strengthened by a broad-based system rather than a centralized one. She was a housewife as well, and she appealed to other housewives across the country. She was elected president of NOW in a heated battle and became one of the women's movement's most beloved and effective leaders. She built NOW into a mass-membership organization and led a nationwide campaign for the Equal Rights Amendment. She also initiated NOW political action committees at all levels of government. The first to identify the gender gap in voting, Smeal popularized the use of the term in the media. She led the organization back to the streets to fight for abortion rights in the 1980s. In 1987 she cofounded the Feminist Majority and the Feminist Majority Foundation. Since then, as the president of the Feminist Majority, Smeal has put her considerable strategic skills to work for the Feminization of Power Campaign, which recruits women to run for public office. Also, she works for gender balance in government appointees, and on education and research projects that empower women in business and public leadership.

Gloria Steinem (1934–)

Steinem was born in Toledo, Ohio, but moved often until the age of twelve, when her parents separated and she settled with her mother in Toledo. Steinem spent most of her teen years caring for her mother, who suffered from severe depression and anxiety. She moved to Washington, D.C., to live with her older sister for her last year of high school and then attended Smith College, graduating in 1956 with a B.A. in government. She became a journalist, writing for major magazines such as *Esquire* and *Vogue*, and didn't begin to seriously focus on feminism for another ten years. At a speakout on abortion held by the Redstockings in 1968, Steinem, who had had an illegal abortion herself, felt a connection to the movement. She quickly became an unofficial spokesperson for the movement and in 1971, along with Shirley Chisholm, Betty Friedan, and Bella Abzug, founded the National Women's Political Caucus. She next helped found the Women's Action Alliance. She is founding editor of *Ms.* magazine, which debuted in 1972. The magazine gave feminists a forum to circulate their thoughts and ideas on a broad, national level, and it was immediately successful. Since those early years of the second wave of feminism, Steinem has continued to be a high-profile spokesperson for the women's movement, sometimes accepted as an insider by feminists, sometimes an outsider, more a journalist than a political organizer. She is a founder of the Ms. Foundation for Women and Voters for Choice. She has written numerous essays, combining her considerable journalistic skills with her innate wit to reveal the patriarchal culture's more ridiculous underpinnings and to simultaneously undermine them as well. She has compiled several of these essays into books. Her best-known to date include *Outrageous Acts and Everyday Rebellions* (1984), *Revolution from Within* (1992), and *Moving beyond Words* (1994).

Alice Walker (1944–)

Born in Eatonton, Georgia, Alice Walker grew up in a working-poor family. Her father was a sharecropper and dairy farmer. Her mother worked as a maid as well as farm help. Walker deeply admired her mother, a strong and capable woman. A BB-gun accident in 1952 left Walker blind in one eye, and scar tissue formed a disfiguring layer over the eye. The scar tissue wasn't removed until she was fourteen, and she spent her adolescent years feeling like an outcast from other children, who taunted her. Her work as an adult feminist and author has often addressed outcasts and the unnecessary scars of life. She graduated from Sarah Lawrence College in 1965 and worked for civil rights. She married Melvyn Leventhal, a Jewish civil rights lawyer, and moved to Mississippi; they were the first legally married interracial couple in Jackson, Mississippi. (They divorced in 1976.) Walker published essays on the civil rights movement and began her fiction writing with *The Third Life of Grange Copeland* (1970). She lectured at Wellesley College and the University of Massachusetts and wrote poetry and short stories, building a body of work that focused more and more on the lives of African American women. Her third novel, *The Color Purple* (1982), brought her a Pulitzer Prize, an American Book Award, and celebrity status. The novel focuses on a black woman dominated and oppressed by a black man and her successful struggle to become her own woman. Walker coined the term "womanist" for a feminist woman of color. In 1992 she tackled the subject of female genital mutilation (FGM) in her book *Possessing the Secret of Joy*. The following year she and Pratibha Parmar made the film *Warrior Marks*, which revealed the practice of FGM and was accompanied by a book, *Warrior Marks: Female Genital Mutilation and the Sexual Blinding of Women*. Her writings also include poetry and the book *Anything We Love Can Be Saved: A Writer's Activism* (1997).

Faye Wattleton (1943–)

Wattleton was born in St. Louis, Missouri, to a fundamentalist Christian family. Her mother was in the ministry and, though supportive of her daughter, has stood in philosophical opposition to Wattleton's work for women's reproductive freedom. Wattleton graduated with a nursing degree from Ohio State University in 1964 and a master's degree from Columbia University with a specialty in midwifery in 1967. During her nursing training she witnessed the results of botched illegal abortions, and these experiences awakened her to the hardships faced by women. In 1970, she became executive director of the Dayton Planned Parenthood board. During her tenure there, abortion became legal throughout the United States with the *Roe v. Wade* Supreme Court decision. Antiabortion militancy grew, and Wattleton witnessed the violence that women's clinic workers faced: arson attacks, bombings, death threats, and personal assaults.

Wattleton was appointed president of the national Planned Parenthood Federation of America (PPFA) in 1978 and held that position until 1991. She was the first woman and the first African American president of PPFA. Wattleton brought Planned Parenthood from its cautious position of noncommitment on abortion into the role of advocate for the pro-choice movement. She also brought the organization into the media spotlight as a pro-choice voice standing in opposition to the vocal antiabortion groups. During the Reagan administration, Wattleton led Planned Parenthood in opposing federal budget cuts to family planning in the United States and in the international arena. After the 1989 Supreme Court decision *Webster v. Reproductive Health Services* gave states rights to restrict abortions, Wattleton led a state-by-state campaign to protect women's abortion rights. She left Planned Parenthood in 1992 and established the Center for Gender Equity, a think tank focusing on women's issues. She has won numerous awards for her humanitarian service and has published her memoir, *Life on the Line* (1996).

Naomi Wolf (1963–)

Wolf has been heralded as a voice of the third wave, and she has been a controversial one. A native of San Francisco, she earned a bachelor's degree from Yale University in 1984, won a Rhodes scholarship, and studied at Oxford University from 1984 to 1987. She left Oxford before completing her doctoral research on the use of beauty in nineteenth- and twentieth-century literature. Her first book, *The Beauty Myth: How Images of Beauty Are Used against Women* (1991), was a controversial best-seller. It presented her theory that a requirement that women maintain a level of male-defined beauty and style is one way that the culture holds and traps women in a second-place position. Though she was careful not to present her thesis as a conspiracy of men working purposely to oppose women, it was interpreted that way by many of her critics. Others, however, agreed with her, and her ideas have since been incorporated into general feminist discourse. Her second book, *Fire with Fire: The New Female Power and How to Use It* (1993), again struck a chord of controversy. In it, she urges women to put their full political and personal power to use. It is a strong feminist message intended to boost women onto the next tier of equality. She was taken to task by many feminists for a section in the book that reflects her stance on abortion. She is staunchly pro-choice, she wrote, yet she adds: "But I would need to be able to talk about an abortion, if I had one, as the death of something, if of no more than a fragment of the self, or the ghost of a human union, or a fingerprint of incarnation. I would have to be allowed to cast it into the realm of the spirit" (p. 131). With this statement, and with subsequent essays, she called on feminists to add a moral dimension and a dialogue about life and death, and right and wrong, to their defense of abortion. *Ms.* magazine responded in 1997 by presenting a panel discussion on abortion that grappled with the complexities of the rights of women to determine the uses of their own bodies, as well as the life of a fetus. Wolf has written numerous articles for national publications. Her third book, *Promiscuities: The Secret Struggle for Womanhood* (1997), deals with the cultural barriers and distortions that face young women in America and keep them from reaching confident adult sexuality.

References

Faludi, Susan. 1996 (March/April). "I'm Not a Feminist But I Play One on TV." *Ms.*, p. 33.

Lorde, Audre. 1978. Comments at the Personal and the Political Panel, Second Sex Conference, New York, September 29, 1978. Reprinted, 1984, in *Sister Outsider.* Freedom, Calif.: The Crossing Press, p. 112.

Schneir, Miriam, ed. 1994. *Feminism in Our Time: The Essential Writings, World War II to the Present.* New York: Random House.

Facts: Feminist Issues, Social Changes, and Education

4

Feminists

Defining Feminism

Feminists identify themselves as people who support political, economic, and social equality for women. This is a tidy definition and fits the ideals that feminists espouse. Most people in the United States say they agree with the idea of equality for women: 71 percent of women and 61 percent of men agreed in a 1995 National Women's Equality Poll conducted for the Feminist Majority. That would make them feminists by definition. Yet, in that same poll only 51 percent of the women volunteered to identify themselves as feminists.

Feminism for much of mass culture has become equated with lesbianism, male bashing, or male hating; for many it has also come to be defined narrowly as encompassing only women of European heritage. Yet, these views contradict feminist history. The feminist movement has never been as monolithically one-noted as it has been portrayed. From the beginning, women have differed in their approaches to change and in their worldviews. Ideologically, feminists have always been divided into "equality" and "difference" feminism. Today the movement is more varied than ever, with feminists also identifying themselves according to race and ethnic heritage as well as to political or social agendas. In the following few pages we will take a look at each of the subgroups, or "schools," of feminist ideology.

Liberal (Equality) Feminism

Liberal feminists are individualists who stress the importance of freedom, especially the freedom to choose. They see more similarities between women and men than differences and envision a community of equitable opportunity for both sexes. They also see most stereotypically masculine or feminine traits as culturally imposed. They view choice as an absolute right, and they seek control over the body and social circumstance. They strive to avoid the imprint of gender codes and the gender socialization of children, looking instead for an authentic, unengineered, and individual approach to life (Elshtain 1991). Some of today's liberal feminists describe themselves as equality feminists and see a link between themselves and first-wave or early second-wave feminists. Rene Denfeld calls herself an equality feminist, explaining, "I believe women should have the same opportunities and rights as men. What they do with those opportunities and rights is their business; the point is that they have them" (Denfeld 1995, 267). She eschews the alternative feminist trend of focusing on differences.

Cultural (Difference) Feminism

Emerging in the 1970s and becoming a strong voice by the 1980s, cultural feminism attempts to revalue the feminine aspects that have been devalued in society. It celebrates all things female, whether these derive from social, class, or biological circumstances of women's lives. But difference feminists, too, see many gender traits as biological, or at least deeply structured cultural, traits. They celebrate the differences between women and men, seeing feminine qualities as a source of personal strength and pride and providing the affirmation that women occupy the moral high ground. Instead of political change, cultural feminism focuses on cultural transformation, stressing the role of the nonrational, intuitive, collective side of life (Freeman 1995). This thread of reasoning can be traced through feminist history to first-wave debates within feminist circles. Those debates centered on the need for women's input in government as guiding, moral voices—the conscience of the nation. (First-wave difference feminists also argued for protective labor legislation for women.)

Radical Feminism

Also stressing the differences between females and males, radical feminism values women and likens males to a separate species. Whether the difference is biological or gendered by society is not at issue; the results of male difference and dominance are. According to the radical feminist ideology, the violence of the heterosexual male has led to the patriarchal and hierarchical cultures of today. Further, the male has oppressed and victimized the female through pornography, violence, and the militarization of the world.

Marxist and Socialist Feminism

Feminists who agree with the tenets of Marxist and socialist feminism believe women are seen as a sex-class, gendered by society into a secondary position through a systemic sex gender system that dictates social roles, purposes, and norms. These feminists believe that women are exploited as both a sex and a class, and that women are consigned to reproduction and their natures tethered. Men take the roles of goods production and potentially reach freedom (Elshtain 1991). To change this situation, Marxist and socialist feminists seek an end to gendered socialization, an alliance of oppressed groups, and a beginning of a sharing of the wealth.

Ecofeminism

Growing from the idea of women's values as separate from men's and also as closer to nature, ecofeminism revalues and defines feminine traits. Women are seen as in tune with nature and seeking to work in conjunction with it; men have a hierarchical relationship to nature and seek to control it. This view poses the idea that men's control of nature up to now has created a crisis, an ecocide, in much of the world. Ecofeminists look for life-affirming and nonviolent solutions to world problems. They would endorse sustained development but condemn clear-cutting of forests. Ecofeminists see feminine values as virtues needed by the world's patriarchy to survive and evolve. Ecofeminists may also subscribe to liberal, radical, or Marxist/socialist thought, but they focus on the environment and nature (Elshtain 1991, Merchant 1990).

Racial, Ethnic, and Gendered Feminist Identity
Black Feminism

Though African American feminists may not have been included in early mainstream second-wave feminism, they have
always been a vocal presence in feminist criticism and ideology.
Racism, they have said, is a problem that lives alongside sexism.
And so is classism (the hierarchy created by a caste-like economic and social class system). They have demanded that feminists consider the problems of racism and classism along with
sexism; further, they have explained the interlacing interconnec-
tions from racism to sexism to classism. Sexism cannot truly be
understood without understanding its racist undertones; by the
same token, racism embodies sexism. They have refuted the
stereotypes of black women as matriarchs and superwomen and
have spearheaded movements to gain economic and political
clout for women of color. African American women support numerous feminist and women's issues organizations, some of
them chiefly for women of color. They are also part of the general feminist movement and leadership, both in the United
States and globally.

Feminism with Other Racial or Ethnic Heritage

Many women in the United States hesitated to join the mainstream of second-wave feminism at first. Women of color, along
with women with strong ethnic and religious ties, had more to
consider than Euro-white women in their quest for liberation.
Latina, Puerto Rican, Native American, and Asian American
feminists have all had to balance the needs and demands of
their cultures with their feminist desires. These needs and demands vary from culture to culture and are often met by separate organizations and activities. Some feminists also form
coalitions and networks and maintain active memberships in
mainstream feminist organizations. Women in religious organizations, especially Catholic, Jewish, and Muslim women, have
worked to balance their feminism with the doctrines of their religions. Many also continue to seek religious reform. The myriad of views that these women are now bringing to feminism in
America is adding depth to the feminist movement, and it is
also adding wisdom to the American feminist voice in the
global feminist movement.

Male Feminists

Men can be feminists, too, and have been from the beginning of the women's movement. Frederick Douglass, Henry Stanton, and Lucy Stone's husband, Henry Blackwell, were some of feminism's greatest early allies. Men have continued to be allies, supporters, and mentors of feminists. They may, of course, also consider themselves to be ecofeminists, cultural feminists, liberal feminists, and so on. Usually, their goal is to see beyond the accepted stereotypes of males that they have grown up with, to create nonsexist relationships, to join in the battle to end violence against women, and to develop partnerships with women instead of hierarchies.

Feminist Eras

In this book and elsewhere, feminism is often discussed in terms of eras, or "waves." Following is an explanation of the three waves of American feminism.

First Wave

The feminists who fought for suffrage in the United States and beyond, beginning with the meeting in Seneca Falls, New York, in 1848 and culminating with winning the right to vote in 1920, are today called the first wave. These were women who broke through the barriers of their day to speak in public, to demand property rights, and to claim a political voice. Susan B. Anthony, Elizabeth Cady Stanton, Lucretia Mott, Sojourner Truth, and Lucy Stone are the women most well known for their leadership in the first wave.

Second Wave

Taking up the cause of women's rights in the early to mid-1960s, these feminists—Bella Abzug, Betty Friedan, Gloria Steinem, and others—founded feminist organizations and raised the consciousness of the women and men of the country. The second wave focused on winning pay equity for women, access to jobs and education, recognition of women's unpaid labor in the home, and a rebalancing of the double workload of family and outside work for women in the paid labor force. The wave began with the founding of women's liberation groups that took New

Left political groups such as the Students for a Democratic Society as their models. Soon after, they were joined by other groups that sought political change within the system and through political organizations of their own, forming feminist groups and the mass of the second wave. This second wave is usually considered to have begun about 1963 and run until the backlash of the 1980s, when feminism is seen as having stagnated.

Third Wave

The third wave consists of many of the daughters and sons of the second wave. These feminists grew up with many of the advantages that the second wave fought for, and their issues are today's issues—parental leave and day care for the children of working parents, gaining decision-making positions in corporate and governmental high offices, worldwide sustainable development, and a global awareness of feminist causes. The third wave is a global surge, with coalitions and networks forming to support individual feminist advances. Many second-wave feminists are a part of this third wave. In the United States, the third wave is multicultural and inclusive, supporting women of all heritages as well as the rights of lesbian women and gay men.

Some of these third-wave feminists are issuing a challenge to the older feminists. They see feminist rhetoric as entrenched in victimization, with an emphasis on the oppression engendered by a patriarchal system. They grew up in a country transformed by second-wave feminist leaders, with established equal employment and education laws, access to birth control and legal abortion, support within police departments for prosecution of rapists, and women holding a vocal presence in politics. Much is different for the third wave, and their self-image is distinctly different from that of second-wave feminists. Many third wavers see women as fundamentally strong, confidant, brave individuals. They seek to establish that image of women within the public consciousness, and they look for greater integration of women into politics, economics, and social forums.

Feminist Issues in the United States

The primary goal of feminists in the United States is fairness. No matter what avenue they use to seek fairness, most feminists will agree on a few basic issues of concern. One group of issues has to do with access, the other with control.

Feminists seek access to:

- *Education.* Fair consideration for scholarships, inclusion in athletic programs, and equal treatment in the class-room head the feminist list. Feminists also seek access to programs and institutions that women have tradition-ally been steered away from, such as engineering and science programs.
- *Economics.* Feminists seek equal access for women to jobs and careers, equal pay, and equal consideration for pro-motions and career enhancement once they are on the job. Many also seek a more flexible, family-friendly workplace and a less hierarchical management structure.
- *Politics.* Feminists seek a 50 percent voice for women in decision making at all levels of government, from local school boards to the White House.

Feminists seek a change in control over:

- *Reproduction.* Feminists seek reproductive freedom for all women. For most feminists, this means an end to laws restricting women's access to abortion. It also means reproduction and sexuality education and avail-ability of birth control to females.
- *Sexuality.* Most feminists support the right of a woman to define her own sexuality and to be free as a heterosexual or a lesbian. In today's society, lesbians face continued discrimination and subtle—as well as blatant—forms of restrictions to their lives. Heterosexual feminists and les-bian feminists share common goals: to unlock women from their male-defined roles and to end the power of the threat of being labeled a lesbian, a threat that has si-lenced many women, lesbian and heterosexual alike.
- *Violence.* The various forms of violence against women exercise control over women's mobility and personal freedom. Feminists seek to end the prevalence of do-mestic violence, sexual harassment, and rape. Some also see pornography as a contributing factor to violence against women, and they seek to control it.
- *Society.* Regardless of how they envision society today, most feminists agree on a desire for a transformation of it, one that values women equally to men. Because con-

trol over women is exercised by norms (standards of acceptable behavior and expectations) established by men, feminists seek to redefine the norms. They seek to change society's vision of women as "the other" and to give women equal voice and status in the outside world as well as in the home.

Feminist Issues Globally

Globally, feminists seek change in many of the same categories as feminists in the United States, with the same issues of fairness on the forefront of global feminists' agendas. Feminists worldwide also are concerned with the same issues of access and control. In many European and developed countries, feminists have led women to similar changes as the American feminists have wrought. In most of the developing countries, though, the work of feminists is on a more fundamental level.

In some regions the feminist issues are simply the right of a woman to earn and carry her own money, the right to own property, the right to drive a car, or the right to a divorce. In countries where literacy of girls lags behind that of boys, the issue may be the right of females to attend school. In some, it is the right of women to be included in government programs for development of land and business; in others, the issue is environmental sustainability and inclusion of women in the decision making concerning these programs. For almost all feminists, an issue of great concern is political influence and representation, along with economic independence.

Globally, feminists seek greater control for women over their own lives, including reproductive freedom. They seek an end to the violence against women in their homes and regions. This violence includes wife beating, incest, marital rape, and forced prostitution. In some regions it includes female genital mutilation; in others, it includes rape and torture as war crimes.

The variety of women's lives and concerns on a global level is multitudinous, for women live in a myriad of social, economic, and political systems. But feminists are connected globally by the threads of the issues that concern all—access and control.

Equal Rights Amendments

An Equal Rights Amendment (ERA) was first proposed in 1923 by the National Woman's Party (NWP), a militant suffrage organization led by Alice Paul. To win suffrage for women, the NWP staged hunger strikes and picketed the White House; after attaining suffrage, NWP members saw the ERA as the next step toward equality. When they first introduced it in Congress in 1923, the amendment met with immediate opposition from labor unions and many women's organizations. The women's organizations were chiefly motivated by fears that the Equal Rights Amendment would overturn protective labor laws, such as maximum hour laws, that they had fought so hard to obtain for women and children. Labor unions were motivated by fears that those laws, which kept women out of many jobs, would force them to allow women to compete on an equal basis, or to extend the protections to men.

The ERA was turned down in 1923, but the NWP and feminists supporting it did not give up. Every year, they came back to Congress to introduce the amendment again. And every year, they were turned down, not even coming close to winning Congressional approval through the 1920s, 1930s, and 1940s. But the amendment did gain some popular support, winning the endorsements in the 1930s of the National Federation of Business and Professional Women's Clubs (BPW) and the National Association of Women Lawyers. In 1940, the Republican Party included it in its platform; in 1944, the Democratic Party added it. In 1950 and 1953, the Senate approved the ERA but attached a rider to it excluding protective labor laws; in the House, Rep. Emmanuel Celler, the chair of the House Judiciary Committee and a staunch opponent of the ERA, made sure the amendment never left his committee; the amendment seemingly could go no further. Yet, feminists would not let the issue die.

In 1967, Betty Friedan brought up the Equal Rights Amendment at the National Organization for Women's (NOW) annual convention. Many NOW members were afraid they would lose union support for their other efforts if they endorsed the ERA, but Friedan argued for the amendment's essential importance to women. Even more effective, however, was that in the front row of the convention hall sat a line of elderly suffragists who had fought for the right to vote. They spoke to the young women present, and that seemed to turn the tide: NOW voted to support the amendment. Work on getting the amendment through Congress and into states for ratification began in earnest. Finally, on March 22, 1972, the amendment was overwhelmingly passed by the U.S. Senate with a vote of 84 to 8. On that same day, Hawaii ratified it. By the end of 1977, 35 of the necessary 38 states had ratified it (see Figure 4.1).

Figure 4.1

Ratification of the Equal Rights Amendment, 1972–1977

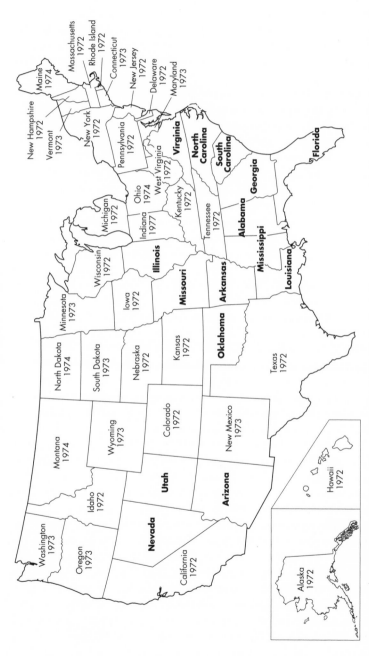

Note: In 1977, the U.S. Justice Department under President Carter's administration issued an opinion that a state's recision of its ratification of the Equal Rights Amendment was in violation of the law and of the Constitution. Three states had voted for recision: Idaho, Tennessee, and Nebraska.

Sources: Toni Carabillo, Judith Meuli, and June Bundy Csida, *Feminist Chronicles: 1953–1993* (Los Angeles: Women's Graphics, 1993); Jane J. Mansbridge, *Why We Lost the ERA* (Chicago: University of Chicago Press, 1986).

ERA supporters were confident, and public opinion polls showed that American voters supported the amendment. On average, a series of surveys taken during the years between 1970 and 1982 found that 57 percent supported the ERA, 32 percent opposed it, and 11 percent had no opinion (Mansbridge 1986). The opposition that was present, though, was building a strong coalition of politicians. The opponents were chiefly religious and political conservatives who feared that the ERA threatened traditional lifestyles, and they were active on many levels.

Conservative politician and lobbyist Phyllis Schlafly's efforts to thwart the passage of the amendment is what most feminists point to as embodying the most successful attack against feminist goals and the most effective tool against the ERA. Schlafly, a Harvard-educated lawyer and a two-time Congressional candidate (1952 and 1970), launched the Stop ERA campaign to save "the marvelous legal rights of woman to be a full-time wife and mother in the house supported by her husband" (Faludi 1991, 239). A good speaker with a smart style of turning a phrase, Schlafly took on the ERA and is credited with creating momentum and cohesion for the amendment's opposition. She succeeded in redefining the debate over the Equal Rights Amendment. Before long, feminist leaders on television found themselves arguing not over women's human rights but over women being forced to share public restrooms with males.

Schlafly lobbied legislatures, too, with her own brand of ultrafeminine antifeminism. She delivered apple pies, jars of homemade jam tied with ribbons, and steaming loaves of home-baked bread to state legislators; her slogan: "From the breadmakers to the breadwinners" (Cohen 1988, 260). She testified before 30 state legislatures. She touched on the hidden fears of women who were untrained for the working world and unwelcome if they chose to venture there. But she was not fighting the battle singlehandedly. Behind her were powerful interests such as insurance companies, real estate lobbies, and other special interests.

When the 1979 deadline for ratification arrived and the number of ratified states still stood at 35, feminist leaders managed to get the deadline extended to 1982. By this time, a clear picture of conservative versus liberal forces had emerged. In 1980, the Republican Party reversed its endorsement of the ERA, leaving it out of its platform for the first time in 40 years. Meanwhile, the Southern states, joined by a few others, held out against ratification. Feminists concentrated their efforts on states that seemed to offer some hope of ratification: Illinois, North Carolina, Oklahoma, and Florida. In the end, some feminists would say that the decision to ratify or not ended up in the hands of just a few men. The Florida discussion ended with a vote of 22 to 16—in defeat of ratification.

Most of the laws that the ERA would have overturned have since been struck down—many during the ERA battle. In the end, many feminists saw the defeat of the ERA as a symbolic defeat. Feminist writer Miriam Schneir explains: "To most women it seemed a matter of simple justice and self-respect that the keystone of the nation's legal edifice should extend to female citizens the same protection and rights as it offered to male citizens" (Schneir 1994, 371). The symbolic point of the word "women" in the Constitution was the loss. But other feminists see the defeat differently. Political scholar Jane J. Mansbridge sees it as "a major setback for equality between men and women." The direct effects of the amendment would have been minimal, she explains, "but its indirect effects on both judges and legislators would probably have led in the long run to interpretations of existing laws and enactment of new laws that would have benefited women" (Mansbridge 1986, 2).

Today, some states have passed their own versions of the Equal Rights Amendment. These states include Alaska, Colorado, Connecticut, Hawaii, Illinois, Maryland, Massachusetts, Montana, New Hampshire, New Mexico, Pennsylvania, Texas, Utah, Virginia, Washington, and Wyoming (Feminist Majority Foundation 1995a).

Equal Rights Amendment—1923 Version

Men and women shall have equal rights throughout the United States and in every place subject to its jurisdiction. Congress shall have power to enforce this article by appropriate legislation.

Equal Rights Amendment—1972 Version

1. Equality of rights under the law shall not be denied or abridged by the United States or by any state on account of sex.
2. The Congress shall have the power to enforce, by appropriate legislation, the provisions of this article.

3. This amendment shall take effect two years after the date of ratification.

Global Commitment to Equal Rights

A feminist-inspired global commitment to equal rights for women has been gathering force over the past 20 years. Some of the strongest instruments of change have been the global women's conventions (see Global Feminist Meetings in Chapter 5). At these conventions, women have had the unprecedented opportunity to reach across cultural boundaries and find shared understanding and need for change. They leave the conventions with renewed hope and energy, backed by proven strategies, for work in their own countries and regions.

Measuring women's equality in countries around the world has been based on a combination of several factors: access to education, access to jobs and inclusion in economic spheres, representation in government, women's own control over their health and reproduction, and freedom from domestic violence and institutionalized, gender-based violence and restrictions. (Refer to the sections in this book on these issues for information on the global status of women.)

One of the tools for effecting change toward equality is the Convention on the Elimination of All Forms of Discrimination Against Women (CEDAW) that was passed by the United Nations in 1979. (It has been ratified by 139 of the 185 UN members, not including the United States.) Feminists studying global equality point out that other conventions have also been passed by the UN. These address equal pay, equal marriage rights (free consent, minimum age), maternity leave rights, and political rights. The CEDAW, however, is the most comprehensive convention on women's rights.

These global conventions and the work of activist women are affecting change for women in many societies, but real equality is still an unattained goal. In many countries, religious and customary laws take precedence over CEDAW, and these customary laws are instructive of women's position. For example, more than 40 countries in the world have majority Muslim populations, and an Islamic legal system rules in at least half of them. These systems include laws that govern family behavior, condone purdah (the exclusion of women from public observance), and support or require sex segregation at all levels, unequal inheritance based on gender, and divorce regulations favoring men. Muslim women often are required to wear a *hijab,* the dark, voluminous covering that conceals a woman's shape and face from view. Also, in Sub-Saharan Africa, many countries allow exceptions to the equality they express in their national constitutions; for example, Kenya exempts inheritance of property from gender equality; Burundi allows a wife to work only with the consent of her husband; Zimbabwe rules that the oldest son inherits a father's property, even if an older daughter is living; and Somalia officially permits female genital mutilation (Sivard 1995).

In addition, in countries everywhere, from Asia to South America, to Europe and North America, equal rights for women are unachieved goals. Women hold fewer seats than men in government everywhere; women lag behind in education, spending less time in school in developing countries and earning fewer degrees in the sciences in developed countries; women hold fewer high-paying jobs, whether that means being paid well in a factory or earning top executive salaries; and women have less control over their own health than men, facing more responsibility for, and restrictions over, their reproductive freedom and health.

Redefining women's rights as human rights will, feminist activists hope, help all women. That redefinition began at the 1993 World Conference on Human Rights in Vienna, Austria. It has continued through subsequent conferences, and feminist activists hope that women's rights as human rights will be a strong foundation for future equal rights.

Lesbian Rights

Lesbians have been a powerful, though initially denied, force in the feminist movement. Their contributions to feminism helped form the basis of feminist philosophy, and their activism helped form the political base for feminist change. In the early days of second-wave feminism a few dates stand out as significant for lesbian feminists:

1969   The modern lesbian and gay rights movement begins when patrons at the Stonewall Inn fight back against New York City police who come to harass them.

1970   Betty Friedan, president of the National Organiza-
            tion for Women, names lesbians the "lavender men-
            ace" threatening the feminist movement. She views
            lesbian rights as a distraction from the main issues of
            women's rights.

            At the Second Congress to Unite Women, in New
            York City, at the end of the evening's program, the
            lights dim, and when they come on again, the 400
            women gathered there see 20 women before them, all
            with T-shirts that say "Lavender Menace." They de-
            mand attention to lesbian issues and call on feminists
            to come forward in support. The Lavender Menaces
            form the Radicalesbians, a separatist lesbian group
            that allows nonlesbians to join. They write a paper ti-
            tled "The Woman-Identified Woman," which is
            printed in the underground magazines *Rat* and *Come
            Out!* They want recognition within the feminist
            movement, and the fight that ensues is bitter.

            NOW "purges" lesbians from its organization lead-
            ership by actively working to keep lesbians from
            being elected or reelected to national or New York of-
            fices. The purge is led by Betty Friedan. Many femi-
            nists resign from NOW during this period, including
            author Rita Mae Brown.

            After a December 14 *Time* magazine article mentions
            Kate Millett's bisexuality, several women demon-
            strate their support for Millett at a rally for abortion
            and child care. Someone hands everyone a lavender
            arm band to wear; feminists Gloria Steinem and Flo
            Kennedy wear them, but Betty Friedan refuses.

            Feminists hold a "Kate is Great" press conference on
            December 18, with a banner stating, "We Stand To-
            gether as Women Regardless of Sexual Preference."
            Gloria Steinem sits beside Millett, holding her hand
            in support. Kate Millett's statement reads, in part:

                Women's liberation and homosexual liber-
                ation are both struggling towards a com-

1970
(cont.)

mon goal: a society free from defining and categorizing people by virtue of gender and/or sexual preference. "Lesbian" is a label used as a psychic weapon to keep women locked into their male-defined "feminine role." The essence of that role is that a woman is defined in terms of her relationship to men. A woman is called a lesbian when she functions autonomously. Women's autonomy is what women's liberation is all about. (Cohen 1988, 250)

1971

NOW votes to include lesbian and gay rights as feminist issues. The organization issues a Lesbian Rights resolution, which begins by admitting that NOW has been silent on the issue of lesbianism, acknowledges the double oppression of lesbians, and concludes with:

> BE IT FURTHER RESOLVED: That a woman's right to her own person includes the right to define and express her own sexuality and to choose her own lifestyle, and
> BE IT FURTHER RESOLVED: That NOW acknowledges the oppression of lesbians as a legitimate concern of feminism. (Carabillo, Meuli, and Csida 1993, 223)

1972

The Furies collective, a Washington, D.C., lesbian feminist group, is established. Early leaders include Charlotte Bunch and Rita Mae Brown. The women of the Furies withdraw from the feminist movement to develop a lesbian-feminist political analysis, culture, and movement. The group helps define lesbian feminism but is torn by political disagreement and disbands a year later.

1975

NOW includes lesbian and gay rights as a national priority. Betty Friedan helps lead a successful campaign to include lesbian rights in NOW's U.S. Plan of Action (Ireland 1996).

1977   Lesbian and gay rights are included as one of the three main issues facing feminists at the National Women's Conference in Houston, along with passage of the Equal Rights Amendment and abortion rights.

1979   The first National March for Lesbian and Gay Rights is held in Washington, D.C.; over 100,000 people attend.

Though meetings of straight and lesbian feminists often have been fraught with argument, even acrimony, most feminist leaders today have embraced the feminist lesbian contingent's quest for an equal voice within feminism's meetings, as well as for equality in the greater world. And today lesbian rights and gay rights are supported by the National Organization for Women and other major women's groups with the same fervor with which the organizations support other minority rights. History is now beginning to clarify that lesbians, many of whom "came out of the closet" as they worked for the feminist cause, have been a valuable part of the women's movement. Their homosexuality has been used, though, as a way of discrediting them and, by extension, the women's movement. When *Time* magazine revealed Kate Millett's bisexuality to the nation, for example, it added: "The disclosure is bound to discredit her as a spokeswoman for her cause, cast further doubt on her theories, and reinforce the views of those skeptics who routinely dismiss all liberationists as lesbians" ("Women's Lib" 1970). Through the years, lesbians' persistence in the women's movement—and the return support of straight feminists for the lesbian cause—has mitigated the effect of accusations of homosexuality. Yet the accusations continue.

The ideological contribution of lesbian feminists includes some in-depth critiques of the patriarchal, heterosexual culture. The Radicalesbians in "The Woman-Identified Woman" clarified the roles that women have played, noting that all feminine roles are male-identified. The male "confirms our womanhood—as he defines it, in relation to him," the Radicalesbians wrote, and added, "As long as we are dependent on the male culture for this definition, for this approval, we cannot be free" (Radicalesbians 1972, 166).

Lesbian feminist Adrienne Rich calls heterosexuality a compulsory institution of modern society that reinforces and enforces male dominance while tying women to male concepts of womanhood and to economic dependency on males (Rich 1986). She and other lesbian feminists issued a challenge to these institutional assumptions. Their challenges helped not only lesbians dealing with stereotypes but heterosexual feminists attempting to develop equitable female-male relationships.

Out of these writings and others developed the ideology of woman identification and separatism from male institutions. Also came the affirmation of the concept of women as essentially different in temperament from men. In this the lesbian feminists separated from many of the feminists of the 1970s, who at that time espoused an androgynous philosophy and equality feminism. This ideology of difference contributed to the growing base of cultural feminism, which was a strong force of the 1980s (Ransdell 1995). In the 1990s, many lesbians continue to be activists for the feminist cause, and feminists continue to support lesbian rights.

Reproductive Freedom

Women's reproductive freedom is at the heart of the feminist consciousness—so it has been since the beginning of the second wave, and it continues to be today. Faye Wattleton, former president of Planned Parenthood Federation of America, describes the feminist position succinctly: "The bottom line is that if you can't control your reproduction, you're not likely to be controlling anything else. There is a centrality about that that we must not obfuscate. . . . It really is about the fundamental power of a woman to control her life and her body" (Wattleton 1997, 65). Adds Patricia Ireland, president of NOW, "If we can control our reproduction, we can control our lives"(Ireland 1996, 166).

Second-wave feminists began to debate control of women's bodies in 1969 with speakouts on abortion. At first, they focused their arguments on back-alley abortions and the deaths of women who underwent them. They disclosed the underside of the lives of America's women, including the difficulty of obtaining birth control. The arguments quickly moved to the arena of women's rights in general. If a woman does not control her body, who does? Judges? Congress? Priests, Rabbis, or other religious leaders? And why is it that women are not deemed capable and morally wise enough to make decisions about their reproduction whereas the men (the U.S. Congress is still over 88 percent male) making laws are trusted with these decisions?

In the 1960s, feminists demonstrated for abortion rights and soon began to call themselves pro-choice. The issue of abortion rights seemed clear-cut to many white feminists, but it was not so clear-cut to many African American women. In fact, abortion rights became a divisive issue between white women and women of color early in the second wave.

The country's history of sterilization filtered the perspective of many African American women. They remembered a eugenics movement in the early part of the twentieth century, a movement aimed at reducing the number of "unfit" mothers giving birth. Whereas well-to-do white women were encouraged to have children, "unfit" women—often immigrants or women of color, and usually poor—were candidates for sterilization and might be coaxed or strong-armed into it. In fact, by 1932, 26 states had compulsory sterilization laws, and the federal government provided assistance to states to pay for sterilization (Wilson and Russell 1996). The women who began the feminist second wave, most of them educated, middle-class, white women, had no knowledge of the effect that sterilization laws and eugenics attitudes had had on women of color. They had little understanding, either, of the humiliation and lifelong bitterness felt by an individual as she sat listening to a doctor suggest sterilization—her future offspring being unwanted by the world around her.

Some analysts of the feminist cause believe that more women of color would have joined in the feminist fight to make abortion legal if whites had been sensitive to the sterilization issue. Also, according to some, the issue of sterilization is not dead. "Even today when such women [women on welfare, many of whom are women of color] arrive at hospitals and clinics for abortions, they may find themselves being persuaded into getting sterilized at the same time," say feminist analysts Midge Wilson and Kathy Russell. Nevertheless, women of color today do support women's rights to abortion in similar proportions as do white women (Wilson and Russell 1996, 208).

African American feminists have played an important part in expanding the rhetoric surrounding the abortion debate to bring its current focus to reproductive freedom. Partly as a result of African American influences, feminists have revised the terms used in the debate. "Abortion rights" and "a woman's right to choose" were the terms originally used, but today, "reproductive freedom" more accurately defines the goal of the multicultural, multiracial feminist movement. Reproductive freedom encompasses feminist goals of improved health care for women, reproductive health education for young women, and insurance-covered access to birth control information and resources, as well as availability of legal abortion. What's more, feminists call for the empowerment of women in all aspects of their lives, with the vision that empowered women, with access to resources, will have more control over their reproductive lives and abortion will become an infrequent necessity—safe, legal, and rare.

The feminist vision of empowered women seems acceptable on the face of it, but it has met with intense opposition from its beginning. As women's access to abortion in the 1960s was just becoming a hope on the horizon, antiabortion forces were already mobilizing. The opposition came from many sides. The Catholic Church restated its ban on the use of artificial birth control in 1968 and, after organizing the National Right to Life Committee in 1970, supported local demonstrations against Planned Parenthood clinics in an attempt to stop the legalization, and then the procedure, of abortion. Faye Wattleton tells the story of protesters lining up in front of Planned Parenthood clinics even while Planned Parenthood officials were still debating whether they would offer abortions.

In 1973 the U.S. Supreme Court ruled in *Roe v. Wade* in favor of a woman's right to an abortion in the first trimester of pregnancy. The same ruling provided, though, that states could pass laws to prohibit abortion after viability, except to protect the woman's life or health. Most feminists considered the ruling a compromise. They sought a prohibition of all laws governing women's access to abortion; nevertheless, thinking the abortion issue was closed, most feminists moved on to other issues. The National Council of Catholic Bishops, however, warned that Catholics who had abortions or who performed them could be excommunicated from the church; the council also urged Catholics to work to outlaw abortion. Other groups formed, too, with the purpose of curtailing abortion rights. Many of them came from the conservative wings of political parties; others arose from the fundamentalist sectors of Christian denominations. Possibly the most well known has been Operation Rescue—a relative latecomer, having been formed in 1988—but the Pro-Life Action League, the Prolife Nonviolent Action Project, and others have been active, too.

Opponents to abortion have mobilized many legal and legislative efforts to hinder or regulate a woman's access to abortion. These have included, for example, state laws imposing mandatory counseling and waiting periods, spousal and parental consent laws, limitations on public funding, and stringent regulation of clinics that result in costly outlays of money for the clinic. Feminists, meanwhile, have spread out to the states to work against any imposed regulations, have worked at the national level to maintain the legality of abortion, and have lent support to the medical facilities and staffs of clinics. Battles have raged over allowing the abortion-inducing drug RU-486 into the country and over pro-life efforts to outlaw specific abortion procedures. Meanwhile, information about abortifacients (drugs that induce abortion) and abortion techniques has been uploaded onto Web sites, providing abortion supporters with their greatest weapon yet: mass communication.

Antiabortion protests have garnered a great deal of attention over the past two decades. What began as legal vocal demonstrations staged outside of clinics has since turned violent. In 1977, the Planned Parenthood offices in St. Paul, Minnesota, were set on fire, and soon thereafter bullets were fired into the building and a bomb (unexploded) was found in front of the clinic's windows. Kidnap threats were made against Planned Parenthood board members (Wattleton 1996). That same year, a clinic in Omaha, Nebraska, was set on fire. In 1978, a chemical bomb was thrown through the window of a clinic. Vandalism became a commonplace hazard, as did telephoned death threats to clinic staff members. In 1982, three members of the Army of God kidnapped a doctor and his wife, holding them for eight days, until the doctor agreed to stop performing abortions (Ireland 1996). Between 1977 and 1983, 149 violent incidents at clinics were reported to the National Abortion Federation. These included bombings, arson, clinic invasions, vandalism, assault and battery, death threats, kidnapping, and burglary. Pro-life "direct action" activists have publicly advocated using force. Doctors and staff members have been harassed, and women entering clinics often face a gauntlet of shouting protesters. Others face clinic blockades. The Feminist Majority Foundation's National Clinic Access Project lists some of the recent violence: In 1991, a clinic receptionist was shot and paralyzed from the waist down; in 1993, a doctor was murdered outside an abortion clinic and another doctor was shot in both arms; in July 1994, a doctor and a volunteer clinic escort were killed; in December 1994, two clinic receptionists were murdered. In 1997, newspapers reported that two bombs were set off at an Atlanta clinic, the second one timed to explode as fire fighters were entering the area.

Feminists seemed at first to be taken by surprise at the violence of the pro-life movement. Indeed, much of the American populace, unaccustomed to terrorist activities on American soil, were stunned by it. Feminists mobilized their forces, forming "human shields" to walk women into the clinics and holding their own protests in support of reproductive rights. They also pursued legal action against pro-life activists who made death threats or used violence. (See Table 4.1.)

Today, feminists are frustrated that the debate between pro-choice advocates and pro-life adherents has become one-dimensional. Pro-life people argue that a life begins with conception, and many believe a fetus should possess legal rights that override the rights of the woman who carries it. Pro-choice arguments have focused on the individual's right to make decisions about her body. Here the debate is stalled. Feminists claim that medical advances should be making the debate more complex. Issues that seemed clear-cut 30 years ago are not today. With the increasingly commonplace use of procedures such as ultrasound, amniocentesis, and in-utero diagnostic procedures, feminists claim that the debate should be going deeper than its current simplistic levels. But it is not, and neither side is giving in.

For feminists, the issue is too essential to concede, and the curtailing of women's reproductive rights is seen as just part of the system of societal control over women. Says Marcia Ann Gillespie, editor of *Ms.* magazine, "Women's reproductive freedom must not be taken for granted, and should never be dis-

Table 4.1
The Number and Intensity of Incidents of Violence
and Disruption Against Abortion Providers Since 1977

	1977–1985	1986–1989	1990–1993	1994–1997	Total
Violence					
Murder	0	0	1	4	5
Attempted Murder	0	0	3	10	13
Bombing	30	4	3	10	47
Arson	27	21	39	29	116
Attempted Bomb/Arson	21	18	25	8	72
Invasion	149	98	98	7	352
Vandalism	119	125	299	104	647
Assault and Battery	25	33	30	10	98
Death Threats	49	21	96	113	279
Kidnapping	2	0	0	0	2
Burglary	7	13	11	12	43
Stalking	0	0	188	150	338
Total	429	333	793	457	2,012
Disruptions					
Hate Mail and Harassing					
Phone Calls	58	134	1,260	1,248	2,700
Bomb Threats	116	121	60	84	381
Picketing	406	441	5,514	6,895	13,256
Total	580	696	6,834	8,227	16,337
Clinic Blockades					
No. of Incidents	0	385	224	41	650
No. of Arrests	0	24,380	9,064	357	33,801

Note: Numbers represent incidents reported to the National Abortion Federation (NAF) as of June 1, 1997; the NAF reports that actual incidents are most likely higher. *Stalking* is defined as the persistent following, threatening, and harassing of an abortion provider, staff member, or patient *away from* the clinic. Tabulation of stalking incidents began in 1993. The *number of arrests* represents the total number of arrests, not the total number of persons arrested; many blockaders are arrested multiple times.
Source: National Abortion Federation, "Incidents of Violence and Disruption Against Abortion Providers, 1997," June 1997.

cussed as if it were isolated from all the conditions that women's equality depends on" (Gillespie 1997, 1).

Laws of the Land

Since the passage of *Roe v. Wade,* many bills concerning reproductive freedoms have been proposed, discussed, and voted on.

Some have been vetoed; some have gone to court and been overturned; others have been enacted into law. Following is a synopsis of the major court cases and legislation concerning reproductive freedom in the past 25 years.

1973   The U.S. Supreme Court in *Roe v. Wade* establishes that abortions are legal in the first trimester and can be regulated in the second trimester only to protect maternal health, but allows states the authority to limit abortion after fetus viability.

1977   The Hyde Amendment to the Health, Education, and Welfare Labor appropriations bill passes. It prohibits the use of federal funds to pay for abortions except in cases of promptly reported rape and incest, where the life of the mother is endangered, or where severe damage to the mother would result from carrying the pregnancy to term.

1989   The U.S. Supreme Court in *Webster v. Reproductive Health Services* upholds a Missouri law that declares life to begin at conception, requiring tests of fetal viability prior to abortions after 20 weeks of pregnancy, and prohibiting the use of public facilities or public employees for abortions. This antiabortion stance serves as encouragement for numerous state-level efforts to curtail abortion access.

1992   In *Planned Parenthood v. Casey*, the U.S. Supreme Court reaffirms a woman's right to abortion but allows restrictions that do not unduly burden a woman. Following the ruling, legislation to make abortion more difficult to obtain is introduced in nearly every state.

1994   The Freedom of Access to Clinic Entrances Act (FACE) passes. The act makes blocking access to abortion clinics a federal crime and provides criminal penalties for using force or threat of force to injure, intimidate, or block anyone entering an abortion clinic.

1996   President Clinton vetoes legislation that would out-
        law abortions done by the dilation and extraction
        method, which pro-life forces rename the "partial
        birth method."

1997   The U.S. Supreme Court in *Schenck v. Pro-Choice Net-
        work* does away with the "floating buffer zones" that
        were part of the FACE protections. Blocking access
        to clinics is still a crime, and protesters must stay 15
        feet away from clinic doors and driveways, but they
        once again can shout directly into the faces of
        women entering the clinics. The case was prompted
        by a series of demonstrations in New York in 1990 in
        which Operation Rescue and other groups tried to
        block the driveways and doors of abortion clinics.
        The Court finds that women seeking abortions had
        been surrounded, grabbed, pushed, and yelled at,
        and local police were harassed. Though the Court
        does away with a "floating buffer zone" around pa-
        tients, it upholds a fixed buffer zone that keeps
        demonstrators at least 15 feet away from clinic door-
        ways, driveways, and driveway entrances. The
        Court also upholds a part of the federal judge's
        order requiring so-called sidewalk counselors who
        approach patients within the fixed buffer zones to
        retreat when patients indicate a desire not to be
        counseled.

        In *Leavitt v. Jane L.* the Court refuses to hear argu-
        ments on a circuit court ruling that strikes down a
        Utah law forbidding abortions after 20 weeks ex-
        cept to save the mother. Thus, the U.S. Supreme
        Court once again lets it be known that states may
        regulate the practice of abortion only so long as
        they do not place an undue burden on the right of
        women to choose abortion within the first six
        months of pregnancy.

        The National Abortion and Reproductive Rights Ac-
        tion League (NARAL) Foundation reports that for
        the first time since *Roe v. Wade,* nearly one-quarter of

1997   all states are enforcing three or more significant abor-
(cont.)   tion restrictions, including mandatory waiting peri-
            ods and counseling requirements, parental consent
            and notification laws, Medicaid funding restrictions
            for low-income women, bans on insurance coverage
            for abortion, and prohibitions on the use of public fa-
            cilities or the participation of public employees in
            abortion services. (See Figure 4.2.)

Global Perspectives

The reproductive freedom of women worldwide has long been a
focus of the global women's movement and recently has taken on
new direction, along with feminists' emphasis on women's rights
as human rights. Gender equity is part of the new human rights
paradigm, and women's sexual and reproduction rights are part
of this paradigm. Women activists are seeking inclusion at all levels of international decision making, and they are working to add
the female voice to transform discussions about women's reproductive lives.

In past discussions of women's health issues, women were
defined in terms of fertility, a narrow outlook that ignored the
lives and bodies of girls and women apart from their child-bear-
ing functions. In international terms, women's health and empowerment over reproduction were seen as instruments of population control. Redefining the terms from fertility to reproductive
freedom implies human rights and personal control.

Although women's rights are being established as human
rights on an international level, the reality is that women in developing regions throughout the world are restricted from control over their sexuality and reproduction. A variety of cultural
and legal barriers against women taking control are placed in
front of them, ranging from female genital mutilation to legal
marital rape to "domestication"—keeping girls inside the household and restricting their education. Overcoming these barriers is
almost impossible on an individual level; feminists hope that international conventions, new laws, and pressure from nongovernmental organizations will bring the barriers down. In addition, feminists hope for a cumulative effect of their efforts. A
woman's reproductive freedom is associated with her status in

Figure 4.2
The Number of Abortion Providers
in the United States, 1982 and 1992

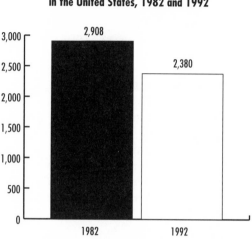

Note: The numbers reflect an 18 percent decrease between 1982 and 1992, with a few states — Alabama, Iowa, Missouri, North Dakota, and West Virginia — losing at least 50 percent of their providers.
Source: National Abortion and Reproductive Rights Action League (NARAL), *Who Decides? A State-by-State Review of Abortion and Reproductive Rights,* Fifth Edition, 1995.

her community, and efforts to empower women on economic, social, political, and personal levels all work to increase her say over reproduction and sexuality as well.

In 1994, the International Conference on Population and Development endorsed women's reproductive freedom as a human right. The conference's Programme of Action states that reproductive rights rest on "the basic right of all couples and individuals to decide freely and responsibly the number, spacing and timing of their children and to have the information and means to do so, and the right to attain the highest standard of sexual and reproductive health . . . [and the right] to make decisions concerning reproduction free of discrimination, coercion and violence, as expressed in human rights documents" (United Nations 1995, 78).

Indicators and evidences of women's health and their reproductive freedom throughout the globe include maternal mortality rates, fertility, contraception, abortion, and restrictive practices. We will look at each of these indicators in turn.

Maternal Mortality Rates

The rate of maternal mortality is high in the developing world. Researchers report that "virtually all maternal deaths and most maternal illnesses occur in the poorer countries: of the half million women who die each year from causes related to pregnancy and childbirth, 99 percent are in developing countries" (Sivard 1995, 28). According to United Nations studies, an African woman's lifetime risk of dying from pregnancy-related causes is approximately one in 23; a North American woman's is one in 4,000. In developing countries, lack of prenatal, delivery, and postnatal care contribute to women's deaths. Lack of emergency care is a major factor in the deaths of many women in labor, but unsafe abortions, pregnancy disorders, infections, and obstructed labor (one of the chief complications of female genital mutilation) also cause women to die.

Fertility

Women's health is linked to the number of children they bear, and overall, world fertility is decreasing. Since 1960, it has dropped from six children per woman in the poorer countries to less than four. In developed countries, it averages less than two. But there is great contrast among the women of the world. In Spain, women's fertility rate is 1.4; in Mali, it is 7.1 (Sivard 1995). The life expectancy for women in Spain is 80 years; in Mali, 49 years. In Latin American and Caribbean countries, the fertility rate is 3.2; in southern Asia it is 5.3; in eastern Asia it is 2.3. Birth rates in urban areas generally are lower than in rural areas, a fact attributed to education, economic opportunity, and other factors that present women with options. Also, declining fertility could be a reflection of gains in gender equality, but in surveys it also is explained as a response of women who work outside the home to their lack of domestic help from men at home.

Contraception

Women's desire for contraception in the developing world exceeds their access to it, with the result that a considerable number of women bear more children than they choose to. The forms of birth control available to women depend on their wealth and location. Urban women have greater access than do rural women, who may have to walk for miles to reach a clinic. Sterilization is the most common form of contraception in the developing world; in eastern Asia it is chosen by 33 percent of the women and 10 percent of the men; in Latin America and the Caribbean, 21 percent of the women choose it, but only 1 percent of the men. Intrauterine devices (IUDs) are also common, chosen by 31 percent of women in eastern Asia. The birth control methods of pills and condoms are difficult for many developing world women to obtain. Not only are they expensive but they need to be regularly replenished. Programs that provide women with contraception have begun to offer Norplant, a progestin-based hormonal contraceptive in tiny capsules that are implanted under the skin and are effective for five years. During a test of Norplant use in Bangladesh, women aggressively sought it as a means of controlling their fertility. A researcher studying the case saw Norplant as a gauge of women's desperation to gain access to birth control. She recalls "the case of a woman in Bogra, who insisted on retaining Norplant when she went to the hospital, even after suffering severe side effects and after doctors advised removal" (Huq and Azim 1995, 430). Yet, many women in India, Bangladesh, and other developing countries have reported being coerced by government-sponsored medical personnel into the use of IUDs or Norplants and then not being able to get them removed when they reported side effects and requested removal. Aggressive government programs to control population growth have used coercive measures, including bribery, to convince women to agree to sterilization.

Abortion

It is estimated that 50 million abortions are performed each year, and almost half of them are done outside a regular health care system. Estimates on the number of maternal deaths from abortions are unreliable, ranging from 70,000 to 200,000 per year. The risk of death from abortion is one in 3,700 in developed regions where it is legal and done by trained health providers; the risk of death in developing regions is one in 250 (United Nations 1995). Access to legal, safe abortions is one part of the global feminist agenda. Feminists face opposition to this agenda by conservative forces within countries, from religious fundamentalists to simple traditionalists. Forces within the United States, too, have sought to limit abortions in the rest of the world by tying foreign aid for family planning to restrictions on abortions.

Restrictive Practices

Many of the systematic and institutionalized methods of controlling women use their sexuality or reproductive capacity. Where early marriages are encouraged, women's sexual choices are limited; they are more often subject to marital rape, and in the case of many young girls often left with lifelong injuries. Arranged marriages, popular in some regions of the world, take the freedom of choice out of a woman's hands. Countries that limit women to domestic roles end up with unsophisticated, uneducated women who are at a tremendous disadvantage in marriage relationships. These uneducated women are more likely to have numerous children and high infant and maternal mortality rates. (Every country's statistics show that the best form of birth control and family health is the education of women.) Cultures that allow female genital mutilation institute lifelong controls over women's sexuality and also leave many with severe physical disabilities; systems that condone FGM usually also have extremely male-oriented laws, leaving women with little recourse or ability to change their lives (see Global Violence later in this chapter). Systems that encourage domestication or segregation of women control women's ability to seek objective medical help and reproductive health information.

The Medical Community

A small discussion group of women met in Boston in the spring of 1969. They talked about their health and about doctors. "We had all experienced similar feelings of frustration and anger toward specific doctors and the medical maze in general, and initially we wanted to do something about those doctors who were condescending, paternalistic, judgmental and non-informative," they report (Boston Women's Health Book Collective 1979, 11). The women embarked on a course that would change women's place in the medical establishment. They wrote a book, the first edition entitled *Women and Their Bodies* (1970), which aimed to demystify medicine and medical institutions. The book was revised and retitled *Our Bodies, Ourselves* and today is known as *The New Our Bodies, Ourselves.*

At a time when almost all physicians were male and were bestowed with a godlike omnipotence in health matters and decisions, the Boston women's challenge to them was revolutionary. The book presented mainstream American women with medical and physiological information that wasn't heretofore available to them. And it was presented "in a new way—an honest, humane and powerful way of thinking about ourselves and our lives" (Boston Women's Health Book Collective 1979, 11). Women were taking back the power over their bodies that they had lost to the medical establishment. They were taking it back by disseminating knowledge and information. They knew that once more women understood how their bodies worked, they would question their doctors. This would be the beginning of the end of "condescending, paternalistic, judgmental and non-informative" medical visits. The Boston collective of women, and then other feminists, began to look "critically, and with strength" at the medical institutions that served them (1979, 11).

The demystification had begun. It continued through the years, as women began to analyze the "medicalization" of childbirth and of women's bodies in general. Feminists reached back into European history to study the healers of the Western world. They traced the power of women as healers and midwives and noted the importance of the women's roles in their communities and villages. They traced those healer women to the "burning times" that began in the fifteenth century, when thousands (estimates range from hundreds of thousands to several million) of women were tortured until they confessed to witchcraft and then were burned at the stake (Daly 1978). They noted the rise of universities and medical training institutions in the eighteenth century and thereafter, as men took over the role of healer from women. Women were not allowed to study in the universities, though they still acted as midwives, and their skills were denigrated by the professional doctors while also outpaced by new medical discoveries. By the end of the nineteenth century, doctors were calling for an end to female midwives, insisting that a license was needed to practice medicine—and women were still excluded from almost all medical schools that could give them the license.

As feminists spoke out in the 1970s, they complained first about the medicalization of childbirth. It was common for women to be on their backs, on a table, with their legs in stirrups while they were giving birth—a convenient position for the doctor, but an obviously difficult one for the woman. The rebirth of midwifery began, along with calls for "natural" childbirth and methods, especially the Lamaze method and the Bradley method, for empowered birthing. Feminists saw these changes as passing the power of childbirth back into the hands of women.

They pointed out the medicalization of women's bodies in general, with women's cycles described in the same terms as chronic diseases and conditions. They focused on revising the medical establishment's view of women, and they focused on revising women's view of themselves. As feminists continue this demedicalization, they are today revealing past and current deficiencies in medical testing, care, treatment, and physician training. Also, they are directing the medical community and the public away from a focus on crisis medical intervention and toward "well care"—preventing illness before it happens.

Recently, the United States government has taken steps to rectify some of the problems in the medical establishment. In 1990, the National Institute of Health (NIH) established the Office of Research on Women's Health (ORWH) to ensure that women would be included in medical tests. Studies showed that they had not been: Male researchers often took the male body as the "norm" in research, then applied their findings to women; their reason for doing so was not that men and women are the same but that with women, the menstrual cycle, pregnancy, and pre- and postmenopausal phases present additional factors to a study. Feminists pointed out that these factors also were present when the results of the study were applied to female patients. In 1991, Congress passed the Women's Health Equity Act, ensuring federal funding for research on women's health issues. In 1993, Congress made what had previously been policy into public law with a section in the NIH Revitalization Act of 1993 entitled "Women and Minorities as Subjects in Clinical Research."

The sociopolitical constructs that underlie medical care have also been challenged by feminists, who have pointed out the imbalance of power between women and men in the medical establishment. Women are a small percentage on decision-making boards in both hospitals and medical schools. For example, the Feminist Majority reports, "the American College of Obstetricians and Gynecologists (ACOG), whose sole mission is to provide health care to women, has never had more than two women in its top 17 offices at any one time in its 41-year history" (Feminist Majority 1995b). These imbalances underlie and help to perpetuate problems in health care.

Reproductive Health

Feminists have objected to the medicalization of women's reproductive processes and organs, and they point to history to explain
the development of modern medicine's relationship to women.
The normal cycles of a woman's life, from the onset of menstruation, through pregnancy, lactation, and menopause, have been
the subject of much controversial medical labeling and intervention. Women's ovaries and uteruses have been seen as disruptive
influences in an otherwise normal body and mind. In 1978, feminist writer Barbara Ehrenreich analyzed some of the most egre-
gious examples of contemporary medical attitudes toward
women. From the late eighteenth century until the 1940s, she
wrote, women who were aggressive or erotic, who masturbated,
or were deemed "unruly" by their husbands (i.e., not "normal")
were subject to oophorectomies (removal of the ovaries) to nor-
malize them. "The operation was judged successful," she wrote,
"if the woman was restored to a placid contentment with her domestic functions" (Ehrenreich 1978, 112). Clitoridectomies (removal of the clitoris), though frowned on by most doctors, were
also performed by physicians in the United States to calm a
woman's sexual drive. Through these and other practices, the
medical community securely linked women's emotional health
and needs to their reproductive organs, a link that has some scientific basis but is easily exaggerated for political use.

Today, premenstrual syndrome (PMS) is a controversial
topic among feminists. Says one feminist: "There is much debate
about whether PMS is a true medical entity or a social phenome-
non that medicalizes the menstrual cycle in order to enforce social control over women" (Rothman and Caschetta 1995, 72). Although the medical community and many suffering women
believe in the medical reality of PMS, feminists question if it has
been exaggerated until it is assumed that all women suffer from
it. They also question why anger—the foremost symptom of
PMS—is considered biological in origin in women but considered
to be caused by outside circumstances in men.

Feminists point to a few particularly devastating medical
practices that stand out as symptoms of the greater problem of
the medical community's treatment of women. One of these is the
prescribing of DES (diethylstilbestrol), a synthetic estrogen, to
three to six million American women between 1941 and 1971, and
to women in Canada and Europe. The drug was prescribed to

prevent miscarriage, and it has been linked to vaginal or cervical cancer in daughters of the women who took DES. Testicular and sperm abnormalities also have been found in the sons of some women who took the drug. (For more information on DES, contact DES Action USA, 1615 Broadway, Suite 510, Oakland, CA 94612; (510) 465-4011.)

Feminists have also alerted women to the number of hysterectomies done in the United States. According to the Boston Women's Health Book Collective (1992), approximately 650,000 women in the United States have hysterectomies each year. At least 30 to 50 percent are unnecessary, and another 10 percent might be avoided by using alternative therapy. The majority are elective surgeries. Doctor's wives have more hysterectomies in proportion to other groups. The highest rates are in the southern and western states. Women of color traditionally have had twice as many hysterectomies as white women, a reflection of hysterectomy once used as a form of sterilization abuse. The rate in the United States is twice that in England and Sweden. Feminists have questioned the prevalence of hysterectomies in the United States and have mobilized studies and informed American women about the problem. (One source for information on hysterectomies is Hysterectomy Educational Resources and Services (HERS), 422 Bryn Mawr Avenue, Bala Cynwyd, PA 19004; (215) 667-7757.)

Cesarean births also have come under feminist scrutiny. The rate of Cesarean births in the United States rose from 5 percent of all deliveries in 1968 to 25 percent in 1987. Feminists have questioned the necessity of some Cesarean surgeries and have pointed to factors that make physicians more likely to perform them: physicians' fear of lawsuits should a birth go wrong, a lack of medical training for physicians in standard cervical births, financial incentives (Cesarean births cost more than cervical births), birthing positions that favor physicians rather than women (i.e., lying on one's back), and physicians' attitudes. (The Cesareans Support, Education and Concern Association, 22 Forest Rd., Framingham, MA 01701, (508) 877-8266, has been instrumental in humanizing childbirth and empowering pregnant women.)

Disease

Feminists have worked to empower women and to redefine women's health and bodies as a norm and not a deviation from the male body. They have succeeded in moving menopause from the "disease" category to the "normal cycle" category. But women still face a bias formed by both sexism and racism in the medical system when it comes to true diseases. Feminists have fought for more research in breast cancer and uterine cancer, for including women in heart and lung disease research, and for more attention to symptoms of diseases.

In the case of AIDS (Acquired Immune Deficiency Syndrome), feminists have worked in medical, political, and social arenas to empower and educate women, thus helping them avoid infection. Even so, women are being infected with HIV (human immunodeficiency virus) and AIDS at a growing rate. Feminists point to the politics of AIDS: Those who suffer the most from it are not usually the ones in control of resources for research and treatment. The disease was well-established in the homosexual male population before the government began to adequately fund AIDS research; some say it is still underfunded. The World Health Organization (WHO) estimates that 40 percent of those infected with HIV worldwide today are women. In sub-Saharan Africa the number is between 52 and 55 percent. WHO estimates that worldwide 16 million adults are HIV infected, and three million have AIDS (United Nations 1995). Women are more susceptible to infection through sexual intercourse than are men, and women in many developing countries have little power over when, how, and sometimes with whom they have intercourse. Part of the feminist agenda of empowering women worldwide is to give women in developing countries the rights to refuse sex and to negotiate for safe sex with their partners. In developed countries, feminists work toward empowerment in personal relations through education.

Violence against Women

Feminists early in the second wave seized on an understanding of violence and its function as part of a patriarchal system. Feminist writers Andrea Dworkin and Susan Brownmiller focused on the profound effects that the images and realities of violence have on women's lives. Their theories and arguments have continued as a thread through the feminist movement. Feminist Carole J. Sheffield has stated that "the right of men to control the female body is a cornerstone of patriarchy" (Sheffield 1995, 1). She further declares that control is exerted through "sexual terrorism," the kind of terrorism that makes a woman nervous if she walks across an empty parking lot—even in broad daylight—because rape and assault can happen at any time, anywhere, and statistics say that the chances of them happening to a woman are high. In 1990, *Newsweek* magazine reported that three out of four American women would be victims of at least one violent crime during their lifetime (Salholz 1990).

Feminists have redefined violence against women, refusing to accept violent acts as isolated incidents and happenstance and putting them instead into the context of male domination and power in society. Violence against women comes in many forms, they assert: through images in pornography and prostitution, sexual harassment, spousal battery, rape, and culturally sanctioned violations or attacks. It is part of a system of control that keeps women frightened and judiciously cautious about rising above their secondary status. It colors their decisions on where they live, what work they do, and how they spend their recreational hours. It is a pervasive factor in women's lives that has no corollary in men's. And it is a factor sustained by many men.

Not surprisingly, feminists have been in the forefront of efforts to reform laws and the judicial system to make them work for women who have been assaulted. In 1984, feminists lobbied for the Family Violence Prevention and Services Act, which provides funding for domestic violence programs. In 1994, feminists won their battle for the passage of the Violence Against Women Act (VAWA). Enacted as part of the Omnibus Crime Control and Safe Streets Act, commonly known as the anticrime bill, it contains an historic provision for gender-motivated crimes. The new law gives victims of gender-motivated hate crimes the right to sue the perpetrator in federal court. It also provides increased funding for shelters and rape education programs as well as improved enforcement of protective orders and training for judges.

Pornography

In general, feminists agree that pornography negatively affects women's lives, but they disagree over what, if anything, should be done about pornographic images of women. They are divided chiefly into three groups: antipornography feminists seeking laws to stop pornography production, anticensorship feminists who see pornography censorship as endangering the Constitutional rights of all, and pro-erotica feminists who believe that instead of curtailing pornography, it's time to celebrate women's sexuality and add bona fide female sensuality to the media.

Andrea Dworkin, feminist leader in the battle to pass laws against pornography, defines pornography as "the graphic, sexually explicit subordination of women that includes one of a series of scenarios, from women being dehumanized—turned into objects and commodities—through women showing pleasure in being raped, through the dismemberment of women in a way that makes the dismemberment sexual" (Gillespie 1994, 34). And it is not limited to women. Men and children can also be thus used in pornography.

According to the 1986 Attorney General's Commission on Pornography (commonly called the Meese Commission after its creator, U.S. Attorney General Edwin Meese), pornography is divided into four categories: (1) nudity; (2) sexually explicit material; (3) sexually explicit material that includes images of degradation, submission, domination, or humiliation; and (4) sexually explicit material that includes violence (Cowan 1995).

Pornography is considered under the heading of violence in this book (and elsewhere) because studies have consistently indicated links between pornography and violence against women. The overwhelming majority of pornography depicts women in submissive, subordinate positions; much of pornography depicts violent acts against women, including rapes and beatings, with women depicted as enjoying the acts; and some so-called snuff films depict mutilation, torture, and murder of women.

The effect of pornographic, especially violent, images on men's attitudes and beliefs about women has been studied, usually in a laboratory setting. Most commonly, the subjects view pornography and then are tested on their attitudes about violence against women. After exposure to rape pornography, male college students test "more likely to see the victim [of rape] as less injured than those exposed to other types of films or to control groups," according to a 1984 report (Cowan 1995, 353). They are, in other words, desensitized in their attitudes toward rape. But does this cause them to actually commit rape? No study can establish a direct link between pornography and the act of rape. The link is an attitudinal one. Images that depict women as enjoying domination and rape bolster the longstanding myths about rape that feminists have fought to end. Antipornography feminists say those myths, kept alive in society, hamper feminists' attempts to strengthen rape laws, protect rape victims, and end violence against women.

Even when the images are not violent, the effect of pornography is negative and well-documented, according to feminist Gloria Cowan. Her research has uncovered various studies showing that exposure to nonviolent but still degrading or dehumanizing forms of pornography changes women's and men's attitudes. These include "trivialization of rape and increased acceptance of sexual coercion, decreased support of the women's movement, promotion of sexual callousness toward women, and changes in traditional values, such as promotion of pre- and extra-marital sex, increased doubts about the value of marriage and of having female children" (Cowan 1995, 353).

At the head of the movement to pass laws against pornography stands Andrea Dworkin. As author of the 1979 book *Pornography: Men Possessing Women*, Dworkin initiated the national feminist debate on pornography. "The major theme of pornography as a genre is male power," she writes, asserting that pornography presents this male power through images of domination and violence toward women, and also that pornography is a means through which men assert their power over women and a vehicle through which they reaffirm it for themselves (Dworkin 1989, 24). Feminist Norma Ramos adds that pornography "is a central feature of patriarchal society, an essential tool in terms of how men keep power over women" (Gillespie 1994, 34).

Dworkin and feminist attorney Catharine MacKinnon worked together in the 1980s to pass antipornography laws. They were nearly successful in two cases. They wrote a proposed law to define pornography as a violation of the civil rights of women, as sex discrimination, and an abuse of human rights. If the law had passed and stood, people could have sued pornography producers and publishers for injury. In 1983 and 1984, the Minneapolis city council passed the law as an amendment to the city's civil rights laws, but the mayor vetoed it. In 1985, the law was put on the Cambridge, Massachusetts, ballot as a referendum but lost with 42 percent of the vote. In 1988, it won on the ballot in Bellington, Washington, with 62 percent of the vote, but the law was judged unconstitutional in federal court (Dworkin 1989). Dworkin characterizes pornography as "an institution of sexual exploitation" (Gillespie 1994, 37). In regard to concerns over censorship, she argues that the civil laws she proposes are not censorship; they do not place any legal prior restraint on pornography publishers. They instead make them answerable to the women they exploit.

Many feminists have sided with Dworkin but have found themselves in the uncomfortable position of sharing their side of the debate with religious conservatives who have little else in common ideologically with the feminist movement. Feminists who have spoken out against censorship of pornography share their side of the debate with pornographers and the misogynists (those who simply hate and disrespect women) who support the servile images of women presented in pornographic publications.

Anticensorship feminists focus on concerns over First Amendment rights and freedom of speech. Placing government control over images and prose could very well put women in the target zone for censorship, argue some feminists on this side. Marilyn French, feminist novelist and journalist, expresses the concern of many writers that an antipornography law could be used to censor her works. Feminist artists, too, show up in the anticensorship ranks, concerned that any rigid definition of pornography could inhibit their exploration of female images. Part of today's feminist artistic direction is one of repossessing female images that have been the subject of male art for so many centuries. "Feminist art aesthetics, which counterpose the male gaze, necessarily stand in the vanguard as targets of bureaucratic, masculinist censorship," writes Katherine Patterson (Patterson 1994, 103). She is skeptical that any censorship system would be just and fair toward women.

Leanne Katz, 1994 executive director of the National Coalition Against Censorship, adds a more universal perspective of anticensorship feminists: "Women can't achieve equality through repression. Feminism does not set freedom in opposition to equality. We must have both" (Gillespie 1994, 44). Gloria Steinem, who has spoken against censorship, has also called for a distinction between pornography and erotica, defining pornography as demeaning to women and erotica as mutually sexually arousing material. Many leading feminists have been active members of anticensorship organizations. Betty Friedan, for example, has been a member of Feminists for Free Expression and the National Coalition Against Censorship. Rene Denfeld, a third-wave feminist and author of *The New Victorians,* has been outspoken against censorship of pornography as a feminist issue.

Finally, according to Gloria Cowan, are the hale and hardy feminists who declare that instead of seeking to control or prohibit pornography, women need to embrace it—on their own terms. Controlling women's sexuality has always been a hallmark of patriarchy; therefore, celebrating women's sexuality is liberating. Pornography presents women in nontraditional roles, their sexuality not tied to procreation, romance, or commitment. That in itself also liberates women from society's limiting stereotypes.

Sexual Harassment

Prior to the second wave of the women's movement, sexual harassment was just another "problem with no name" that women faced in schools and the workplace. In fact, it wasn't until 1974 that the term sexual harassment was introduced. That year, Carmita Woods, an administrative assistant at Cornell University, with the help of Cornell instructor Lin Farley, filed a claim for unemployment compensation after leaving her job because of the sexual advances of her employer.

Since then, sexual harassment has been identified and defined many times over. It is now established as a violation of Title IX of the Educational Amendments Act of 1972 and as a violation of Title VII of the Civil Rights Act. The U.S. Equal Employment Opportunity Commission (EEOC) defines it as "unwelcome sexual advances, requests for sexual favors and other verbal or physical conduct of a sexual nature." It further states that sexual harassment includes the idea that submission to the conduct is connected to the worker's job as a condition or term, or promotion or job status is implicitly or explicitly predicated on compliance, or the conduct interferes with the worker's performance or creates a hostile environment (Eisaguirre 1993, 57).

The women's business organization Catalyst emphasizes that according to the EEOC definition and refinements in legal precedent, sexual harassment is not limited to quid pro quo harassment (a "trade" of sexual favors for employment benefits) but includes the existence of a hostile work environment. According to Catalyst research, more than 95 percent of sexual harassment involves existence of a hostile environment.

Feminists have worked to define sexual harassment, to identify it in the workplace and in schools, to educate the public about it, to lobby for legal changes, and in court cases to advocate for victims of sexual harassment. Expressing the mainstream feminist view of sexual harassment, feminist author Susan Ehrlich Martin explains:

Understanding sexual harassment requires recognizing that it is central to maintaining women's subordinate social, economic, and sexual statuses and this is closely related to other feminist issues. Along with rape, wife beating, prostitution, and pornography, it is one of the ways in which male control of women's sexuality shapes women's experiences. (Martin 1995, 22)

With the understanding that feminists see sexual harassment as part of the underpinnings of a sexist society, it is not surprising that feminist organizations have been involved in the development of sexual harassment law and in raising public consciousness. Following is a list of events and legislation that helped shape sexual harassment law:

1974   A Cornell University employee files a claim with the EEOC, coining the term sexual harassment.

1975   During the New York City Commission on Human Rights chaired by Eleanor Holmes Norton, Lin Farley, feminist activist from Cornell University, speaks on the problem of sexual harassment. Her words make headlines, and women around the country respond with stories of their own sexual harassment.

1979   Catharine MacKinnon's book *Sexual Harassment of Working Women: A Case of Sex Discrimination* presents her argument that sexual harassment is not just a personal harm done to a woman but is sex discrimination. MacKinnon postulates that sexual harassment is, therefore, a violation of the Civil Rights Act, Title VII.

1980   The EEOC issues federal guidelines defining sexual harassment and prohibiting it as a form of sex discrimination under Title VII of the Civil Rights Act of 1964.

1986   The U.S. Supreme Court rules in *Meritor Savings Bank FSB v. Vinson* that sexual harassment is a form of sex discrimination under Title VII of the Civil Rights Act of 1964. Catharine MacKinnon serves as

1986
(*cont.*)

cocounsel. She again refines the definition of sexual harassment. Up to now, it has been defined as quid pro quo; MacKinnon expands the definition to include maintenance of a hostile environment. Although it is a groundbreaking ruling, it still does not resolve whether employers can be held responsible for damages.

1991

University of Oklahoma law professor Anita Hill charges U.S. Supreme Court nominee Clarence Thomas with sexual harassment. While the details of her case hold the nation enthralled, the realities of sexual harassment and the impact harassment can have on women's lives are discussed and argued from coast to coast, and even globally. The image of a panel of white male senators challenging Professor Hill's veracity and seemingly not understanding the reality of sexual harassment for women works as a clarion cry for feminists in the United States. African American feminists voice concerns about racism inherent in the spectacle that the hearings become, as both Professor Hill and Clarence Thomas are African American. Thomas becomes a Supreme Court judge, and women turn out in record numbers at the next election to run for office. "Vote for a woman for a change" is a campaign slogan with direct links to Anita Hill's reception at the Senate hearing. EMILY's List membership jumps from a prehearing 3,000 to a posthearing 15,000. Contributions soar. African American women form several organizations, including the Ain't I a Woman Network and the African American Women in Defense of Ourselves. Also, say feminists Midge Wilson and Kathy Russell, "Women of both races [Negro and Caucasian] were rudely awakened to the truth that the fight for women's rights is far from over" (Wilson and Russell 1996, 215).

The Civil Rights Act of 1991 provides the right to a jury trial and makes employers liable for damages of up to $300,000 to victims of job discrimination, including sexual harassment. Feminists support the act but also point out the inequities of it: No other group

is subject to such severe monetary limitations on possible damages awards.

1992   A claim of sexual harassment at a 1991 Tailhook convention of U.S. Navy pilots raises questions about the
navy's overall integration of and acceptance of women
in its ranks. Twenty-six women speak out, half of them
navy officers. One, Lieutenant Paula Coughlin, continues to pursue the complaint after the navy gives it a
cursory review. Congressional and media pressure finally force an in-depth investigation that ends in the
resignation of several high-ranking officers, including
Navy Secretary Lawrence Garrett and Admiral John
Snyder (Eisaguirre 1993). The navy then initiates "consciousness-raising" training for all of its ranks.

1993   The American Association of University Women
publishes the results of a survey on sexual harassment in grades 8 through 11. Titled *Hostile Hallways:
The AAUW Survey on Sexual Harassment in America's
Schools*, it reports that even in schools girls are overwhelmingly subjected to harassment.

1996   The U.S. Army's policies come under scrutiny when
three male officers at the Aberdeen Proving Ground
in Maryland are accused of rape, assault, and sexual
harassment. Inundated with phone calls on a sexual
harassment hotline following the accusation, the
army is taken by surprise by the number of callers
registering complaints of harassment in the military.

Also in 1996, a six-year-old boy is suspended for sexual harassment after kissing an unwilling girl. Conservatives use the incident to illustrate that sexual
harassment rules have gone too far; feminists see
conservative reaction as using this incident to trivial-
ize the serious problem of sexual harassment.

American feminists join Japanese women in Tokyo
whose protests against sexual harassment on the job
are being ignored by the Mitsubishi Motors Corporation as well as by the Japanese press. The protesters

1996 *(cont.)*	win the media's attention when American feminist Rosemary Dempsey flies to Japan and joins them in their sidewalk demonstration.
1997	The U.S. Supreme Court holds that Paula Jones, who accuses President Clinton of sexual harassment when he was governor of Arkansas, may take him to court while he still holds office. Feminists are accused of hypocrisy for their reluctance to support Jones in her suit against feminist-endorsed Clinton. Feminist reluctance is based on Jones's financial backers, ultraconservatives who are part of the anti-Clinton political faction.
	In what is called the "worst sex scandal in U.S. military history," the number of soldiers at Aberdeen Proving Ground, Maryland, accused of sexual harassment stands at twelve, plus many others both in the United States and at military posts abroad. Before it is shut down in June, the army's sexual misconduct hotline logs in more than 8,300 complaints. The army reports that they initiate investigations in 1,200 of the calls. The hotline is ended partly because the calls have slowed down but also because of military concerns that it is being used as a tool for revenge. Many calls have reported adulterous activity. Adultery is a crime in the military, a fact that the general public learns when the U.S. Air Force discharges First Lieutenant Kelly Flinn, the first female B-52 bomber pilot, for misconduct resulting from adultery charges. Air Force Gen. Joseph W. Ralston, vice chairman of the Joint Chiefs of Staff, is a candidate for chairman of the Joint Chiefs when adultery charges against him are revealed. He withdraws his candidacy (Richter 1997). As the controversy continues—and adultery charges are mixed with sexual harassment charges—the military is forced to review gender bias in its procedures and culture.

Domestic Violence

In the 1970s domestic violence against women was a hidden and silent reality. The law did not adequately address the problem of violence against women in their homes, and women who came forward to charge men with domestic violence were as likely to be blamed for it themselves as to be helped. Feminists can justifiably take credit for opening the curtains on domestic violence in women's homes and giving voice to the women inside.

The modern movement to protect women and end domestic violence against women began in 1971 in London, England, when Erin Pizzey formed a group of activist women and opened a shelter for women and children. A year later, U.S. feminists traveled to London to study the women's shelters that were springing up in the wake of Pizzey's first effort. They brought their research home and opened shelters for battered women in the United States; the first one, Women's House, in St. Paul, Minnesota, opened in 1973 (McCue 1995). Other shelters quickly opened in other cities. Today, shelters for battered women have been established in most cities across the country.

Domestic violence has a history that reaches back to when women were the property of men—when men were answerable for their wives' acts and gave themselves the right to discipline their wives as well. The "rule of thumb," though it has been called a feminist fiction, was a reality for women under English common law and early American law. The rule allowed a husband to beat his wife with a whip or stick as long as it was no bigger in diameter than his thumb. In Alabama in 1871 that right was taken away when the court ruled in *Fulgham v. State* that "the privilege, ancient though it be, to beat her with a stick, to pull her hair, choke her, spit in her face or kick her about the floor or to inflict upon her other like indignities, is not now acknowledged by our law" (Sheffield 1995, 6). Women legally were no longer the property of men, but they still had no legislation meant to protect them from violence and no system in place to help them when it occurred. The violence continued.

Along with setting up programs to help individual women in need, the women's movement during the 1980s worked to educate the public about the extent of the problem, its entrenched position in American society, and its protected position within the legal system. During the 1980s and 1990s, a few cases of abused women gained media attention and helped to inform the public. In 1987, Hedda Nussbaum, abused wife of Joel Steinberg, made headlines when her daughter was beaten to death by Steinberg; debate raged over how much responsibility Nussbaum, though severely beaten and scarred over a period of nine years, bore for her daughter's murder. (See Chapter 2 for details about this case.) After Nicole Brown Simpson was murdered in 1994, news surfaced that she had been battered for years by her husband, football star O. J. Simpson. Her postmortem story of abuse focused national attention on the continuing reality of domestic violence. It was a spark to educate the public further about the extent of abuse in American homes.

Through the years, too, states and districts have passed laws and reforms: Some districts instituted department-wide programs to prosecute and track domestic violence; some followed a pro-arrest policy; today, many states have mandatory arrest laws. A patchwork of protection and law enforcement resulted from these various efforts. Feminists supported these laws and in most cases were instrumental in helping to institute them, but they wanted more.

Feminists sought a federal law to create a national code of protection for women and a recognition of women's human right to protection from violence. In 1994, with the passage of the Violence Against Women Act, women achieved part of that aim.

By the mid-1990s, the statistics on battered women were still staggering but now well known. In the United States, feminist organizations reported that a woman was beaten by a significant man in her life (father, husband, boyfriend, brother, uncle, or other) every 15 to 18 seconds. The U.S. Department of Justice reported that 75 percent of all "lone-offender" violence against women was committed by someone the victim knew; 29 percent of this violence was by an intimate (husband, ex-husband, boyfriend, or ex-boyfriend).

Feminists have approached the problem of domestic violence from several angles. The work that women's shelters do and the changes that women have achieved in reforming laws against women's assailants are one arm of the approach. Most feminists agree that these changes are essential but are not enough. Feminists also seek a transformation of the roots in society that support violence in the home. They approach this transformative goal from many angles.

The terms need to be changed for people to understand the true nature of domestic violence, argue some feminists. Ann Jones, author of several books on violence against women, writes that calling violence against women in the home "domestic violence" "makes the violence sound domesticated" and "less serious" than other categories of violence. She uses the term "violence against women" instead (Jacobs 1994, 56). Jones also takes on the term "battered woman," which she says suggests that there is a category of women who are "batterable" and therefore responsible for their plight. Her studies have shown that battered women are usually strong women who must resist the control of the men in their lives in order to stay alive, as well as to cope with the rest of life's stresses; they are "resisters" (Jacobs 1994). Other feminists have argued against the term "spousal abuse" because it is non–gender-specific and camouflages the hard facts of who is beating whom: Men are beating women in 90 percent of all cases (McCue 1995). The Boston Women's Health Book Collective calls it "woman abuse."

Feminists also argue that domestic violence is one of the forms of sexual terrorism that keeps women in their place—second place. Domestic violence is not an individual act but is part of the continuum of male power over females. Men as the dominant class wield power over women in many ways, but the fact that violence is one way that some men wield power has a controlling effect over all women. "Men as a class benefit from how women's lives are restricted and limited because of their fear of violence by husbands and lovers as well as by strangers," explains writer Michele Bograd. "Wife abuse or battering reinforces women's passivity and dependence as men exert their rights to authority and control. The reality of domination at the social level is the most crucial factor contributing to and maintaining wife abuse at the personal level" (Bograd 1988, 14). Domestic violence will not end, therefore, until society is transformed to embody equality between women and men. Many feminists working toward equality see their work also as an effort toward ending domestic violence.

Feminists also seek a change in society's perception of women's rights as human rights. Those rights are stated simply, as a first principle to all else: "Women have the right to live free from harm," says Ann Jones (Jacobs 1994, 61). That includes life in the privacy of their homes. The feminist quest for human rights, then, is also a quest for women's rights within the home.

Domestic Violence on a Global Level

Globally, women face similar, often even worse, situations of violence as that of American women. According to the United Nations, violence against women cuts across all cultural, religious, and regional boundaries and is a major problem in virtually

every country in the world. Most countries now have nongovernmental organizations devoted to eliminating violence against
women, and these organizations have been instrumental in urging countries to pass antiviolence laws. Many have done so. As of
1995, domestic violence laws had been passed in Australia, the
Bahamas, Barbados, New Zealand, Trinidad and Tobago, and the
United Kingdom (as well as the United States; see above). Usually, the laws define domestic violence and empower the courts to
issue protection for women. In addition, some governments have
budgeted social services for women and launched media campaigns to educate the public about a need to end violence against
women.

These are all early indicators of possible change, but a 1995
UN report on the percentage of adult women who had been
physically assaulted by an intimate partner revealed that violence is a daily reality for millions of women. In 1997, First Lady
Hillary Rodham Clinton listened as Zimbabwe women told her
about the violence in their lives. A reporter repeated the story:
"Husbands routinely beat their wives, even those who are highly
educated. The men, moreover, blame women for causing the violence 'because they have poor manners' or are wearing pants and
'deserve to be beaten for trying to mimic the man's function'"
(Rosen 1997:B15). Also, men in the region infected with the AIDS
virus rarely disclose that information to their wives, another form
of abuse.

Aung San Suu Kyi, Nobel Peace Prize Laureate and nonviolent political leader of Burma, addressed the problem of domestic
violence in her keynote address to the 1995 Nongovernmental
Organization Forum on Women in China. It was presented on
videotape, as Aung San Suu Kyi does not leave Burma for fear
that she will not be allowed to return. Her words: "Traditionally,
the home is the domain of the woman. But there has never been a
guarantee that she can live out her life there safe and unmolested.
There are countless women who are subjected to severe cruelty
within the heart of the family which should be their haven"
(Fisher 1996, 55).

Rape

Feminist Susan Brownmiller broke new ground for women in
1975 when she wrote, "[Rape] is nothing more or less than a conscious process of intimidation by which *all men* keep *all women* in

a state of fear." Rape is ingrained in a system of patriarchal control of women, she argued. "Men who commit rape have served in effect as front-line masculine shock troops, terrorist guerrillas in the longest sustained battle the world has ever known" (Brownmiller 1993, 209). Brownmiller's work brought together the growing feminist perspective of rape as a form of violence tacitly supported by society. Other forms of violence against women have since been studied and seen through this same lens by feminists (see earlier section in this chapter titled Domestic Violence)—violence as a means by which the dominant male class holds females in check. (See Figure 4.3.)

Feminists have sought to redefine rape from a sexual context into a power/control context. They have worked to reform laws to better protect women and prosecute rapists. And they have tried to educate and empower women, attempting to reduce some of the limitations on women's mobility.

Figure 4.3
Reported Forcible Rapes in
the United States, 1976–1995

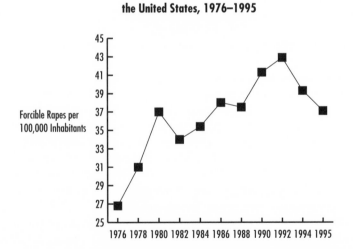

Note: The number of reported forcible rapes dropped from 42.8 in 1992 to 37.1 in 1995, but has been on a general upward trend since 1976. Forcible rape, as defined for this report, is the carnal knowledge of a female forcibly and against her will. Assaults or attempts to commit rape by force or threat of force are also included; however, statutory rape (without force) and other sex offenses are excluded.
Source: U.S. Department of Justice, Federal Bureau of Investigation, *Crime in the United States 1995: Uniform Crime Reports,* October 13, 1996.

One of the earliest demonstrations of women's anger and frustration over the threat of rape under which they live was the 1971 New York Radical Feminists' "speakout" on rape. Forty women stood before a meeting of some 300 people and told the stories of their rapes. They revealed the bias of the police who attended to their cases and noted the blame that was fixed on them for having been raped. What's more important, they broke the traditional silence that surrounded the crime of rape, and they took the blame for the crime off their own shoulders and placed it squarely on the shoulders of the rapists.

Since that first speakout, women have continued to speak up and out against rape and rape laws biased in favor of rapists. In the 1970s, 15 states still had laws requiring corroboration of a rape accusation. Some required witnesses, proof that penetration had occurred (either that the woman was a virgin before the rape or that the man ejaculated), and proof that the woman did not consent. Bruises were necessary to show that she put up a fight. It was also difficult to convince the average jury that a woman was blameless in her attack. Prevailing myths held that raped women were willing victims or brought it on themselves through their provocative clothing, that women sought revenge through rape accusations, or that an unwilling woman couldn't be raped.

In the 1970s police departments were virtually all-male, a fact, Susan Brownmiller argued, that resulted in few rape arrests and little comprehension of the crime of rape. Women who reported they had been raped faced men who trivialized the crime and the women's trauma. Feminists have sought to increase the number of women in law enforcement and have urged women to learn self-defense tactics to enable them to fend off an attacker. (See Figure 4.4.) They note that males are taught to use their bodies to tackle, wrestle, and punch whereas females are instead taught to be polite and graceful. This difference in training puts most women at an immediate disadvantage in an assault.

While white feminists focused on rape and its position in the system of patriarchy, feminists of African American heritage hesitated. Once again, they were in a double bind. The history of rape in the United States is awash in racism, including the rape by white slave owners of enslaved African women, the lynching of African American men for unproven rape accusations, the racism inherent in the stereotypes of African American male sexual violence, and the imbalance in the successful prosecutions of

Figure 4.4
The Percentage of Female Police, Detectives,
Sheriffs, and Bailiffs in the United States, 1976–1996

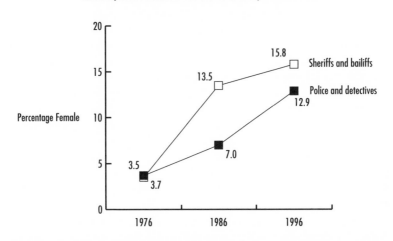

Note: The U.S. Bureau of Labor Statistics revised its protective service categories in 1983. Figures for 1986 and 1996 police and detectives are slightly elevated in comparison to 1976, as they include a small number of inspectors and public administrators. Figures for 1986 and 1996 sheriffs and bailiffs include a small number of guards, marshalls, constables, and police detectives.
Source: U.S. Bureau of Labor Statistics, Division of Labor Force Statistics.

white versus black rapists, as well as the imbalance in legal reaction to a white rape victim versus a black rape victim.

"In general," explains one feminist research team, "white women view rape, harassment, and battering solely in terms of gender. Most African American women, however, view sexual abuse first in terms of race and only second in terms of gender" (Wilson and Russell 1996, 140). An African American woman raped by a man of her own race must decide whether to report the crime and add to the stereotype of the violent African American male. If the accusation is made against a successful or famous African American man, the woman might also face censure within her own community. White women have no such dilemma. This is a fundamental difference in perception and life experience, and one that has divided feminists.

As the feminist movement has progressed and expanded, however, some of these differences are being surmounted. Marcia Ann Gillespie, editor of *Ms.* magazine and an African American, speaks of the need for African American women to hold all men accountable for their violence and urges women of color to support other women who go public when they are victims of violence by African American men (Wilson and Russell 1996, 143). White feminist leaders also urge a continuing, unrelenting reportage of all rapes. The future for a more concerted effort among all women and a bridging of cultural and racial differences is brighter now than it has been in the past.

Feminists can claim some success in their efforts to change the country's perception of rape. By 1990, most rape trial procedures had been revised to leave the rape victim's dignity intact, and evidence-gathering procedures, including obtaining semen specimens, had been revised to show greater sensitivity to the victim. In addition, the crime of rape is now recognized as a crime regardless of the relationship of the victim to the rapist (Sheffield 1995).

The crime of rape has not abated, though; in fact, in 1990, Federal Bureau of Investigation (FBI) statistics showed rape increasing "at four times the rate of other crimes." And this increase came despite the fact that as many as half of all sex crimes even today go unreported (Salholz et al. 1990, 23). Law enforcement officials still advise women to stay off the streets at night, to be wary at all times when in deserted areas, and to walk in pairs. Concerned about the inequity of such a blunted manner of living, feminists remain frustrated. Some feminists like to tell the anecdote about former Israel Prime Minister Golda Meir's response to her counselors during an epidemic of attacks on women. The counselors, all male, wanted to put a curfew on women to keep them off the streets at night. Meir responded: Since the men are the problem, let us put a curfew on them (Kaufman 1990, 59).

The rape rate is 13 times higher in the United States than in Great Britain, nearly 4 times higher than in Germany, and more than 20 times higher than in Japan (Salholz et al. 1990). However, women in many regions of the world are at a greater disadvantage than women in the United States. In many countries women still assume the blame for rape, and many suffer disgrace in their families and communities if they are known to be victims of rape. In a few areas, laws remain that confuse the Western sense of the rapist as criminal. In 1997, Peru's government initiated moves to overturn a well-established custom, one in which rape victims are strongly pressured by family and community to marry the rapists, thus saving the rapists from prison and restoring the honor of the victim and her family. Also in 1997, Mexican feminists were outraged when the Supreme Court of Mexico ruled that marital rape was not rape but was the "undue exercise of a right" (Vedia 1997).

Global Violence

"In virtually every nation, violence or the threat of violence constricts the range of choices open to women and girls in almost every area of life, public and private," says Noeleen Heyzer, director of the United Nations Development Fund for Women (Heyzer 1995, ix). She echoes the words of American feminist Susan Brownmiller, who when speaking about rape pointed out that the personal threats that women face are not just personal but are institutionalized and supportive of the overall system.

Gender-based violence, adds the United Nations, "crosses all cultural, religious and regional boundaries and is a major problem in every country in which it has been studied" (United Nations 1995, 158). Every country in the world lives with condoned or uncondoned but accepted incidences of violence against women.

Much of the knowledge the public has about violence against women worldwide has been publicized by feminists who have dedicated their efforts toward uncovering the facts. The separate efforts of Fran P. Hosken and Alice Walker, for example, brought the practice of female genital mutilation (FGM) to the attention of the world. Other feminists have studied the dowry deaths of women in India, female infanticide, forced marriages of young girls, forced prostitution, sexual abuse of girl children, domestic violence, and rape as a war crime.

As women began to work more in the international community after the 1975 first World Conference on Women in Mexico and turned some of their attention to global issues, they identified numerous abuses against women, many of which are legal in the regions in which they are perpetrated. In the eyes of feminists, these abuses are crimes against women regardless of laws. In addition to the obvious physical abuses, feminists add those of omission—noneducation of girls, starving girls while feeding boys, and providing boys with immediate medical care while girls sometimes go without.

In the past, much violence against women was dismissed as cultural or personal, but with the redefinition of women's rights as human rights in the international community, violence in all its forms has a forum for change. Feminists repeat as often as possible that violence is "profoundly political." Its message is domination. Says feminist Charlotte Bunch, "[violence] results from the structural relationships of power, domination and privilege between men and women in society. Violence against women is central to maintaining those political relations at home, at work, and in all public spheres" (Bunch 1991, 7). The global feminist agenda is bent on reforming those political relations; ending gender-based violence is fundamental to that agenda.

Women all over the world face sexual harassment, domestic violence, and rape. But in addition to these forms of violence, global violence against women includes:

Confinement of Migrant Workers

The UN refers to a study by Middle East Watch that has reported "abuse, confinement, and debt bondage" of Asian women working in Kuwait. Also, a 1991 study revealed 1,400 Filipino domestic servants and hundreds of Bangladeshi, Indian, and Sri Lankan maids working in Kuwait sought refuge in their home embassies in an attempt to escape from abuse (United Nations 1995, 164). There have also been reports of women tricked into prostitution and, in the United States, at least one incident of women held captive and enslaved in a garment sweatshop.

Dowry Deaths

In India, where traditional family custom still includes arranged marriages and bridal dowrys, "bride burnings," or dowry deaths, persist. The women are most often doused with kerosene and burned alive in their kitchens. Motivation for the murder is often an inadequate dowry paid to the husband's family. In 1993, the official count of dowry deaths in India was 5,000; however, according to Amnesty International, the burnings are "notoriously undercounted because they are typically reported as kitchen accidents" (Fisher and MacKay 1996, 32).

Female Infanticide and Sex Selection

Without intervention, about 93 to 96 female babies are born for every 100 males. Deviation from this norm indicates interference from the natural process. Since sex selection has become more accessible through abortion, a few countries that have a cultural male preference show a decrease in their number of female births. Imbalances have recently been reported in China, India, Pakistan, and the Republic of Korea. (See Table 4.2.) The imbalances are an "alarming indication," the UN reports, of the use of modern technology to discover and abort female fetuses. The imbalance in female-to-male births increases when couples already have female children, suggesting that they are even less willing to give birth to a second female (United Nations 1995). Specific evidence of sex selection surfaced in a study of pregnant women in Bombay, India. The study found that women were seeking out ultrasound procedures to determine the sex of their fetuses. Out of 8,000 fetuses aborted after such a test, only one was male (Sivard 1995). Sex-screening tests have since been outlawed in India as well as in China—a country that also shows a pronounced preference for males—but reports and statistics suggest they are still common. Where sex selection through abortion is not possible, female infanticide is used to keep a family free

Table 4.2
Global Violence: Fewer Girls Are Born in Male-Preference Countries

	Girls born per 100 boys	
Country	1982	1988/89
China	93	88
India	92	91
Republic of Korea	94	88
Pakistan	98	92

Girls born per 100 boys, by birth order		
Country and birth order	1982	1988
China		
1st	94	95
2nd	95	83
3rd	91	80
4th	89	76
Republic of Korea		
1st	95	93
2nd	94	88
3rd	91	59
4th	88	50

Source: United Nations, *The World's Women 1995: Trends and Statistics* (New York: United Nations, 1995). United Nations publication, Sales No. E.95.XVII.Z.

from too many female children, which are considered a burden on the family. Unwanted female babies are left to die or are killed outright.

Female Genital Mutilation

The practice of FGM, often euphemistically called female circumcision, involves the cutting off, usually without anesthetic, of the clitoris and some or most of the external genitalia. It can also include infibulation, which means the surface is either stitched together or kept in contact by tying the legs together until it heals, covering most of the vaginal opening. The vaginal opening later is cut open for intercourse (RAINBO 1997). FGM is practiced in a broad region of Africa from the Red Sea to the Atlantic coast, in the southern part of the Arab peninsula, in Malaysia, and in parts of Indonesia. It has been performed, chiefly among immigrants, in Western countries including Europe, Canada, and the United States. Usually the act is performed on girls at the age of puberty, but it is also done as early as infancy and as late as the age of marriage.

Not only is FGM mortally dangerous at the time of the cutting but the results, depending on the extent of the mutilation, include a range of chronic health problems as well as high mortality rates for both mother and baby in childbirth. FGM is a type of violence against women that was protected from international interference because it was labeled a "cultural practice." Feminists, through their lobbying and global re-education, relabeled it an abuse. It was labeled a form of violence against women at the 1993 World Conference on Human Rights in Vienna; its abolishment was included as a goal in the 1995 fourth World Conference on Women Beijing Platform for Action. In 1996, the United States Board of Immigration Appeals ruled that mutilation may constitute grounds for fleeing persecution and thus seeking asylum in the United States. The ruling was based on the case of a West African woman who fled Togo to escape the threat. The United States also passed a federal law outlawing FGM as part of the Illegal Immigration Reform and Immigrant Responsibility Act of 1996. Immigration officials now provide information on the harmful physical effects of FGM and of the law to all who enter from countries where FGM is widely practiced. Laws against FGM also have been passed in most European countries and in Canada. And today, almost all of the countries where FGM is practiced have reported to the United Nations on the occurrence of it and expressed official opposition to it.

Yet, the practice remains entrenched in traditionalist communities. In these areas, patriarchs rule, and women have little or no say in whether they or their daughters will undergo the mutilation. It is estimated that two million females are mutilated annually and that 130 million women alive today have been mutilated (RAINBO 1997). In 1996 FGM was banned in Egypt; in 1997 Islamic scholars and doctors succeeded in overturning the ban; then finally the ban was reinstated by Egypt's highest court. Arguments for FGM in Egypt included keeping women's sexual drives "to acceptable and reasonable levels" and protecting the population from AIDS by reducing promiscuity (Daniszewski 1997). Also in 1996 and 1997, international fashion model Warris Dirie, a Somalian, spoke out about the pain, trauma, and after-effects of her own mutilation, a personal story that reached millions through magazine articles and television.

Female Neglect

Among the daily crimes and offenses against women are feeding girls and women last and least. Women of all ages, including pregnant women, suffer anemia at rates that indicate they are getting an unfairly reduced share of food. Female children often are denied medical care; preference is given to sick male children. The International Center for Research on Women reports in its Global Fact Sheet (1996) that according to a recent study, boys in Bangladesh under age five got 16 percent more food than girls; in India, "girls were four times more likely than boys to suffer acute malnutrition but 40 times less likely to be taken to a hospital" (p. 2). Also, studies of the chores and work done by girls and boys consistently show that girls work more hours in a day than boys, and they are allowed less time for school and studies.

Forced Prostitution

The Japanese government recently admitted forcing tens of thousands of women into prostitution for the Imperial Army during World War II, an admission that came after intense efforts by women's organizations in the Philippines and Korea. In 1993, women who testified before the Vienna Global Tribunal on Violations of Women's Human Rights told their stories of current practices—of being tricked into prostitution and being held captive, both by criminal individuals and by state-supported groups. Though the United Nations reports that the extent of forced prostitution today is unknown, studies are showing that the problem exists in countries all over the world. The Commission on Human Rights Working Group on Contemporary Forms of Slavery estimates that two million women are in prostitution in India, with roughly 400,000 of them under 18 years of age. The commission also reports that 5,000 to 7,000 young Nepal girls are sold into brothels each year. Filipina women, too, have been frequent victims of forced prostitution. The women, usually between the ages of 16 and 23, migrate as entertainers and are tricked into prostitution. Once they are in a foreign country, the women's passports are confiscated and the women are imprisoned, subject to physical violence and threats against their families back home (United Nations 1995). In the Philippines, women have mobilized to combat forced prostitution, forming an information center to help women in Thailand prostitution rings and to warn Filipinas of deceitful ads that entice women into foreign countries.

Rape as a War Crime

The mass rape of women in wartime has been a documented staple of war since biblical times. Yet, very little mention has been made of it in history books, and global concern over it did not mobilize until recently. Reports of mass rapes in the war in the former Yugoslavia surfaced in the early 1990s. At the same time, there were reports of systematic, military-endorsed mass rapes in Rwanda. Human Rights Watch reported that their investigations in the former Yugoslavia, and also in Peru, Kashmir, and Somalia, revealed that the rape of unarmed women and girls was used "as a tactical weapon to terrorize civilian communities or to achieve 'ethnic cleansing,' a tool in enforcing hostile occupations, and a means of conquering or seeking revenge against an enemy" (Human Rights Watch 1995, 2). The Human Rights Watch also found that in Haiti, women activists, members of the opposition, and female relatives of opposition members have been raped. Feminists have lobbied for recognition of rape as a war crime to be prosecuted by war crime tribunals. The fact that women's rights are officially recognized as human rights helps to place violence such as rape into the context of a war crime.

Affirmative Action

The battle over affirmative action has often been one of defining just what affirmative action is. Opponents have called it a quota and preference system that produces reverse discrimination. But feminists have pointed out that affirmative action when applied legally is not discrimination in reverse. Instead, affirmative action is a concept that generally means "positive steps taken by a company, organization, agency, or institution to end discrimination, to prevent its recurrence, and to create new opportunities that previously were denied to qualified women and people of color" (Frye 1996, 34).

A core principle of affirmative action as defined by feminists is that all candidates must have a chance to compete, and the qualifications of all candidates should be evaluated and compared. Also, affirmative action is designed to be temporary and to be in place until the goal of integration is met. Under affirmative action rulings, employers cannot promote unqualified people over qualified ones and thus are prevented from creating "preferences." Also, companies cannot set rigid, inflexible quotas and cannot fire men and whites to replace them with women and minorities.

Examples of legal affirmative action policies would be efforts alerting women and people of color about job openings, training programs that target minorities for scholarships, and goals and timetables to measure and encourage participation by personnel (Costello and Krimgold 1996).

Affirmative action has had a short but contentious life in the United States. While conservatives have fought affirmative action in an effort to hold on to the status quo, feminists have rallied behind the cause and lobbied intensively to promote affirmative action. Following is an overview of affirmative action in the United States.

1961   Federal Plans for Progress, a voluntary program for all contractors doing business with the federal government, is initiated.

1965   President Lyndon Johnson first uses the term "affirmative action" in an executive order, requiring federal contractors to "take affirmative action to ensure that applicants are employed, and that employees are treated during employment, without regard to their race, creed, color, or national origin."

1967   President Johnson extends his executive order, prohibiting sex discrimination by federal contractors.

1970   By the end of the year, the Labor Department issues affirmative action guidelines to all federal contractors to ensure nondiscrimination in hiring.

1978   The U.S. Supreme Court rules in *Steelworkers v. Weber* that employers can sometimes give job preference "to break down old patterns of race segregation and hierarchy."

The U.S. Supreme Court rules in *Regents of the University of California v. Bakke* that diversity constitutes a compelling interest for institutions of higher education to consider race and national origin in their admissions procedures. (In most cases, the courts continue to hold that affirmative action plans can be supported in the interest of diversity in student bodies or to redress past discrimination.)

1987   The U.S. Supreme Court rules in *Johnson v. Transportation Agency* that employers can sometimes favor women and minorities over better-qualified men and whites to correct "a conspicuous imbalance in traditionally segregated job categories" and also to bring its work force in line with the makeup of the labor market (Woloch 1994).

1995   The U.S. Supreme Court rules in *Adarand Constructors v. Pena* in favor of a white contractor who challenges a program that awards contracts to minority-owned businesses. Affirmative action programs must be drawn narrowly and must serve a compelling purpose. This ruling is one indication that official political opinion is shifting.

Anti-affirmative action legislation is introduced in 26 states and in the U.S. Congress. Not a single bill passes (Verhovek 1996).

1996   In *Hopwood et al. v. State of Texas et al.* the U.S. Supreme Court lets stand a lower court ruling that the University of Texas law school's admissions policy discriminates against whites when it considers race as a basis for admission.

In California, voters support Proposition 209, the California Civil Rights Initiative, a ballot referendum that says government cannot discriminate or grant preferential treatment on the basis of race, sex, or national origin in public employment, education, or contracting. Though it never mentions the words "affirmative action," Proposition 209's purpose is to ban state and local government affirmative action programs except where required by federal law. Its passage is a setback for feminists.

Throughout affirmative action's history, feminists have maintained staunch support of its policies and have attributed much of women's inroads into business management and the professions to affirmative action policies. In fall 1995, Kathryn J. Rodgers, executive director of the National Organization for Women Legal Defense and Education Fund, urged women to speak out for affirmative action and to support it in the face of growing opposition. She called it a "critical tool for creating equal opportunity for women in the workplace," adding that, "It says: a woman should apply; if she applies, she will be considered on her merits; when she's hired she can be trained for advancement; and when a promotion is available, she will be considered on her merits" (Rodgers 1995, 2). "Affirmative action is every woman's issue," added Irma D. Herrera, a feminist with the Equal Rights Advocates in San Francisco, as she was rallying women to fight California's Proposition 209 (Herrera 1996, 2).

Feminists faced opposition in the mid-1990s that said affirmative action had done its job; the time had come to end it and move on. But feminists argued that though women have made inroads, progress is not a synonym for success; women still have a long way to go to achieve equity. They also warn that "the elimination of affirmative action will mean an erosion of the gains made by women" (Frye 1996, 42).

Although polls showed that most Americans in the mid-1990s supported creating opportunities for women, Americans rejected the idea of quotas and preferences. The forces supporting California's Proposition 209 appealed to this antipreference sentiment; they defined affirmative action in terms of quotas, preferences, and reverse discrimination.

Eleanor Smeal, president of the Feminist Majority, called Proposition 209 "the opening war to roll back civil rights and women's rights in this nation" (Boxall 1996). Feminists mobilized alongside minority groups and other political allies for an all-out effort to defeat Proposition 209. Feminists asserted that passage of Proposition 209 would weaken California's sex discrimination laws and jeopardize school athletics for girls and education and job programs for women (Boxall 1996). Irma Herrera warned that the proposition would eliminate girls' math and science programs, girls' sports that were less well-attended than boys' sports, and courses in rape prevention, sexual harassment, and self-defense offered by campus women's centers.

Nevertheless, Proposition 209 passed. Votes in favor of the proposition were heavily Republican (80 percent), male (61 percent), and white (63 percent). Democrats, liberals, African Americans, Latinos, and Asian Americans came out strongly against the proposition, with three-fourths of Latino and African American Californians opposed. Women were divided, at 52 percent against and 48 percent for (Stall 1996).

Proposition 209 immediately went to court, winning at the U.S. Circuit Court of Appeals level; it is, however, expected to be taken all the way to the Supreme Court. After the circuit court victory, California Governor Pete Wilson, who supported the proposition, said, "With this ruling, California comes one step closer to assuring the kind of society which will afford genuine equality and access to opportunity to all of its citizens" (Dolan 1997:A-1). Speaking for the forces in support of affirmative action, Mark Rosenbaum, American Civil Liberties Union legal director, disagreed: "[The ruling] does not just move minorities and women to the back of the bus, it boots them off all together" (Dolan 1997:A-1). The national impact of Proposition 209 was immediate. Across the country, affirmative action opponents pledged to work to reignite their battles to end affirmative action in their states.

As feminists faced growing opposition to affirmative action in the 1990s, the debate settled into a predictable set of pros and cons.

ANTI: Affirmative action is no longer necessary for women.

PRO: Discrimination continues to deny women opportunities in many fields. Examples of discrimination: In 1995 only 2.1 percent of the construction workforce was female; also in 1995, though women were 46 percent of the national workforce, they were only 5 percent of top management at Fortune 1000 industrial and service firms. White men were 43 percent of the workforce but 95 percent of senior management.

ANTI: There are already laws against discrimination in employment. We do not need affirmative action.

PRO: Civil rights laws don't address subtle institutional discrimination. Affirmative action is a tool that opens doors to qualified individuals who might otherwise be excluded because of prejudice.

ANTI: Affirmative action gives preference to undeserving women and people of color solely on the basis of their gender or race.

PRO: Preferential treatment, quotas, and hiring of unqualified people are activities prohibited by law. Affirmative action allows women and minorities to compete and excel on the basis of their qualifications, not gender or race, in areas where they are, or have been, underrepresented.

ANTI: Affirmative action results in reverse discrimination against white men.

PRO: A report by the Department of Labor found that of more than 3,000 discrimination opinions in federal district courts from 1990 to 1994, fewer than 100 were claims of reverse discrimination. Of these, reverse discrimination was established in only six cases.

ANTI: Affirmative action is bad for business.

PRO: Affirmative action widens the labor pool of qualified candidates, introduces more competition for jobs, and provides a workforce that reflects the diversity of the markets that businesses serve.

ANTI: Affirmative action undermines an employer's ability to make employment decisions based on merit.

PRO: Affirmative action was created precisely because decisions were not being made based on merit. In seeking to achieve an end to discrimination, an employer is never required to hire a person who does not have the qualifications needed to perform the job successfully or to hire a less qualified person over a qualified one.

ANTI: Affirmative action should be based on social and economic disadvantage rather than on race and gender.
PRO: This idea ignores the reason that affirmative action was created—to prevent race and sex discrimination and ensure inclusion of all qualified individuals. It would be illogical to bring an individual's economic or social situation into employment decisions about hiring, promotion, and pay. (Women Employed Institute, 1995)

Education

Up until about the time of the American Revolution, an educated woman in the colonies was likely to be seen as a "monstrosity" who was unattractive to men and unmarriageable in the extreme—marriage being a woman's sole rightful role in life. The war caused colonial women's roles to shift and their expectations to rise. As a result of their active role in running households and communities while the men went off to battle, many women began to see themselves—and be seen—as rational creatures. They also came to identify themselves as "republican mothers." This identity outlined a new civic role for women, that of molding the values and minds of their sons, the future decision makers of the land, and of their daughters, the future mothers of sons who would be decision makers. Doors to education slowly began to open to white females. By 1830, women's literacy reached almost the same rate as men's (Woloch 1994). By the end of the nineteenth century, a few colleges for women had been established, and women were being accepted in a few others, with restrictions. Lucy Stone, the noted feminist, attended Oberlin Collegiate Institute (later renamed Oberlin College) in Ohio in 1843, where she joined other women students in the laundry room to wash the male students' clothes; she and her female classmates also waited on the men at dinner. Her studies were separate from the men's, and though she won the right to write the commencement address, a man read it at the ceremonies: Women then did not speak in public (Sadker and Sadker 1994). Yet, the women's movement for suffrage was underway, and it would affect education as well as politics.

As the twentieth century progressed, more and more women attended high school, and growing numbers were accepted into colleges. By the onset of the second wave of feminism, educational opportunities seemed to be equal between the sexes. However, though there were few written policies discriminating against females, women's experiences taught them that they were far from equal. Most textbooks ignored women's impact in the sciences, literature, and other subjects—either as individuals or as a group—instead presenting a male-oriented view of all events. Girls in high school were encouraged into home economics programs while boys were pointed toward vocational skills with earning potential. Young women interested in engineering, architecture, physics, or any of the hard sciences and higher mathematics were discouraged, and sometimes they simply were not allowed into the programs. Women were still often admonished by school officials that they were selfishly taking the seat of a male student who would be supporting a family one day.

Well into the 1960s, many prestigious colleges and universities maintained a closed-door policy toward women. Harvard College opened its curriculum to women in 1943 through its sister college, Radcliffe, but did not allow women to earn Harvard degrees until the 1960s (Franck and Brownstone 1995). By 1969 Princeton University had opened its doors to women. In 1976 the U.S. Army, Air Force, Navy, and Coast Guard military academies admitted women.

Almost twenty years later, in 1995, Shannon Faulkner became the first woman to be admitted to the Citadel, a 154-year-old South Carolina military college. She fought a feminist-supported legal battle to get in—but dropped out after only six days. Citadel males cheered victoriously at her failure. Nevertheless, in 1996 four more women joined the freshman Citadel class. Two dropped out after one semester, reporting that freshman hazing of them had included being smeared with fingernail polish and set on fire (Gleick 1997, 38).

Today, women and girls have access to educational opportunity, and feminists have turned much of their attention to residual gender bias in the classroom. Studies in the early 1990s showed that girls were receiving an inferior education. Though the achievements of women and minorities had been added to class materials, often they were presented as additions or sidebars to the real action of the text. History or politics from a woman's point of view had not surfaced in mainstream texts, and children still received a male-biased worldview. Further gender inequities in the elementary school classroom existed: Girls were called on less than boys even when their hands were raised, girls received less personal instruction and less feedback and encouragement when giving answers, and girls were rewarded for neatness while boys were praised for ingenuity. In colleges, female students faced a similar situation. Women spoke up less in the classroom and were interrupted by males more; males received more of their professors' attention and feedback. And universities had a "glass wall" that separated the majority of female students into the "softer" humanitarian disciplines, with only a minority of females entering the hard sciences, especially on the graduate level (Sadker and Sadker 1994).

Feminists have focused on the problems of gender bias in educational materials and in classroom instruction, backing studies of the problems and educating the public and educators about gender inequities. They have also focused attention on educating girls and women in nontraditional disciplines, in urging girls to join school sports teams, and in encouraging scholarships and grants to include women.

The Title IX Generation

During the 1996 Summer Olympic Games, women won 38 of the 101 medals awarded to U.S. athletes. They took home medals in soccer, softball, swimming, track, and other sports. This was a record high for the women, and the whys and wherefores of such an event were quickly analyzed. The conclusion arrived at by virtually every observer: Blame it on Title IX.

The 1996 Olympics presented the world with the first full generation of Title IX women, defined as those who grew up after the 1972 Education Act Amendment was passed with Title IX attached. Because of this piece of legislation, girls were raised with the opportunity to join baseball teams, play in soccer leagues, and have access to school basketball and volleyball courts and softball diamonds. Pre-Title IX generations of girls seldom had equitable gym facilities in schools and were often budgeted what was left over after the boys' programs were organized. Their equipment was inferior (often hand-me-downs from the boys), their playing fields second-rate, and organized team sports often unavailable.

In 1972, as Rep. Edith Green introduced Title IX in Congress, she was well-supported by feminist organizations. She was well-opposed, too: Her most vocal opposition came from school sports departments across the country, and her most bitter opposition arose from college football coaches who feared having to share their budgets with women athletes. The National Collegiate Athletics Association (NCAA) led a campaign to have football exempted from Title IX on the grounds that football produced revenue for other sports, an argument that feminists punctured. Football supports football, writes feminist athlete Mariah Burton Nelson, and most programs run at a deficit. She adds, "in 91 percent of all colleges, the football program does not make enough money to pay for itself" (Nelson 1994, 124). Forty-five percent of Division I-A university football programs lose money on football; so do 94–99 percent of other universities (Nelson 1991). The myth of football as a great revenue producer lingers, however, and feminists continue to battle it while also battling the football coaches who continue to fight to get football exempted from Title IX.

Feminists have consistently struggled to achieve enforcement of Title IX in the years since it became law. The federal government, they charge, has almost always been reluctant to enforce Title IX and has never pulled federal funding from schools or colleges that discriminate against women and girls. The Office of Civil Rights (OCR), which has responsibility for interpreting and implementing Title IX, is part of the Department of Education (previously the Department of Health, Education, and Welfare) and therefore is subject to political reappointments as presidential administrations change.

In the 1970s, though the OCR was not proactive in implementing Title IX, it did interpret it to mean that if any part of an institution received federal money, the entire institution was bound by Title IX's nondiscrimination requirement. During those years, feminists sought enforcement of Title IX through individual lawsuits challenging discriminatory school policies. The courts ruled in favor of Title IX implementation, but suing for gender equity on a case-by-case basis was an expensive and time-consuming avenue to parity, achieving only a patchwork result. What's more, in the 1980s, as the political climate took a swing to the right, Title IX met with disfavor from the conservatives in the Reagan and Bush administrations. The OCR continued to be overwhelmingly inactive, and it reversed its earlier interpretation of Title IX as being all-inclusive for an institution: Enforcement of Title IX became only program-specific. This meant that only the select programs that discriminated in an institution would lose federal funding; the institution itself would continue to benefit directly from federal coffers and from federal student loans. The Supreme Court agreed with this interpretation in 1984.

Feminists and other leaders took the battle back into the U.S. Congress, winning a new law, the Civil Rights Restoration Act, that passed both houses by large margins. President Reagan vetoed the law but was overridden by Congress, and Title IX was restored.

The focus of Title IX has been on sports, but the significance of it reaches beyond the baseball diamonds and soccer fields and into the classroom itself. Because of Title IX, previously discriminatory admissions policies were revised, educational programs and classes that had been closed to high school girls were opened, and budgets throughout institutions were examined for gender equity. Title IX addressed many areas of potential and ongoing discrimination, including student activities and organizations, counseling, academic advising, financial assistance, testing, physical and mental health facilities, institutional rules and policies, treatment of students, publications, facilities, housing, and employment (Durrant 1992). Nevertheless, most of the opposition to the amendment has come from sports departments.

Men's sports coaches continue today in a campaign to limit or retract the law. In early 1995, the American Football Coaches Association asked Congress to revisit Title IX, arguing that Title IX was hurting football funding. In addition, coaches of men's sports such as wrestling, golf, and gymnastics joined together to lobby against Title IX, which they argued is hurting their sports by taking opportunities away from men—another argument that feminists refute. As more women become athletes, they do not displace men in athletic programs; instead, the total number of athletes increases.

According to the Feminist Majority Foundation, in 1972 there were 31,852 women athletes and 172,447 men athletes at NCAA institutions. In 1993, there were 99,859 women athletes and 187,041 men athletes. (See Table 4.3.) Meanwhile, a 1991 study revealed that men at NCAA campuses received 70 percent of athletic scholarship money, 77 percent of operating budgets, and 83 percent of recruiting money. In high schools, while boys'

Table 4.3
Opportunities to Participate in Many College Sports Have
Increased for Women, as Shown in Selected Major Sports

Sport	Percent of Colleges Offering Each Sport to Women					
	1977/1978	1980	1985	1990	1995	1996
Basketball	90.3	97.5	96.8	96.2	97.5	98.3
Cross-country	29.4	46.6	75.2	82.1	83.0	85.2
Gymnastics	25.9	25.6	20.4	15.5	11.1	11.2
Soccer	2.8	8.2	26.8	41.3	61.8	68.9
Softball	48.4	62.3	68.4	70.9	74.5	77.0
Tennis	80.0	88.6	87.0	88.8	86.4	87.8
Track	46.1	58.6	63.8	68.6	63.7	65.8
Volleyball	80.1	87.8	86.3	90.6	90.9	92.4

Note: Figures are for National Collegiate Athletic Association (NCAA) colleges. Though gymnastics was offered in only 11.2 percent of all NCAA colleges in 1996, it was offered in 25.4 percent of Division 1 colleges. Other sports in which there has been an overall decrease include archery, badminton, bowling, fencing, field hockey, and synchronized swimming.
Source: R. Vivian Acosta and Linda Jean Carpenter, *Women in Intercollegiate Sport: A Longitudinal Study—Nineteen Year Update 1977–1996* (Brooklyn: Brooklyn College, 1996).

participation has remained relatively steady, girls' participation has risen from 7 percent of interscholastic athletes in 1972 to 32 percent in 1977, and 37 percent in 1992 (Feminist Majority Foundation 1995a). Nevertheless, the National Association for Girls and Women in Sports reports that in 1992, when asked to name three great athletes, 83 percent of girls aged 9 to 13 named all males. The battle over Title IX continues. Following is a brief chronology of Title IX legislation and effects.

1972   Title IX is passed as part of the Education Act; it reads: "No person in the United States shall, on the basis of sex, be excluded from participation in, be denied the benefits of, or be subjected to discrimination under any education program or activity receiving Federal financial assistance."

1974   The NCAA, which governs men's athletics, files legal action in an attempt to invalidate Title IX.

1975   Title IX regulations are finalized. All school districts, colleges, and universities must complete a self-study

1975 (cont.)	to identify noncompliance, develop strategies, and set timelines for compliance.
1978	The deadline for all institutions to be in compliance arrives. Few have achieved parity, many have not tried.
1979	In *Cannon v. University of Chicago,* the U.S. Supreme Court finds that private lawsuits may be filed as an alternative to the administration's complaint process. This allows pro-Title IX forces to go around a foot-dragging Office of Civil Rights to sue for enforcement of Title IX.
1980 (approx.)	The Office of Civil Rights reinterprets Title IX to be program-specific, rendering the law virtually powerless.
1984	In *Grove City College v. Bell,* the U.S. Supreme Court rules that Title IX is program specific, essentially neutering the law. Fifty members of Congress file a brief in protest stating that the law's intention was institution-wide.
1988	Over President Reagan's veto, Congress passes the Civil Rights Restoration Act in reaction to Supreme Court decisions that have reduced the effectiveness of Title IX and other laws. The act reaffirms that Title IX applies institution-wide, regardless of whether all programs draw federal funds directly.
1992	In its decision on *Franklin v. Gwinnett County,* the U.S. Supreme Court strengthens Title IX by ruling that plaintiffs may sue for monetary damages. The case involved a high school woman who said she was sexually harassed and abused by a teacher.
1993	In *California NOW v. Board of Trustees of the California State University,* the two parties reach a settlement. The California State University (CSU) system of 20 campuses agrees to raise participation rates and scholarships so that women are within 5 percent of their proportion by 1998–1999.

1994   Senators Carol Moseley-Braun (D.-Ill.) and Edward
        Kennedy (D.-Mass.) introduce an amendment to the
        Elementary and Secondary Education Act requiring
        colleges and universities to disclose funding and par-
        ticipation rates. The amendment is passed; the re-
        quirement takes effect in 1996.

1997   Title IX is upheld when the U.S. Supreme Court al-
        lows a lower court ruling, *Brown v. Cohen,* to stand.
        The case is a suit brought by female students against
        Brown University when its athletic department de-
        cided to cut women's gymnastics and volleyball
        (plus men's golf and water polo) in a budgeting ef-
        fort. The women charge that Brown has fewer
        women than men overall in sports and was in viola-
        tion of Title IX when it dropped women's programs.
        Women, who make up 51 percent of the student
        body, are only 38 percent of intercollegiate varsity
        athletes. The university complains that gender dis-
        parity exists because more men than women are in-
        terested in sports; the law calls for gender parity be-
        tween student body and athletic lineup. The decision
        sets no legal precedent but has practical effects, reaf-
        firming the Court's expectations for Title IX compli-
        ance (National Association for Girls and Women in
        Sports 1997). Christine Grant, athletic director at the
        University of Iowa, is quoted by the Associated Press
        as saying, "I think the message that goes across the
        country today is that those who have been dragging
        their feet [on Title IX compliance] are duly warned
        that the time is now. It's a very clear message and
        long, long overdue" (Associated Press 1997).

        The results of the 1993 suit against the California
        State University system take effect. The time arrives
        to budget for the 1998–1999 school year, and at least
        one campus, CSU at Northridge, creates a furor
        when it cuts men's baseball, volleyball, swimming,
        and soccer, but not its football team, to achieve gen-
        der equity. The media focuses on the great loss of
        athletic opportunities suffered by male athletes
        (Wharton and Henson 1997).

Second-Wave Changes

Feminists lobbied extensively for passage of Title IX of the Education Acts Amendments. They saw the possibilities of far-reaching changes that equity in the classroom could reap for women. And the changes have been tremendous. Many are directly traceable to Title IX, but other factors have played into the equation throughout the years, too. A change in consciousness inspired by second-wave feminists helped women see the limitations in schools, and the activist spirit of the second-wave feminists inspired women to stop accepting what they saw.

One of the changes has been the addition on many campuses of women's history classes and women's issues curriculums. The first women's studies course, Women in Contemporary Society, was offered in 1970 at the State University of New York in Buffalo. By 1974, an array of 2,000 women's studies courses were offered at 500 colleges. By 1976, San Francisco State University offered a B.A. major in women's studies. By the mid-1980s, 30,000 courses in women's studies were offered nationwide, and virtually every college campus taught one or more courses on the subject (Wilson and Russell 1996; Woloch 1994). Groundbreaking textbooks such as *All the Women Are White, All the Blacks Are Men, but Some of Us Are Brave* (1982) were published. The programs increased awareness of women's history and politics, but they also helped to reshape what is being taught at all grade levels and, what's more, influenced the method of teaching. Women's studies programs have been innovative in changing classrooms from teacher-directed to participatory environments, with greater use of oral histories, biographies, journals, and discussion groups (Hahn 1997). This methodology now can be found at all grades, in all subjects.

Another change on campuses has been an attempt by textbook buyers to find texts for all departments that include women's contributions. In English departments, *The Norton Anthology of Literature by Women* (1985) was added to a canon that previously included a sparse representation of women's works. The 1974 third edition of *The Norton Anthology of English Literature*, a standard text in college English classes, for example, included just eight women writers in its list of more than 170. Virginia Woolf's influential work was given two pages. In 1993, *The Norton Book of Women's Lives* was published, chiefly for college use, and includes works by Judith Ortiz Cofer, Joan Didion, and

Maxine Hong Kingston. Even today, though, many textbooks still include women's contributions and events as sidebars to the action, whether it be history, anthropology, or literature. Progressive professors look for texts that do more—they want texts that include women not just as sidebars but as integral factors in the narrative. *A History of Their Own: Women in Europe from Prehistory to the Present* is a 1988 work that has shown professors new ways to narrate history, one that discusses women's roles in history and illustrates how history books can be organized to include both women and men.

Teachers have also taken gender-equity awareness seminars, and major organizations have surveyed and studied gender equity at all grade levels of classrooms. Many studies report surprise at the heretofore unnoticed bias of many classrooms as evidenced in, for example, the attention and respect given to male college students as opposed to female students. As Myra Sadker and David Sadker reported in 1994, "men [in college classes] are more than twice as likely to monopolize class discussions, and women are twice as likely to be silent" (p. 170). In their research, the Sadker team also encountered blatant sexist comments in class by both professors and students, professorial preference toward males, and de facto segregation of females and males in the sciences and humanities. Feminists, therefore, point out that as these studies show, despite great achievements in the past twenty years there is still much to be done by third-wave feminists seeking equity.

American women have been, however, gaining ground in disciplines traditionally dominated by men. According to the National Center for Education statistics, the percentage of bachelor's degrees in architecture earned by women went from 17.4 percent in 1974 to 35.8 percent in 1993. In business too, women made a dramatic leap, from 16.3 in 1974 to 47.6 in 1993. Even in fields where female representation remains low, such as engineering and computer sciences, the numbers have increased from previous years. And overall, women are earning postsecondary degrees in greater numbers than men at every level except the doctoral. (See Tables 4.4–4.5 and Figures 4.5–4.6.)

Global Education of Females

In 1993, almost a quarter of the world's adult population was illiterate, and 65 percent of those illiterate were women. (See Fig-

Table 4.4
Percentages and Totals of Women Enrolled in
U.S. Colleges, by Ethnic Background, 1976, 1988, 1994

Women Students	1976	1988	1994
Non-Hispanic White	39.6	43.9	41.8
Non-Hispanic Black	5.2	5.4	6.5
Hispanic[a]	1.6	2.9	4.2
Asian or Pacific Islander	.8	1.9	2.8
American Indian/Alaskan Native	.3	.4	.5
Total Percentage[b]	47.6	54.6	55.9
Total Number, in thousands	5,191.2	7,044.9	7,906.9

[a]Hispanics include Mexicans, Puerto Ricans, and various Central and South American nationalities
[b]Percentages may not add up to total because of rounding
Source: National Center for Education Statistics, *Digest of Education Statistics 1996*, Table 203.

ure 4.7.) In some countries, girls still count themselves lucky if they receive a primary school education and extremely fortunate if they attend secondary school. In many regions of the world, girls are routinely kept home to care for the house; they watch as boys in the family are given educational priority. But there have been advances for women. A 1993 study showed that approximately 885 million children were attending school that year, and about 400 million were girls (United Nations International Children's Fund 1994).

In fact, girls and women are being educated in greater percentages and numbers than ever before. In developed nations, access to education for girls is virtually equal to that for boys. Differences in education in these nations still appear, but they are more apparent in the upper levels, as women's numbers fall off in comparison to men's in postgraduate education and faculty standings. Differences also appear in choice of subjects, with women underrepresented in mathematics, sciences, and other technical fields.

In many developing nations, the primary level of schooling no longer shows any significant gender gap; these countries include some parts of Latin America, South America, and the Caribbean. Differences in these regions appear in secondary and higher education. But in other regions—for example, South Asia, the Arab nations, and sub-Saharan Africa—the education gender gap is more pronounced. The gender gap is especially wide in

Table 4.5
Women Earning Degrees in U.S.
Colleges and Universities, by Field, 1974–1994

	Percentage of Total Degrees Earned		
	1974–1975	1984–1985	1993–1994
Architecture and Related Programs			
Bachelor's	17.4	35.5	35.8
Master's	20.3	34.4	38.4
Doctor's	15.9	25.8	31.1
Business Management and Administrative Services			
Bachelor's	16.3	45.1	47.6
Master's	8.5	31.0	36.5
Doctor's	4.2	17.2	28.2
Computer and Information Sciences			
Bachelor's	18.9	36.8	28.4
Master's	14.7	28.7	25.8
Doctor's	6.6	10.0	15.4
Education			
Bachelor's	73.3	75.9	77.3
Master's	62.3	72.5	76.7
Doctor's	30.4	52.0	60.8
Engineering			
Bachelor's	2.2	13.1	14.9
Master's	2.4	10.7	15.5
Doctor's	2.1	6.4	11.1
Mathematics			
Bachelor's	41.2	46.2	46.3
Master's	30.1	32.9	38.1
Doctor's	10.7	15.5	21.9
Physical Sciences			
Bachelor's	18.2	28.0	33.6
Master's	14.4	23.2	29.2
Doctor's	8.3	16.2	21.7
Psychology			
Bachelor's	52.6	68.2	73.1
Master's	46.4	65.1	72.1
Doctor's	32.1	49.6	62.2
Social Sciences and History			
Bachelor's	37.3	44.1	46.1
Master's	30.1	38.4	44.0
Doctor's	20.8	32.2	36.1

Source: National Center for Education Statistics, *Digest of Education Statistics 1996*, Tables 272, 275, 277, 278, 279, 285, 286, 288, and 290.

Figure 4.5
The Number of Women Earning Postsecondary Degrees, 1969–2001

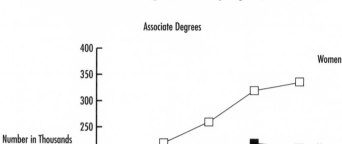

Associate Degrees

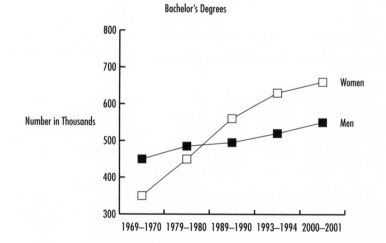

Bachelor's Degrees

(continues)

**Figure 4.5
(continued)**

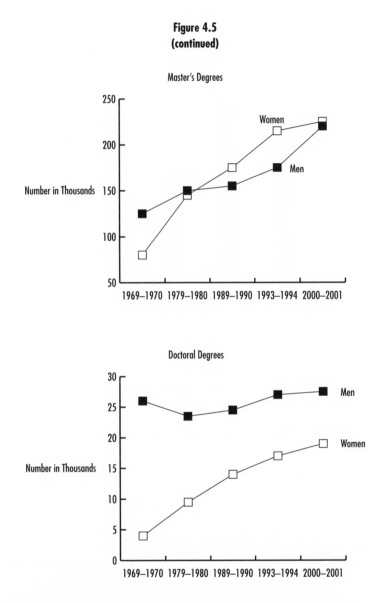

Master's Degrees

Number in Thousands

Women

Men

1969–1970 1979–1980 1989–1990 1993–1994 2000–2001

Doctoral Degrees

Number in Thousands

Men

Women

1969–1970 1979–1980 1989–1990 1993–1994 2000–2001

Note: Numbers for 2000–2001 are National Center for Education projections. Overall, more women earned postsecondary degrees than did men at all but the doctoral level.
Source: National Center for Education Statistics, *Digest of Education Statistics 1996,* Table 239.

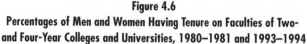

Figure 4.6
**Percentages of Men and Women Having Tenure on Faculties of Two-
and Four-Year Colleges and Universities, 1980–1981 and 1993–1994**

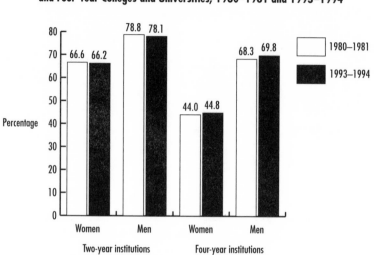

Source: National Center for Educational Statistics, *Digest of Education Statistics 1996,* Table 235.

rural areas. What's more, young women can face formidable political and social barriers to obtaining an education. Parents in
fundamentalist and conservative cultures that restrict women's
roles and career choices can be reluctant to invest in a daughter's
higher education; she is likely to leave the family and marry
whereas her brothers will earn incomes for the family. Her housework today is valued higher than her limited future possibilities.

The societal benefits of educating women are well-documented by the United Nations, its commissions, and nongovernmental organizations and are used to convince nations to
institute policy changes. The United Nations International Children's Fund (UNICEF) reports the following benefits of educating females:

- The education of females correlates with improved
  health for the family. Across the globe, with few exceptions, nations that show a rising educational level of
  women also show a lowering of infant mortality rates
  and of maternal mortality. A recent United Nations

Figure 4.7
Illiteracy Rates Show That Globally Women
Have Less Access to Education than Do Men

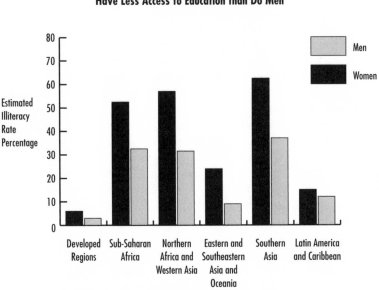

Note: The percentage for developed regions is based on limited data. Data for Northern Africa and Western Asia includes Djibouti, Mauritania, and Somalia. All are for adults of fifteen years and over.
Source: United Nations, *The World's Women 1995: Trends and Statistics* (New York: United Nations, 1995). United Nations publication, Sales No. E.95.XVII.Z.

Population Fund report put the difference in child mortality as high as 9 percent for every year the mother spends in school.

- The education of women correlates with lower population growth. It's long been an axiom that women have fewer children as they become more educated, and this continues to be true in all parts of the world. A 1993 study showed, for example, that in Brazil, uneducated mothers had an average of 6.5 children; those with a secondary education had 2.5.
- The education of women correlates with improved productivity, both in the workplace and at home. Educated women work more effectively, and they pass their earnings onto their families.

- When educated, women in all cultures tend to make more independent decisions and to stand up for themselves and their families. They also begin to know their rights and to speak out for them.

All of these benefits of education help the individual woman as well as her family and society and, in addition, give her a more "feminist" consciousness—encouraging her to seek equality. Fundamentalist and conservative forces throughout the globe are doing their best to subvert women's status change in this direction. In fact, women's education was halted in Afghanistan in 1996 when Islamic fundamentalist forces (the Taliban) took over much of that nation. Conservative societal and cultural forces come into play against women's improved education, too. Marriage is the one expected role for women in many regions, and education may actually hinder a woman's marriageability. "Women who talk back to men stay unmarried," explained an African male attendee at a UNICEF/nongovernmental organization conference in the early 1990s, and educated women talk back.

While feminists have engaged in the struggle to improve global educational opportunities for women, they have been well-supported by the international community in their efforts to end educational inequities. "Gender apartheid is an obscenity," says UNICEF's executive director, James P. Grant. "It won't end without educating girls" (United Nations International Children's Fund 1994). He and other international leaders have long supported the goal of equal education.

In 1948, the countries of the world, establishing the goal of achieving an equitable global society, drew up the Universal Declaration of Human Rights, declaring that such a society cannot be achieved if fundamental rights (including education) continue to be denied to half the world's population. In 1962, the United Nations Educational, Scientific and Cultural Organization (UNESCO) drew up the Convention Against Discrimination in Education, calling firmly for gender equity in schooling. In 1975, education was identified as a key issue on the agenda of the first World Conference on Women; in 1985, at the third World Conference on Women, education for women was described as a basic tool necessary for women to become full members of society; in 1990, designated the International Literacy Year, education for girls was given top priority; in 1995, at the fourth World Conference on Women in Beijing, China, access to education was identified as one of the twelve critical areas of concern.

Hillary Rodham Clinton, in her speech at the Beijing Conference, included this statement:

> What we are learning around the world is that, if women are healthy and educated, their families will flourish. If women are free from violence, their families will flourish. If women have a chance to work and earn as full and equal partners in society, their families will flourish.
>
> And when families flourish, communities and nations will flourish. (September 5, 1995)

References

"Abortion in America." 1996. *Los Angeles Times.* August 12: A15.

Associated Press. 1997. "Supreme Court Rejects Appeal of Bias Rulings." *Ventura County Star Free Press.* April 22: A-10.

Bograd, Michele. 1988. "Introduction." *Feminist Perspectives on Wife Abuse.* Newbury Park, Calif.: Sage.

Boston Women's Health Book Collective. 1979. *Our Bodies, Ourselves: A Book by and for Women, Second Edition.* New York: Simon & Schuster Touchstone.

Boxall, Bettina. 1996. "Women's Advocates Assail Prop. 209" *Los Angeles Times.* October 1: A-3.

Brownmiller, Susan. 1993. *Against Our Will: Men, Women and Rape.* New York: Fawcett Columbine (originally published by Simon & Schuster, 1975).

Bunch, Charlotte. 1991. "Women's Rights as Human Rights: Toward a Re-vision of Human Rights." *Gender Violence: A Development and Human Rights Issue.* New Brunswick, NJ: Rutgers Office of University Publications: Center for Women's Global Leadership.

Carabillo, Toni, Judith Meuli, and June Bundy Csida. 1993. *Feminist Chronicles: 1953–1993.* Los Angeles: Women's Graphics.

Cohen, Marcia. 1988. *The Sisterhood: The True Story of the Women Who Changed the World.* New York: Simon & Schuster.

Costello, Cynthia, and Barbara Kivimae Krimgold, eds., for the Women's Research and Education Institute. 1996. *The American Woman, 1996–97: Women and Work.* New York: W. W. Norton.

Cowan, Gloria. 1995. "Pornography: Conflict Among Feminists." In Jo Freeman, ed., *Women: A Feminist Perspective, Fifth Edition.* Mountain View, Calif.: Mayfield Publishing.

Daly, Mary. 1978 (reprint 1990). *Gyn/Ecology: The Metaethics of Radical Feminism.* Boston: Beacon Press.

Daniszewski, John. 1997. "Female Circumcision Ban Nullified." *Los Angeles Times.* June 25: A-4.

Denfeld, Rene. 1995. *The New Victorians: A Young Woman's Challenge to the Old Feminist Order.* New York: Warner Books.

Dolan, Maura. 1997. "U.S. Panel Upholds Prop. 209" *Los Angeles Times.* April 9: A-1.

Durrant, Sue M. 1992 (March). "Title IX—Its Power and Its Limitations." [*Title IX at Twenty.*] *Journal of Physical Education, Recreation and Dance.*

Dworkin, Andrea. 1989. *Pornography: Men Possessing Women.* New York: E. P. Dutton (paperback reprint of original 1979 edition with a new introduction).

Ehrenreich, Barbara. 1978. *For Her Own Good: 150 Years of the Experts' Advice to Women.* New York: Doubleday.

Eisaguirre, Lynne. 1993. *Sexual Harassment: A Reference Handbook.* Santa Barbara, Calif.: ABC-CLIO.

Elshtain, Jean Bethke. 1991 (May). "Ethics in the Women's Movement." In Richard D. Lambert, ed., *The Annals of the American Academy of Political and Social Science.* Newbury Park, Calif.: Sage.

Faludi, Susan. 1991. *Backlash: The Undeclared War against American Women.* New York: Crown.

Feminist Majority Foundation. 1995a. *Empowering Women in Sports.* Arlington, Va.: Feminist Majority Foundation.

———. 1995b. "The Feminist Majority Foundation's Empowering Women in Medicine Report." *Women's Health.* Feminist Internet Gateway: New Media Publishing, Inc.

Fisher, Elizabeth, and Linda Gray MacKay. 1996. *Gender Justice: Women's Rights Are Human Rights.* Cambridge, Mass.: Unitarian Universalist Service Committee.

Franck, Irene M., and David M. Brownstone. 1995. *Women's World: A Timeline of Women in History.* New York: HarperPerennial.

Freeman, Jo. 1995. "The Revolution for Women in Law and Public Policy." In Jo Freeman, ed., *Women: A Feminist Perspective, Fifth Edition.* Mountain View, Calif.: Mayfield Publishing.

Frye, Jocelyn C. 1996. "Affirmative Action: Understanding the Past and Present." In Cynthia Costello and Barbara Kivimae Krimgold, eds., for the Women's Research and Education Institute, *The American Woman, 1996–97: Women and Work.* New York: W. W. Norton.

Gillespie, Marcia Ann. 1994 (Jan./Feb.). "Where Do We Stand on Pornography?" *Ms.*, pp. 33–45.

———. 1997 (May/June). "Editor's Page: I'm Not Eve." *Ms.*, p. 1.

Gleick, Elizabeth. 1997. "And Then There Were Two." *Time.* January 27: 38–39.

Hahn, Susan K. 1997. Associate professor of English, DePauw University and California Lutheran University. Personal interview.

Herrera, Irma D. 1996 (Spring). "Affirmative Action: What Do Women Think?" *Women and Philanthropy News* 19, 1.

Heyzer, Noeleen. 1995. "Foreword." In Margaret A. Schuler, ed., *From Basic Needs to Basic Rights: Women's Claim to Human Rights.* Washington, D.C.: Women, Law & Development International.

Human Rights Watch. 1995. *Human Rights Watch Women's Rights Project.* New York: Human Rights Watch.

Huq, Nasreen, and Tasneem Azim. 1995. "Reproductive Technologies and State Policies: Norplant in Bangladesh." In Margaret A. Schuler, ed., *From Basic Needs to Basic Rights: Women's Claim to Human Rights.* Washington, D.C.: Women, Law & Development International.

International Center for Research on Women. 1995. *Where Women Stand.* Fact sheet. Washington, D.C.

Ireland, Patricia. 1996. *What Women Want.* New York: Dutton.

Jacobs, Gloria. 1994 (Sept./Oct.). "Where Do We Go from Here?" *Ms.*, pp. 56–63.

Kaufman, Lois L., ed. 1990. *Women on Men: Views on the Opposite Sex.* New York: Peter Pauper Press.

Mansbridge, Jane J. 1986. *Why We Lost the ERA.* Chicago: University of Chicago Press.

Martin, Susan Ehrlich. 1995. "Sexual Harassment: The Link Joining Gender Stratification, Sexuality, and Women's Economic Status." In Jo Freeman, ed., *Women: A Feminist Perspective, Fifth Edition.* Mountain View, Calif.: Mayfield Publishing.

McCue, Margi Laird. 1995. *Domestic Violence: A Reference Handbook.* Santa Barbara, Calif.: ABC-CLIO.

Merchant, Carolyn. 1990. "Ecofeminism and Feminist Theory." In Irene Diamond and Gloria Feman Orenstein, eds., *Reweaving the World: The Emergence of Ecofeminism.* San Francisco: Sierra Club Books.

National Association for Girls and Women in Sports. 1997. Press kit.

Nelson, Mariah Burton. 1994. *The Stronger Women Get, the More Men Love Football: Sexism and the American Culture of Sports*. New York: Avon Books.

Patterson, Katherine J. 1994 (Fall). "Pornography Law as Censorship: Linguistic Control as (Hetero) Sexist Harness." *Feminist Issues* 14, 2: 91–115.

Radicalesbians. 1972. "The Woman-Identified Woman." In Miriam Schneir, ed., *Feminism in Our Time: The Essential Writings, World War II to the Present*. New York: Random House.

RAINBO (Research, Action and Information Network for Bodily Integrity of Women). 1997. *Female Genital Mutilation: A Fact Sheet*.

Ransdell, Lisa. 1995. "Lesbian Feminism and the Feminist Movement." In Jo Freeman, ed., *Women: A Feminist Perspective, Fifth Edition*. Mountain View, Calif.: Mayfield Publishing.

Rich, Adrienne. 1986. "Compulsory Heterosexuality and Lesbian Experience." In Miriam Schneir, ed., *Feminism in Our Time: The Essential Writings, World War II to the Present*. New York: Random House.

Richter, Paul. 1997. "Army Mothballs Phone Hotline for Reporting Sex Misconduct Charges." *Los Angeles Times*. June 14: A11.

Rodgers, Kathryn J. 1995 (Fall). "Affirmative Action: A Women's Issue." *In Brief*, NOW Legal Defense and Education Fund newsletter.

Rosen, Ruth. 1997. "Hillary Makes Her Case, but Abroad" ["Column Left"]. *Los Angeles Times*. May 1: B15.

Rothman, Barbara Katz, and Mary Beth Caschetta. 1995. "Treating Health: Women and Medicine." In Jo Freeman, ed., *Women: A Feminist Perspective, Fifth Edition*. Mountain View, Calif.: Mayfield Publishing.

Sadker, Myra, and David Sadker. 1994. *Failing at Fairness: How Our Schools Cheat Girls*. New York: Simon & Schuster Touchstone.

Salholz, Eloise, with Eleanor Clift, Karen Springer, and Patrice Johnson. 1990. "Women Under Assault." *Newsweek*. July 16: 23–24.

Schneir, Miriam, ed. 1994. *Feminism in Our Time: The Essential Writings, World War II to the Present*. New York: Random House.

Sheffield, Carole J. 1995. "Sexual Terrorism." In Jo Freeman, ed., *Women: A Feminist Perspective, Fifth Edition*. Mountain View, Calif.: Mayfield Publishing.

Sivard, Ruth Leger, with Arlette Brauer and Rebecca Cook. 1995. *WOMEN . . . A World Survey*. Washington, D.C.: World Priorities Inc.

Stall, Bill. 1996. "Outcomes on State Propositions Yield Paradoxes and Contradictions." *Los Angeles Times*. November 7: A3.

United Nations. 1995. *The World's Women 1995: Trends and Statistics.* New York: United Nations.

United Nations International Children's Fund. 1994. "Women and Literacy" Web site.

Vedia, Eduardo Molina y. 1997. "Mexico: Supreme Court Legitimises [sic] Rape of Spouses, Critics Say." InterPress Service, June 19.

Verhovek, Sam Howe. 1996. "Prop. 209 Win Bolsters Affirmative-Action Foes." *Ventura County Star* [New York Times News Service]. November 11: A1.

Wattleton, Faye. 1997 (May/June). [moderator of published panel discussion] "Speaking Frankly." *Ms.,* p. 65.

Wharton, David, and Steve Henson. 1997. "4 Men's Sports Dropped from CSUN Lineup." *Los Angeles Times.* June 12: A1.

Wilson, Midge, and Kathy Russell. 1996. *Divided Sisters: Bridging the Gap between Black Women and White Women.* New York: Anchor Books, Doubleday.

Woloch, Nancy. 1994. *Women and the American Experience, Second Edition.* New York: McGraw-Hill.

"Women's Lib: A Second Look." 1970. *Time.* December 14: 50.

Economics, Politics, and Choice Words

5

Economics

Economic opportunity and equality has long been a quest of both feminist and nonfeminist women workers. In fact, one of the first major steps toward equality for women in the United States was the passage in 1848 of the New York Married Woman's Property Act. Prior to this legislation, all money that married women earned was legally the property of their husbands. A few other states soon followed New York's example and passed similar property laws, but the reality of women's need to support themselves and their families conflicted sharply with the American ideal of family—which by this time, as the country industrialized, had become a woman at home and a man in the paid labor force. "Employment of women," warned Edward P. O'Donnell, expressing the views of many of the time, "must gradually unsex them [women] of that modest demeanor that lends charm to their kind" (Mofford 1996). Enough women disagreed with O'Donnell to create a steady increase in the number of women in the workforce.

Women faced society's discouraging attitude toward them as paid workers but found, too, that they were sought out as employees during times of need, like wartime, and during years of high industrial or business growth, when the demand for workers was great. Meanwhile, feminists led the struggle for equitable wages and job opportunities for women. Early economist and feminist Charlotte Perkins Gilman, ahead of her time in 1898, presented a case not just for women's access to paid work but for their economic autonomy, and also for equality between women and men in domestic and child-raising tasks. In 1926, feminist Suzanne LaFollette argued that women's sexual equality could only be achieved with economic independence.

Other feminists joined the movement toward economic independence, and groups formed to protect and expand women's place in the working world. Labor unions did not immediately embrace the new women workers but instead were openly hostile to women in the labor pool, seeing them as threats to high wages (women worked for less pay than men) and as direct competition for jobs that men might want. Partly through union support, protective labor laws were passed in the early part of the this century. Many feminists celebrated such laws, seeing them as protection for women against exploitation in low-paying industries that were dominated by women, such as the garment-sewing industry. However, the laws made women less competitive because they required employers to improve working conditions for women, limit their hours, and raise their wages. On these terms, men were cheaper, or at least less trouble, than women workers, and this was an excuse to hire men for the more desirable jobs.

In response, feminist groups lobbied the government for equitable laws, wanting either no protective laws or protective laws that covered both women and men, thus creating a level playing field. Finally, the Fair Labor Standards Act of 1938, a product of Eleanor Roosevelt's work, established minimum wages and maximum hours equally for men and women; it did not, however, end sexual discrimination in hiring and promoting or "protecting" workers. The feminist camp remained divided over protective legislation and, during these same years, divided also into those supporting the Equal Rights Amendment—thinking it would create an absolutely equal working world and would do away with discriminatory laws—and into those who sought separate protective laws but equitable treatment in the workplace for women.

In 1960, as the second wave of feminism gained force, women's economic status was one of the first considerations of the new generation of feminists. By 1960, two out of five American women worked for pay, double that in 1940. And by 1970, almost half of adult women were working for wages, either full- or part-time (Woloch 1994). More and more, too, the working woman was married and had children under the age of 17. This was a major structural change, and it contributed to establishing a more vocal, long-standing, and assertive group of working women. Despite some labor law improvements, though, women still faced discrimination, even in hiring. In fact, the first major success for the National Organization for Women (NOW) in the 1960s was its campaign to end sex-segregated employment advertising. NOW led feminists in achieving an Equal Employment Opportunity Commission ruling that ended separate male and female "want ads" in 1968.

Sexual discrimination on the job had been legally ended in 1963, when the Equal Pay Act was passed, but equality in earnings was still far from achieved. In the late 1960s, feminists rallied around the cry of "59 cents!"—approximately the median amount women workers earned to the male worker's dollar in 1963. The National Committee on Pay Equity reports that in 1995 the median for full-time working women is at 71.4 cents to the male's dollar, and among some groups of women and in some fields of work it reaches equity or near-equity. Feminists point to these figures as partial successes; antifeminists point to them as reason to call an end to affirmative action and feminism in general.

Many women still face "ghettoization" of their labor, however, so that some occupations are considered "women's work" and are consistently low-paying—this situation is what inspires feminists to call for equal pay for *comparable* work. Also, while feminists celebrate the rise in women's earnings, at the same time they are busy seeking real parity, with women earning dollar for dollar to men. Many call, too, for changes in the workplace that go further than earnings equity, harking back in some ways to the work of Charlotte Perkins Gilman and looking forward to new work paradigms in the twenty-first century.

Many feminists are calling for women-friendly workplaces. In addition to earnings equity, they seek changes that include parental and family responsibility leave policies, day-care considerations or facilities, flexible time for women and men, and an end to sexual harassment on the job. In much of this, the feminists are in the mainstream of American thinking. Day care, for example, was a controversial topic that feminists fought for in the 1970s (overcoming the characterization that women who used day-care facilities were irresponsible); in the 1990s, women expect to use day care for their children if they need to and are not stigmatized for it. Women and men seek out employers who provide child care on-site, and many employers provide day care for children in order to attract the brightest and the best of workers.

Women's expectations have changed dramatically, too, in the way they map out their lives. Most expect to work outside the home, either as single or married women. And most do. Three out of every four women age 25 to 54 are now in the labor force. Women with children work, too. Three-fourths of the women with children ages six to 17 work outside the home, as do more than half of mothers with children below age one (Costello and Krimgold 1996). These women and the adult men in their families are changing America's corporate image of the average worker.

On a less tangible level, women, having attained the legal status of equality in the workplace, have begun to examine the very structures of the business world. Its traditional hierarchical organization catered to males who had no responsibilities at home; a dependent female there did the parenting and the domestic labor. The traditional worker could put in long hours, be sent on extended business trips, and be expected to give his undivided loyalty to his job. Women, on entering the workplace, lived up to these expectations in the 1970s and 1980s but found themselves then with the disadvantage of two jobs—still expected to run the household and parent the children even when working full-time outside the home. The 1980s "superwoman" was born, and women strove to achieve this new ideal. In the 1990s, most women rejected this unachievable goal and turned their attention instead to integrating men into the household chores and parenting joys and responsibilities.

Feminists have also begun to question the traditional hierarchical organization of the business world at its very foundation. The traditional flow chart of corporate responsibility is a pyramid of power, with lower echelons reporting to the levels above them. It is a hierarchy built on a military ideal of authority, and it tends to be rigid and slow to react. Women, socialized to work cooperatively as well as competitively, have set up and encouraged work environments that are organized around hubs, or are weblike, with an active interchange of ideas and information and with fewer strict authority rulings. Fortuitously, these kinds of environments mesh well with today's independent spirits and with the fast-paced, technological industries of the 1990s.

Not everyone has agreed that the changes wrought by feminists have been positive. A backlash against women's growing economic independence has been examined and analyzed by feminist writers, especially by Naomi Wolf and Susan Faludi. Wolf theorized that a new "beauty quotient" has become part of professional American women's needs: Working women are expected (though men are not) to appear youthful, attractive, trim, and well-dressed. She describes this as part of an undercurrent of a backlash that attempts to hold women in their place, putting sexual desirability first and job capability second (Wolf 1991). Faludi, in her best-selling book *Backlash,* points to numerous instances of attempts to turn back the tide of feminist economic advances. She writes that "the backlash decade [the 1980s] produced one long, painful, and unremitting campaign to thwart women's progress" (Faludi 1991, 454).

The backlash has become an established part of feminists' quest for equality in the workplace. Even as women begin to crack the glass ceiling of corporate management, they have lost battles to maintain affirmative action, and they face the reality that white males still hold 98 percent of the top earning positions in Fortune 500 companies in the United States (Catalyst 1996a). Pay equity is still an unachieved goal for many American women. And women are still doing most or all of the housework.

Numerous laws have been passed that affect women's place in the working world. Many have had a tremendous impact, including:

1963   The Equal Pay Act: The first federal law against sex discrimination, the Equal Pay Act prohibits unequal pay for equal or "substantially equal" work. It was first introduced in Congress in 1943.

1964   The Civil Rights Act of 1964 and Title VII: The Civil Rights Act prohibits discrimination in employment on the basis of race, color, religion, or national origin. Title VII, an amendment, prohibits discrimination in employment on the basis of sex. The Equal Employment Opportunity Commission (EEOC) is created to enforce the new law.

1974   The Equal Credit Opportunity Act (ECOA): Prohibits financial discrimination on the basis of sex or marital status. Before ECOA, single women were often refused loans; upon marriage, a woman's account was automatically switched to her husband's name; when a woman divorced, her credit stayed with her husband and she started over; a wife's income was often ignored when a couple applied for a mortgage; and sometimes a wife was asked for a note certifying that she was on birth control or sterile and would therefore not be quitting her job.

1978   The Pregnancy Discrimination Act: An amendment to Title VII, it states that pregnancy discrimination is sex discrimination. Pregnancy must be treated in the workplace in the same way disabilities are treated. The act seeks to change policies of companies that fire women when they get pregnant or that do not cover pregnancy in health plans.

1993   The Family and Medical Leave Act: Requires companies with more than 50 employees to provide unpaid time off for the care of a newborn or adopted child, for a medical condition, or to care for a sick family member. Employees are eligible for up to 12 weeks of leave in a 12-month period, with a guaranteed reinstatement to the same or a similar position.

Women's Work at Home

Though change has come in the paid labor force, change in the unpaid domestic force has been slow and halting. What was once considered women's sphere—the care and maintenance of the home, family, and children—is today still considered women's responsibility. Though some men help with the daily drudgery of laundry, dish washing, floor mopping, and child caring, most still rely on women to keep the house and home in order. (See Figures 5.1 and 5.2.)

Feminists have called on fathers to take a more active role in the day-to-day raising of their children. Studies done in the mid-1990s have shown that men *think* they do more household chores

Figure 5.1
Household Responsibilities in Dual-Earner Families

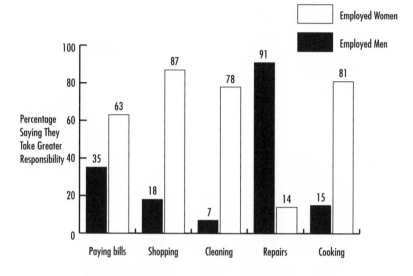

Source: Ellen Galinsky, James T. Bond, and Dana E. Friedman, *The Changing Workforce: Highlights of the National Study* (New York: Family and Work Institute, 1993). (© Family and Work Institute) Reprinted by permission.

now than before—more than the women think the men in their households do. Certainly, though, if feminists have achieved anything in this arena it is the acknowledgment of an inequality in the amount of household work that women in families do in a week's time versus the amount done by men.

Feminists point out that women also generally take responsibility for "kin care"—all those letters, gifts, thank-you notes, telephone calls, and special occasion arrangements that are part of maintaining social and family ties. The time women devote to these responsibilities explains some of the gap in women's leisure time versus men's. And there is a gap. When her family and home responsibilities are added up, explains feminist Jo Freeman, "a typical woman has more tasks to perform in a typical day than a typical man and thus has less time" (Freeman 1995, 397). Freeman and other feminists call for a complete reorganization of labor in

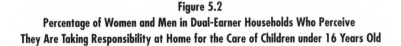

Figure 5.2
Percentage of Women and Men in Dual-Earner Households Who Perceive
They Are Taking Responsibility at Home for the Care of Children under 16 Years Old

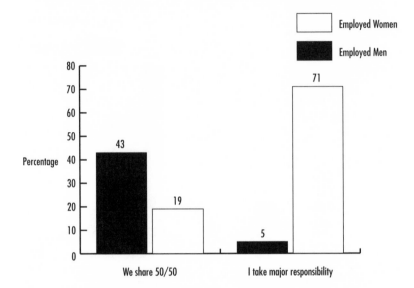

Note: Percentages are the result of a telephone survey of 155 women and 134 men, one per household. Each individual was asked to respond for her/himself only, with a yes or no; therefore, percentages do not sum to 100. *Source:* Ellen Galinsky, James T. Bond, and Dana E. Friedman, *The Changing Workforce: Highlights of the National Study* (New York: Family and Work Institute, 1993). (© Family and Work Institute) Reprinted by permission.

the home, one that is fair and equitable for male and female members and that replaces stereotypical gender roles with individualized roles.

The traditional division of labor that places greater responsibility on women in families with both spouses working full-time has an obvious impact on the women involved. They are more tired than men. But another, less obvious, impact gives men an advantage in the working world and produces a disadvantage for women. Men who depend on women to run the household are freer to focus on their work, freer to put in long hours on the job, and freer to pursue whatever is necessary to secure job promotions. They are less frequently interrupted during their workday with questions from home, and consequently their on-the-job concentration is high. Also, they seldom miss a workday to tend to a sick child. The other side of this coin, of course, is the woman's side. She suffers a disadvantage in her career as she is the one who is interrupted, does not have the freedom to pursue her career without consideration of domestic responsibilities, and loses ground when she takes time off with her sick children. (See Table 5.1.)

Some prognosticators are finding hopeful signs of family men becoming more active fathers and adjusting their focus from the job to the home, and there is growing societal support for such changes. The Family and Medical Leave Act, for example, applies to both men and women. But another sign of the times is a conservative, antifeminist message that calls for a return to "family values" and blames working women for the problems of delinquent teens and the drug culture among the young. Though evidence has shown that children of working mothers fare as well as children of women who do not work outside the home, the backlash message has persisted, and many working mothers carry an additional burden to work with them—guilt.

Women's Work outside the Home

In the United States, 58.8 percent of women age 16 or older work outside the home (see Figures 5.3–5.4). Their equal status in the working world is legally protected through such laws as the Equal Pay Act and Title VII of the Civil Rights Act of 1964.

But are women equal in the working world? Chief among the inequities in working women's lives is the assumption that a

Table 5.1
**Percentage of Employed Mothers and Fathers Who
Stay Home from Work to Take Care of Sick Children**

	Percentage Who Say They:		
	Stay Home	Go to Work	It Depends
Employed mothers	26	9	65
All fathers	12	34	55
Fathers with employed spouses	12	25	62

Source: Ellen Galinsky and James T. Bond, *Work and Family: The Experiences of Mothers and Fathers in the United States Labor Force* (New York: Family and Work Institute, 1993, as cited by the Women's Research and Education Institute in *The American Woman 1996–97.* (© Family and Work Institute) Reprinted by permission.

Figure 5.3
Percentage of Women Participating in the
Labor Force, Relative to Men, 1950–1990

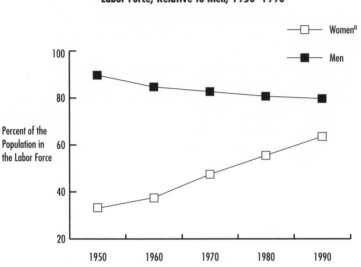

[a]Age 16 and over
Source: Institute for Women Policy Research, "Are Mommies Dropping Out of the Labor Force? *No!*" *Research-in-Brief,* fact sheet derived from Bureau of Labor Statistics. Reprinted by permission.

man has a right in life to goals and ambitions for a career outside the home, whereas a woman has no assumed right to a career. Still underlying the American mythology of women's and men's roles in life is that motherhood and wifehood are a woman's primary goals in life. Fatherhood and husbandhood are typically seen as secondary to career goals for men, and good wage-earning capabilities, in turn, are seen as attributes of a good father and husband but not necessarily of a good mother and wife. This mythology, left over from the late 1800s—when a woman's sphere was solely the household and when women were indeed financial dependents on fathers and then husbands—gives rise to a certain amount of antifeminist resentment at women's advances in the workforce.

Feminists point to the many financial inequities that women face in the paid labor force. A "ghettoization" of women's labor exists today—a concentration of women in low-paying jobs.

Figure 5.4
Percentage of Mothers in the Labor Force, 1950–1990

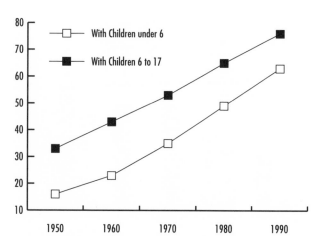

Source: Institute for Women Policy Research, "Are Mommies Dropping Out of the Labor Force? *No!"* Research-in-*Brief,* fact sheet derived from Bureau of Labor Statistics. Reprinted by permission.

Women entered the labor force in the early 1900s through such low-paying mill or garment industry jobs. It is still the way many enter today, and many stay there. According to the National Committee on Pay Equity, women are still segregated into a few low-paying occupations. In 1994, a full 61 percent of all women workers held sales, clerical, or service jobs, all job categories that pay lower-than-average wages. And within these job categories, men's earnings outstripped women's, as men tended to work in higher-paying jobs such as wholesale sales, and women in lower-paying jobs such as retail cashier sales (National Committee on Pay Equity 1997).

Another discriminatory factor built into the system, say feminists, is a lack of equal pay for comparable jobs. Certain jobs pay less because they are held by women, asserts the National Committee on Pay Equity. And they counter the familiar argument of the impossibility of comparing apples and oranges by asserting that it is indeed possible to compare different jobs. Business firms and various government agencies have always evaluated jobs to discern relative value based on skill level, educational

170

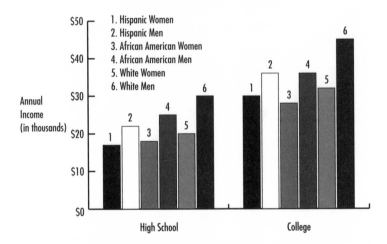

Figure 5.5
Gender, Race, and Educational
Achievement Affect the Wage Gap

Source: National Committee on Pay Equity, "Background on the Wage Gap," fact sheet based on U.S. Census Bureau data, 1995. Reprinted by permission.

Table 5.2
Women's Annual Earnings as a Percentage of Men's (selected years)

Year	Median Annual Earnings (Year-round, full-time)	Median Weekly Earnings (Usually work full-time)
1955	63.9	
1960	60.7	
1965	59.9	
1970	59.4	62.3
1975	58.8	62.0
1980	60.2	64.4
1985	64.6	68.2
1990	71.6	71.7
1995	71.4	75.4

Source: National Committee on Pay Equity, "Background on the Wage Gap," fact sheet based on U.S. Census Bureau data and U.S. Department of Labor, Bureau of Labor Statistics, annual averages. Reprinted by permission.

Table 5.3
Average Weekly Wages for Women and Men
and Percentage Wage Gap in Select Occupations, 1995

Occupation	Women's Weekly Wages	Men's Weekly Wages	Percent Wage Gap
Occupations with Estimated Annual Earnings of $33,000+			
Managerial	$570	$833	68.4
Professional	632	827	76.4
Technical	480	641	74.9
Occupations with Estimated Annual Earnings of $20,000 to $32,999			
Sales	330	579	57.0
Administrative Support	384	489	78.5
Precision Production, Craft, Repair	371	534	69.5
Operators, Fabricators, Laborers	297	413	71.9
Transportation, Material Moving	354	482	73.4
Occupations with Estimated Annual Earnings of Less Than $20,000			
Service	264	300	88.0
Handler, Equipment Cleaner, Laborer	284	328	86.6
Farming, Forestry, Fishing	249	294	84.7

Source: National Committee on Pay Equity, "Profile of the Wage Gap by Selected Occupations and Class," derived from 1995 annual averages, U.S. Department of Labor, Bureau of Labor Statistics. Reprinted by permission.

requirements, and responsibility. Therefore, business has proven itself able to place relative price values on job categories. Now it is time, say feminists, to get rid of the gender bias inherent between categories of jobs. Why, for example, are a secretary's skills worth less on the job market than a mechanic's when both require comparable years of education and commitment to the job? (See Figure 5.5 and Tables 5.2–5.3.)

In some job categories not traditionally female, women earn near-equal wages to men. Women who worked as electrical and electronic equipment repairers, for example, earned about as much as men in those categories in 1994. And women engineers reported 86.5 percent of the earnings of men, which is better than the overall average (Costello and Krimgold 1996, 64).

Feminists see some hopeful signs of parity within age categories of workers. Women between the ages of 20 and 24 years earned an average of 94.5 percent of men's earnings in 1994, and the next group, age 25 to 34, earned 82.9 percent of men's earnings. Younger workers are benefiting from hiring practices that are more equitable than in past years, according to the Women's

Research and Education Institute, and this may explain some of the near parity. It might partly explain, too, why women face a sharp drop in comparative earnings to 72.6 percent in the next category of years, age 35 to 44. Another explanation, however, is that feminism has achieved a level playing field on the entry level, but cumulative factors such as fewer promotional and training opportunities catch up to women as they age, so that as men reach their peak earning years in their 40s and 50s, benefiting from successive promotions and business relationships, women face reduced opportunities.

In 1986, the media coined the term "glass ceiling" to describe the invisible barrier between women workers (and also people of color) and top management positions. It was found that as women reached the age and experience level to be eligible for upper management, their careers mysteriously slowed. They were offered fewer advancement enhancing opportunities such as training seminars and conferences; they were included in fewer business networking activities; and, in short, they had to be better than their white male competition to be considered equal. The glass ceiling was the result of this subtle and unspoken discrimination in business practices. (See Table 5.4.)

Table 5.4
**Reasons Given by Executive Women and Chief Executive Officers (CEOs)
to Explain What Prevents Women from Advancing to Corporate Leadership**

Reasons Given	Executive Women (%)	CEOs (%)
Male stereotyping and preconceptions of women	52	25
Exclusion from informal networks of communication	49	15
Lack of general management/line experience	47	82
Inhospitable corporate culture	35	18
Lack of mentoring	30	34
Women have not been in the pipeline long enough	29	64
Lack of awareness of organizational politics	19	4
Commitment to family responsibilities	18	23
Few women can or want to do what it takes to get to the top	15	16
Ineffective leadership style	11	4

Note: Information is from a 1994/1995 survey of Fortune 1000 companies. As of 1996, a total of five women were CEOs of Fortune 1000 companies.
Source: Catalyst, "Women in Corporate Leadership: Progress and Prospects, Executive Summary," 1996. Reprinted by permission.

The U.S. Department of Labor's Glass Ceiling Commission reported in 1995 that though women were 46 percent of the overall workforce, they were less than 5 percent of senior managers (vice president and above) in Fortune 1,000 companies. The glass ceiling was still intact. Meanwhile, corporate boards of the Fortune 500 companies showed an increase in women members, with women directors holding 10.2 percent of the total board seats in 1996. (See Figure 5.6.) Interestingly, the 83 companies (out of the 500) that had no women on their boards also lacked women in their highest-level corporate offices. John Bryan, chairman and CEO of Sara Lee Corporation, partially attributed the lack of women on these boards to male reluctance to include women (i.e., sex discrimination). He expressed a belief that could bode well for feminists in the future: "Those 83 boards without women are losing out on invaluable input," he told Catalyst reporters. (Catalyst is a nonprofit organization for research and advocacy of professional and executive women.) Bryan continued, "Companies with all-male boards lack the diversity of perspectives needed to excel in our global business environment" (Catalyst 1996b, 2). Feminists would agree.

Second-Wave Changes

Though parity in the workforce has not yet been achieved, feminists can point to some improvements that are apparently due to their efforts. Women earn more today, on average, than they did before the second wave of feminism hit, going from 59 cents for every dollar earned by men in 1963 to 71 cents in 1996. Women are "in the pipeline" for top jobs, too, and have entered professions that previously were virtually men-only domains. Today's women who enter the job market do not face overt discrimination—no segregated "want ads," no *written* corporate policies that direct males into management "tracks" and females into support personnel "tracks," no "men-only" signs on carpentry, engineering, or law enforcement fields. Subtle discrimination, however, still exists for today's activists to overcome.

Feminists take note of the differences in backgrounds of today's young women versus the young women entering the job market in the 1960s. Today's women have been allowed entry into university educational programs that previous generations were denied—so they have formal training. Today's women also have a lifetime of expectations of equal treatment in areas such as

Figure 5.6
Corporate Leadership and Earnings of
Women and Men in Fortune 500 Companies, 1995

Women represented 1.9 percent of the top earners at Fortune 500 companies[a]

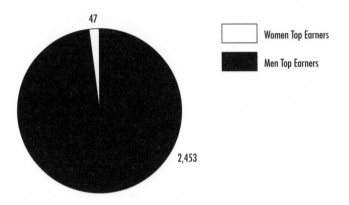

Eighty-nine percent of corporate officers in Fortune 500 companies were men

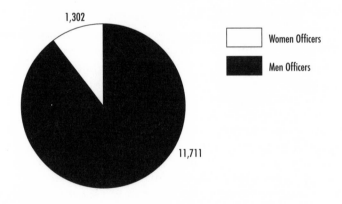

[a]Top earners were defined as the five most highly compensated officers at the companies
Source: Catalyst, "Fact Sheet: 1996 Catalyst Census of Women Corporate Officers and Top Earners."

school sports and academic clubs—so they have practice in team-work and confidence in their leadership skills. Today's women have different expectations—and realistically so—than did the young women of the 1960s. The young women of the 1960s had hope; the young women of today have access.

Global Women's Work

In many parts of the world, men have first priority when there is a shortage of food because they are considered the heavy work-ers. But in reality, it is women who are the heavy workers of the world. They work longer hours and carry heavier work loads—working in their households, in the paid labor force, and in their reproductive child-rearing roles. The annual value of women's unpaid work has been estimated at $11 trillion, nearly half the world's entire economy, according to the 1995 Human Develop-ment Report for the United Nation's Development Program. Men's unpaid work is valued at $5 trillion (Stahura 1996). In fact, it is a misconception that women play only a minor share in the world's economic production: They are majority players. Con-ventional measurements of work and production, however, do not include the unpaid labor of women throughout the world.

Women's unpaid labor is only now becoming recognized as a fundamental part of a nation's economic picture. As global fem-inist Ruth Leger Sivard explains:

> [Women's] traditional responsibilities—bearing and caring for children, maintaining the household, guard-ing the family's health, protecting the elderly, and in rural areas of the developing world, growing and pro-cessing food and providing fuel and water for the household as well—undergird all productive activities of society, but are seldom counted among them. (Sivard 1995, 10)

Global census takers still omit unpaid household work from their calculations but are attempting to broaden their per-ception of labor to include more of women's labor, such as their work on family farms and in family businesses. The political im-portance of showing women's economic value lies in its possible impact on the allocation of development monies to regions and to women. At the same time, world economists are beginning to tabulate the inequities in women's and men's unpaid labor. Men contribute far less unpaid labor to their households than do women. On average, men spend 10 to 15 hours per week on housework; women spend 30 or more. In fact, worldwide, women are shouldering from two-thirds to three-fourths of the household work. In some countries, such as Japan, women do almost 90 percent of the work. And the workload is picked up by females from an early age, with even young girls given more chores and household responsibility and less free time than boys (United Nations 1995).

However, women are today entering the paid labor force, and feminists see this change as critical to women's empowerment. Women who become part of the paid labor force can then break through their veil of relative invisibility and isolation from the world, can increase their prestige and security in society, and in turn can demand that politicians give attention to their concerns. Paid labor, many feminists assert, is one key to women's further advancement. But it is no guarantee of advancement.

The route from paid laborer to empowered individual is not a direct one. Though women's participation in the world's labor force has increased, many feminist scholars point out that their labor has generally been concentrated in the low-wage sectors. Antidiscrimination measures that would assure women of family-support wages and benefits are seen by developing countries as protectionist—that is, they protect *developed* countries from competition with the cheap labor available in developing countries. Many developing countries have welcomed labor-intensive industries, and they have hired women to supply these industries with cheap labor.

Women are almost always the cheapest source of labor (see Table 5.5), and sociocultural factors are usually seen as the reason. In patriarchal societies, women's primary role is seen to be wife and mother, so very little is invested in their education and skill training. Therefore, females, with their lower educational levels, tend to have fewer marketable skills as workers. What's more, they are more apt than men to accept jobs that pay lower wages. Stereotypes such as the belief in women's docility, nimble fingers, and "near-divine patience" further keep them in low-skilled, repetitive, and dead-end jobs (Sewall 1995). So the mere fact that women are working in developing countries does not mean that they are becoming empowered. For answers to the undergirding of empowerment, feminists studying global women's issues have had to dig deeper.

Table 5.5
Women's Nonagricultural Wage as a Percentage of Men's in Selected Countries

Country	Women's Wage as Percentage of Men's
Tanzania	92.0
Vietnam	91.5
Australia	90.8
Sri Lanka	89.8
Iceland	89.6
Sweden	89.0
Norway	86.0
Bahrain	86.0
Kenya	84.7
Colombia	84.7
Turkey	84.5
Jordan	83.5
Costa Rica	83.0
Denmark	82.6
Hungary	82.0
Mauritius	81.3
France	81.0
New Zealand	80.6
Italy	80.0
Egypt	79.5
Zambia	78.0
Greece	78.0
Poland	78.0
Austria	78.0
Finland	77.0
Netherlands	76.7
Portugal	76.0
Brazil	76.0
Paraguay	76.0
Germany	75.8
United States	75.0
Mexico	75.0

Source: United Nations Development Programme, *Human Development Report 1994–1996.* (Oxford: Oxford University Press, 1996). Reprinted by permission.

One factor that has surfaced as a setback for women's financial independence globally have been the programs of economic structural adjustment. Under plans of structural adjustment, loans from the World Bank and the International Monetary Fund (IMF) are offered to developing countries. But the loans have conditions attached that were intended to produce free, market-oriented economies. The conditions include requirements to liberalize trade, downsize government, deregulate business, and greatly reduce overall government spending. To meet these conditions, governments have deregulated wage legislation, reducing many affirmative action programs or job protections for women. They have also, in efforts to downsize government, cut education and social services budgets. Therefore, having suffered a direct loss of benefits-protection as workers, women have also suffered from the loss of government services, especially family health services. In Nicaragua, for example, structural adjustment required drastic cuts in health care. In 1991, Nicaragua spent 68 percent less on public health care than in 1988. The result was a longer waiting period for everyone using the services, including women taking their children to clinics. Even more, the infant mortality rate went from 61 per 1,000 births in the 1980s to 72 in the 1990s, and maternal mortality doubled (Fisher and MacKay 1996).

Women also suffered an indirect loss under structural adjustment, as the programs were delivering money and equipment into the hands of men and not women. Many men were drawn to the cities for jobs, leaving rural women to work the farms—some in areas where women had few or no property rights. Many women were suddenly faced with the complete burden of subsistence farming in addition to the marketing and household jobs they already had; they often saw no money from the men who left for the cities. In addition, resources that were directed to small agricultural holdings typically went to modern equipment, and men were trained to operate the new farm equipment and ride the new tractors. Women were left out of this labor-saving loop of resources. Money and control over the resources of the land was placed firmly in the hands of men. Women grew poorer and less empowered.

Economic security and independence is critical to women's empowerment and advancement in the world, say feminists today. How critical? Feminists point to the lessons learned when the Taliban Islamic fundamentalist forces took over much of Afghanistan in 1996: Women's right to work and their economic independence were stripped from them as the Taliban reasserted fundamentalist control over women and returned patriarchal power to men.

International feminist leaders are pushing for changes in allocation of funds and of economic programs and resources, calling for more to be directed specifically to women. Microloans for women's businesses have recently shown to be good investments from a bank's point of view. Women use the money, often as little as $100, to start up small businesses such as food stands, clothing stalls, or craft enterprises. Contributing countries are now making efforts to direct some of their training program funds directly to women. These, and changes in the structural adjustment program requirements to include social and environmental protections, are some of the changes that are beginning to appear in the global arena of women's economic empowerment.

Politics

Government, the seat of decision-making power, is where feminists have placed much of their emphasis, from the suffragists seeking the vote at the turn of the twentieth century to the feminist women campaigning for political office at the turn of the twenty-first century. Political power has always been recognized as fundamental to educational opportunities and economic independence. And equality in these three arenas—politics, education, and economics—is fundamental to the feminists' goal of full equality in all of life's arenas.

The women and men who gathered at the Seneca Falls Women's Rights Convention in 1848 noted the "absolute tyranny" that had resulted from women's lack of the vote. In the convention's Declaration of Sentiments, Elizabeth Cady Stanton listed grievances—exclusion from education, employment, the trades, professions, and the pulpit, as well as denial of property rights and guardianship of children. Through disenfranchisement, Stanton and the 100 others (68 women and 32 men) who signed the convention agreed, men had tried to destroy women's confidence and self-respect "and to make her willing to lead a dependent and abject life." The vote was in part a symbol of women's oppression, but it was also in fact an instrument of it, one that aided men's tyranny at every level, both public and private. The voice of women was not heard in the halls of justice or in legislative assemblies. Stanton concluded, "In view of the unjust laws . . . and because women do feel themselves aggrieved, oppressed, and fraudulently deprived of their most sacred rights, we insist that they have immediate admission to all the rights and privileges which belong to them as citizens of these United States" (Rossi 1973, 418). They wanted the vote.

Early in the women's movement a few groups formed. The National Woman Suffrage Association (NWSA), founded by Elizabeth Cady Stanton and Susan B. Anthony in 1869, took the radical, militant route. It sought to build a mass movement of American women and held an agenda of changes for every aspect of women's lives. The American Woman Suffrage Association, formed by Lucy Stone and others, broke off to pursue a course of working within the Republican Party for goals that put women's suffrage second to a focus on the full enfranchisement of African Americans.

As the vocal presence of feminists increased, a few doors opened to women. Or rather, women pushed a few doors until they opened. Elizabeth Blackwell earned a medical degree in 1849, the first woman to do so, and Rebecca Lee followed in 1864 as the first African American woman to earn a medical degree. A few colleges formed for women or were opened to them, including Radcliffe College in 1894; also, a few trades and professions began to allow women. But women did not have the vote, and their second-class citizenship was much intact. Their sphere, it was still widely believed, was the home and the family. The rest of the world was men's domain.

The strategy of the feminist groups during this time included state-by-state lobbying for women's voting rights. The women did succeed by 1890 in getting 33 states to enact married women's property laws. In many states, also, they gained equal guardianship over children and the right to keep their own earnings. They weren't able to convince men to grant them full national suffrage, but they gained limited suffrage in 19 states by 1890—they could vote in school board elections or, in some cases, municipal elections.

Full suffrage was elusive. Women did, however, gain suffrage in the territory of Wyoming—an attempt to attract "civilizing" elements to the rough mining territory—and in Utah, an attempt by Mormon men to outnumber non-Mormon voters. The feminists' quest for the national vote finally led to the two women's groups combining to form the National American Woman Suffrage Association (NAWSA). Women's place in the community gradually changed during this same time, from one in which it was a shock to hear a woman speak publicly to one in which women's organizations and clubs were speaking out for temperance and were offering social programs and reforms for the poor.

Antisuffragists continued to put forth their arguments, declaring that a women's vote would endanger traditional beliefs about sex roles that defined women as domestic and maternal beings. Some argued that women were represented already through a household vote by their husbands; others argued that women would vote against their husbands, and families would dissolve as a result. Another argument pointed out that women were incapable—physically, mentally, and emotionally—of carrying out the responsibilities of a voting citizen. The battle itself was emotional, and it cut to the core of many people's beliefs. One thing that both sides seemed to agree on: The political rights of women were the underpinnings of an entire social and political system that defined women's place.

Women did finally win the vote, going first to the polls for statewide elections in a few states and, in 1913 in Illinois, in a presidential election as well. They went to the polls in every state across the nation in 1920. And not much changed because of it. Women voted in lower numbers than, and very similarly to, men.

NAWSA dissolved, having achieved its goal of suffrage, and a new organization formed: the League of Women Voters. Though the world faced many volatile political and social events between the 1920s and 1960—the Great Depression, World War II, the Korean War, space exploration—for feminist issues, the years were uneventful. A few changes occurred in the laws; a few female politicians rose to prominence. Women's place was discussed and projected in movies and on television. But whether the woman was a hard-headed journalist played by Rosalind Russell, a brainy lawyer played by Katherine Hepburn, or a comedic housewife played by Lucille Ball, the fact that "it's a man's world" and "politics is a man's game" was understood. Women chafed at the limitations placed on their lives, but most lived within them.

The second wave brought a newly politicized woman into the public arena. The personal is political, she said. And changes—big changes—needed to be made. Second wave feminists set out to make these changes.

Over the years, feminists have supported individual politicians who share feminist ideals, such as former Rep. Patricia Schroeder (D-Colo.) and Senator Barbara Mikulski (D-Md.). But some have espoused a "wide-seeding" strategy as well. Seeking to win a voice for the woman's perspective on issues, some feminists have celebrated an increase in almost any females in national and state congressional halls. They explain that having women in government (except the most antifeminist women) serves to express some aspect of women's sociocultural perspective. In addition, it opens the doors to other women. It helps the populace grow accustomed to seeing women in powerful political positions, and eventually it makes the female look as natural on the politician's campaign circuit as does the traditional male, therefore breaking down the population's resistance to voting for female candidates.

Representation of Women in U.S. National Government

After obtaining the vote in 1920, women voted in greater and greater numbers as the years wore on, until they outnumbered male voters by almost two million voters in 1964 (see Table 5.8). Yet, female representation in U.S. seats of power has been slim. A 1950s photo of the U.S. Congress shows a sea of gray suits and short-cropped white male heads. In the U.S. Senate, only two women won seats between 1920 and 1960:

- Hattie Wyatt Caraway, 1931 to 1945. A Democrat from Arkansas, Caraway was appointed on her husband's death to fill his seat and was later elected to complete his term and then to two full terms of her own.
- Margaret Chase Smith, 1949 to 1973. A Republican from Maine, Smith was first elected to the House of Representatives to fill her husband's seat upon his death. She served four full House terms, then was elected to four full Senate terms.

Seven other women were appointed to serve out terms caused by deaths, but they were not elected to full terms on their own. One, Rebecca Latimer Felton, served one day in 1922. Two of them never sat in the Senate; three served from one month to six months; one served for a year, when her deceased husband's term was completed.

Women got off to a slow start in the U.S. House of Representatives, too. Three women served in the U.S. House the year after women won the vote. That number dropped to one in 1923. The increase in women in the House has been slow ever since, going from six or seven in the 1930s to a high of 18 in 1961. Interestingly, as the second-wave feminist movement was getting underway, the number of women in the House dropped to a low of ten in 1969. Through the feminist-active 1970s, the numbers increased, but only gradually, and in 1979, the number of women in Congress exactly matched that of 1961. A passage of 18 years and a great deal of feminist work had not yet paid off in congressional representation. But the 1980s, a conservative decade and one that brought an antifeminist backlash to the surface, saw a quiet increase in the number of females in Congress. In 1987, 25 women served in the U.S. Congress. Those numbers took a significant jump in 1992, as the national mood became one of "throw out the bums" and "bring in some new blood." Feminists passed out buttons that said, "Vote for a Woman for a Change." Republican President George Bush, who had hoped to continue the conservative agenda begun by President Reagan, was voted out after one term. Women caught the reins of the nation's new mood and rode into Washington along with Democrat Bill Clinton.

What had galvanized so many women to run for office? Many experts point to the 1991 Senate Judiciary Committee hearings on the confirmation of U.S. Supreme Court Justice Clarence Thomas. Women watched the all-male panel of senators struggling to understand the dynamics of sexual harassment, a problem that most women fully grasped and many grappled with in the working world. The question of whether these men were representing women arose. According to NOW president Patricia Ireland, the number of calls that NOW received during and after the hearings "threatened to blow out the phone lines" (Ireland 1996, 247). New members swelled the ranks of local NOW chapters. Ireland also adds that "the [Anita] Hill hearing was the first time that many women had made the connection between what goes on in Washington and what goes on in their lives, and the first time they had seen such dramatic evidence of what it means that women have been excluded from the Senate and other positions of power" (Ireland 1996, 247). The personal became obviously political, and another "click" in the nation's feminist consciousness was heard.

Women stepped forward to run for Congress—and the Year of the Woman was declared. After the 1992 elections, 48 women served as U.S. representatives and seven as senators for the 103rd Congress. Those numbers increased for the 104th and again for the 105th, so that when Congress convened in 1997, nine out of

100 senators were women, and women occupied 51 of the 435 seats (11.7 percent) in the House. They also held two delegate seats, with Eleanor Holmes Norton (D) representing the District of Columbia and Delegate Donna Christian-Green (D) representing the U.S. Virgin Islands. Feminists celebrated but also reminded the country of a sobering reality: Women, 51 percent of the population of the United States, were nowhere near being equally represented in the national seat of power.

Feminists note that women are underrepresented in another way, too. The U.S. Congress works on a seniority system, and leadership in committees—and even committee membership—is based on time in office. Women, comparatively, are the new guys in town. As the Senate entered its 1997 session, there were no Democrat women in committee leadership positions—even though the women's vote had been an important force in the Democratic party's national elections—and no Republican women leading committees. In the House, Republicans elected just two women to their leadership, and those were to the lower ranks. Democrats elected one woman to their House leadership position, Rep. Barbara B. Kennelly (D-Conn.). Her comment: "The men came earlier and stayed longer" (Hook 1996:A5). The seniority system means that men will continue to fill most of the positions of power until the new congresswomen have served in office several terms.

Women in National Positions

President Clinton appointed five women to his 1993 cabinet, setting a record for the most women in a presidential cabinet. Following his reelection in 1996, Clinton appointed eight women to his 23-member cabinet, a new record. Clinton has appointed women to high-level positions since the beginning of his first administration, thus positioning them as the natural candidates for the senior level and cabinet positions. The recently appointed and reappointed women in the Clinton cabinet include Madeleine Albright, secretary of state; Janet Reno, attorney general; Donna Shalala, secretary, Department of Health and Human Services; Alexis Herman, secretary, Department of Labor; Janet Yellen, chief economic adviser; Carol Browner, administrator, Environmental Protection Agency; Aida Alvarez, administrator, Small Business Administration; and Charlene Barshefsky, a U.S. trade representative.

Only three women have run for president:

- 1872—Victoria Woodhull formed the Equal Rights Party and ran for president. She was a celebrity of her day, supporting women's rights and several liberal causes.
- 1964—Margaret Chase Smith became the first woman to run for the presidential nomination of a major party (Republican). She ran against Senator Barry Goldwater, who won the nomination.
- 1972—Rep. Shirley Chisholm, the first African American to run for the presidency in the primary of one of the two major parties (Democratic). She was endorsed by the National Organization for Women. She helped organize the National Women's Political Caucus in 1971 and supported the Equal Rights Amendment, but she did not win the support of African American males and did not win the nomination; that went to George McGovern.

Representation of Women in State Government

Just as the suffragists sought enfranchisement from the states before the national right to vote was won, feminists today work steadily on the state level to lobby on particular issues and support feminist candidates for office.

The same feminist issues that come up for debate in Washington are frequently issues at the state level. States, for example, have passed legislation to restrict women's reproductive rights. They also exercise control over many aspects of welfare and medical benefits and over labor laws and affirmative action policies.

In addition to seeking a voice in statewide legislation, feminists are building a base of politicians, betting that many future national politicians will come from today's state leaders. Senator Patty Murray (D-Wash.), for example, served in the Washington Senate before running for her national seat, Senator Carol Moseley-Braun (D-Ill.) served in the Illinois legislature, and Senator Diane Feinstein (D-Calif.) was mayor of San Francisco. Feminist political activists keep an eye on state leaders, including state legislators, governors, mayors, and other citywide and statewide offices, with an eye to future national candidacy as well as to the impact these women can have on local issues.

In many ways state offices are more readily accessible to women than are national offices. It costs less to run for a local or state office than it does to run for a national office. And the traditional financing machine of both political parties is still more reluctant to put money into a woman's campaign than into a man's.

Women find more acceptance and support in the community for their work if it involves local school policies, family welfare, and environment—issues that have always been associated with women's roles, and many of which are legislated and overseen at local and state levels. When debating foreign policy, national defense, and other traditionally male issues that are common at the national level, women are faced with overcoming inherent biases of the electorate and their own parties.

In 1997, the Center for the American Woman and Politics reported that the number of women "in the pipeline" and working at the state level was at an all-time high. Women were 21.5 percent of the state legislators in the United States, numbering 1,593 out of 7,424 state legislators. They held 361 of the 1,984 state senate seats (18.2 percent) and 1,232 of the 5,440 state house or assembly seats (22.6 percent). That was a fivefold increase since 1969, when they held just 4 percent of state legislative seats. (See Table 5.6.) Of those holding office in 1997, 58.7 percent were Democrats and 40.2 percent were Republicans (0.8 percent were nonpartisans, and 0.3 percent were Independents).

A few states still report extremely low female representation, with Alabama at 4.3 percent as a glaring example, but most states show at least as much representation as does the national level (at 11.7 percent), and a few have topped 35 percent. Washington state, with 38.8 percent, leads the nation in female participation, and Arizona is not far behind at 37.8 percent. (See Table 5.7.) These are encouraging signs to feminists in search of state impact, though the numbers still reflect an average state-level picture that, overall, is 78.5 percent male.

First Female Governors

Women have made strides in state elective executive offices. In 1995, a record number of 19 women were serving as lieutenant governors; in 1996, 18 lieutenant governors were women. And in 1997, 81 women held statewide elective executive offices (such as attorney general, secretary of state, state treasurer,

Table 5.6
Women in Politics: Women's Representation
in State Legislatures, 1969–1997

Year	Women Legislators	Percentage of Total Legislators
1969	301	4.0
1971	344	4.5
1973	424	5.6
1975	604	8.0
1977	688	9.1
1979	770	10.3
1981	908	12.1
1983	991	13.3
1985	1,103	14.8
1987	1,170	15.7
1989	1,270	17.0
1991	1,368	18.3
1993	1,524	20.5
1995	1,532	20.6
1996	1,539	20.7
1997	1,539	21.5

Source: Center for the American Woman and Politics (CAWP), National Information Bank on Women in Public Office, Eagleton Institute of Politics, Rutgers University, New Brunswick, N.J. Reprinted by permission.

comptroller, chief of state education, and public service commissioners) in a pool of 323.

The office of governor, however, has seldom been held by a female. In fact, in the country's two centuries of elections only 14 women have served as state governors. And it was 1974 before the first one, Ella Grasso, was elected in her own right. Before Grasso, of the three women who held the office of governor, two stood as surrogates for their husbands and one followed a deceased husband into office:

1925   Nellie Tayloe Ross (D) wins in a special election in Wyoming to replace her deceased husband. (Term: 1925–1927.) In Texas, Miriam "Ma" Ferguson (D) is elected as a surrogate for her husband, who cannot run for reelection. (Term: 1925–1927, also 1933–1935.)

1967   Lurleen Wallace (D) is elected as surrogate governor of Alabama for her husband, who cannot run for reelection. (Term: 1967–1968.)

Table 5.7
Percentages and Rankings of Women Serving in State Legislatures, 1997
(w/all = women to overall members)

State	Rank	Senate w/all	House w/all	Overall w/all	Percentage
AL	50	2/35	4/105	6/140	4.3
AK	43	3/20	5/40	8/60	13.3
AZ*	2	8/30	26/60	34/90	37.8
AR	35	1/35	22/100	23/135	17.0
CA	24	7/40	20/80	27/120	22.5
CO	3	10/35	25/65	35/100	35.0
CT	10	9/36	44/15	53/187	28.3
DE	17	6/21	9/41	15/62	24.2
FL	21	6/40	31/120	37/160	23.1
GA	36	7/56	32/180	39/236	16.5
HI*	32	5/25	8/51	13/76	17.1
ID	18	6/35	19/70	25/105	23.8
IL*	13	11/59	35/118	46/177	26.0
IN	28	14/50	14/100	28/150	18.7
IA	27	11/50	20/100	31/150	20.7
KS	9	14/40	35/125	49/165	29.7
KY	49	2/38	11/100	13/138	9.4
LA	47	2/39	14/105	16/144	11.1
ME	15	13/35	35/151	48/186	25.8
MD	8	8/47	48/141	56/188	29.8
MA	22	7/40	39/160	46/200	23.0
MI	23	3/38	31/110	34/148	23.0
MN	7	22/67	39/134	61/201	30.3
MS	46	3/52	17/122	20/174	11.5
MO	26	3/34	40/163	43/197	21.8
MT	20	9/50	26/100	35/150	23.3
NE	12	13/49	Unicameral/1	13/49	26.5
NV	4	5/21	16/42	21/63	33.3
NH	6	8/24	123/400	131/424	30.9
NJ	38	2/40	17/80	19/120	15.8
NM	11	10/42	20/70	30/112	26.8
NY	29	8/61	31/150	39/211	18.5
NC*	32	6/50	23/12	29/170	17.1
ND	37	6/49	18/98	24/147	16.3
OH	25	8/33	21/99	29/132	22.0
OK	48	6/48	9/101	15/149	10.1
OR	16	9/30	14/60	23/90	25.6
PA	45	6/50	25/203	31/253	12.3
RI*	13	11/50	28/100	39/150	26.0
SC	44	3/46	19/124	22/170	12.9
SD*	32	5/35	13/70	18/105	17.1

(continues)

Table 5.7
(continued)
(w/all = women to overall members)

State	Rank	Senate w/all	House w/all	Overall w/all	Percentage
TN	42	3/33	15/99	18/132	13.6
TX	30	3/31	30/150	33/181	18.2
UT	39	1/29	15/75	16/104	15.4
VT	5	10/30	47/150	57/180	31.7
VA	40	7/40	14/100	21/140	15.0
WA	1	22/49	35/98	57/147	38.8
WV	41	4/34	16/100	20/134	14.9
WI	19	9/33	22/99	31/132	23.5
WY	31	4/30	12/60	16/90	17.8
Total		361/1,984	1,232/5,440	1,593/7,424	21.5

*States with the exact same percentages are ranked the same (IL and RI, 13; HI, NC, and SD, 32); since there is a tie, no states are ranked 14th, 33rd, or 34th. States that round out to the same figure (MA and MI) but are not exactly the same are ranked differently.
Source: Center for the American Woman and Politics (CAWP), National Information Bank on Women in Public Office, Eagleton Institute of Politics, Rutgers University, New Brunswick, N.J. Reprinted by permission.

1974	In Connecticut, Ella Grasso (D) becomes the first woman elected governor in her own right. (Term: 1974–1980.)
1976	Dixy Lee Ray (D) is elected governor of Washington state. (Term: 1977–1981.)
1983	Martha Layne Collins (D) is elected governor of Kentucky. (Term: 1984–1987.)
1984	Madeleine Kunin (D) is elected to her first of three terms as governor of Vermont. She is the only woman governor elected to three terms. (Term: 1985–1991.)
1986	In the Nebraska race, Kay Orr (R) becomes the first Republican woman to be elected governor. She also is the first woman to run against another woman for the governorship. (Term: 1987–1991.)
1988	Rose Mofford (D) becomes governor of Arizona by constitutional succession when Governor Evan

1988   Mecham is impeached. She serves until March
(*cont.*)   1991.

1990   In Kansas, Joan Finney (D) becomes the first woman
            to defeat an incumbent governor. (Term: 1991–1995.)
            Barbara Roberts (D) serves as governor of Oregon.
            (Term: 1991–1995.) And Ann Richards (D) is elected
            governor of Texas. (Term: 1991–1995.)

1993   Christine Todd Whitman (R) is elected governor of
            New Jersey. (Term: 1994– .)

1996   Jeanne Shaheen (D) wins the New Hampshire gover-
            norship. (Term: 1997– .) (Center for the American
            Woman and Politics 1997)

The Gender Gap

Fear of the effect that the women's vote would have on the politics of the nation was rampant before women went to the polls
for the first time in 1920. But the women's vote, or at least a
women's voting bloc, didn't materialize. Instead, women voted
much as men had, ranging across the spectrum from liberal to
conservative, and political fears subsided. As the years passed,
the women's vote did slowly separate from men's in one respect:
More women than men voted. Since 1964, women have consistently voted in greater numbers than men, and since 1980, a
greater proportion of women than of men have voted, too. (See
Tables 5.8 and 5.9.)

These numbers and percentages, however, do not constitute the gender gap that has gained so much attention in the past
decade. The gender gap that has concerned and excited so many
pundits on both sides of the feminism issue is the gap between
women's and men's voting patterns. It first appeared in 1980,
with President Ronald Reagan's victory. Reagan's election was
an acknowledged defeat for feminists, but it was also a feminist
victory of sorts—the first significant gender gap among voting
Americans. Women voted against Reagan in greater percentages
than men did. For the first time, in other words, women voted
quite differently than men. (See Table 5.10.)

Table 5.8
Percentage and Number of Women and Men
Voting in Presidential Elections, 1964–1992

Presidential Election Year	Percent of Voting Age Population Who Reported Voting		Number Who Reported Voting (in millions)	
	Women	Men	Women	Men
1992	62.3	60.2	60.6	53.3
1988	58.3	56.4	54.5	47.7
1984	60.8	59.0	54.5	47.4
1980	59.4	59.1	49.3	43.8
1976	58.8	59.6	45.6	41.1
1972	62.0	64.1	44.9	40.9
1968	66.0	69.8	41.0	38.0
1964	67.0	71.9	39.2	37.5

Source: Center for the American Woman and Politics (CAWP), National Information Bank on Women in Public Office, Eagleton Institute of Politics, Rutgers University, New Brunswick, N.J. Reprinted by permission.

Table 5.9
Percentage and Number of Black, Hispanic, and White
Women and Men Who Voted in Presidential Elections, 1984–1992

	Percent of Voting Age Population Who Reported Voting		Number Who Reported Voting (in millions)	
	Women	Men	Women	Men
1992				
Black	56.7	50.8	6.6	4.8
Hispanic	30.9	26.8	2.3	1.9
White	64.5	62.6	52.9	47.6
1988				
Black	54.2	48.2	5.9	4.2
Hispanic	30.1	27.4	2.0	1.8
White	59.8	58.3	47.7	42.7
1984				
Black	59.2	51.7	6.1	4.2
Hispanic	33.1	32.1	1.7	1.4
White	62.0	60.8	47.7	42.4

Note: The data are approximate. The data are derived from the U.S. Bureau of the Census Current Population Reports. Respondents to the survey report their own voting activity and that of other members of their household. The sample systematically overreports both voting and registration by several million people.
Source: Center for the American Woman and Politics (CAWP), National Information Bank on Women in Public Office, Eagleton Institute of Politics, Rutgers University, New Brunswick, N.J. Reprinted by permission.

Table 5.10
Percentage of Women and Men Voting Republican,
Democrat, or Independent in Recent Presidential Elections

Presidential Candidates	Women	Men
1992[a]		
Bill Clinton (D)	45	41
George Bush (R)	37	38
Ross Perot (I)	17	21
1988[b]		
George Bush (R)	50	57
Michael Dukakis (D)	49	42
1984[b]		
Ronald Reagan (R)	55	63
Walter Mondale (D)	45	37
1980[b]		
Ronald Reagan (R)	47	54
Jimmy Carter (D)	44	36
John Anderson (I)	8	8

[a]1992 figures drawn from the Voter News Service, known as Voter Research and Surveys until 1993
[b]1980, 1984, and 1988 figures drawn from an average of *Washington Post, New York Times,* and NBC News surveys
Source: Center for the American Woman and Politics (CAWP), National Information Bank on Women in Public Office, Eagleton Institute of Politics, Rutgers University, New Brunswick, N.J.

Eight percent more women than men voted against Republican Ronald Reagan, creating a gender gap that continued in Reagan's 1984 race, according to the Center for the American Woman and Politics. More women than men voted against Republican George Bush in his 1988 run for the White House, too, but Bush won. When he ran again in 1992, women again voted against him, but this time they were backing a winning candidate, Democrat Bill Clinton. Women voted for Clinton both in greater numbers and percentages than did men. The gender gap, though, was still not highly respected in political circles.

The gender gap came into its own in 1996. That year, the presidential election had feminists cheering. President Clinton was reelected by the women's vote. The gap had done its work. Men split their votes almost evenly between Clinton and his opponent, Republican Robert Dole. But 11 percent more women voted for Clinton than against him. And that had made the difference.

Though it has often been discounted, the gender gap has shown itself in other ways as well. Since the 1980s, more women have identified themselves as Democrats than as Republicans. (See Table 5.11.) And since 1982, a greater percentage of women than of men has voted Democratic in U.S. Congressional elections.

Fundraising Feminists

That men are still in charge of the purse strings in the political arena is a reality that has driven many women—some of whom call themselves feminists, some of whom do not—into the business of campaign funding.

Women entering the political arena come in at a disadvantage. Even today, they are met with greater skepticism of their abilities than are men. Also, though more women are running for office today than ever before and are becoming less of a novelty, they still do not fit the image that many voters hold of a credible, reliable political official, the ones they are accustomed to seeing— male attorneys (Mandel 1995).

Women cannot rely on the age-old campaign financiers—the political party, business, labor, special interest groups, and civic networks that customarily come out to back candidates for every election. These organizations form political action committees (PACs) to fund their political choices, and they like to back winners, being especially drawn to those with proven track records.

Table 5.11
Percentage of Women and Men
Who Identify Themselves as Democrats

	Democrats		Republicans	
	Percent Who Are:		Percent Who Are:	
	Women	Men	Women	Men
1996	44	33	26	29
1994	38	34	25	29
1992	36	29	32	34
1990	38	28	30	32
1988	41	32	29	31
1986	40	35	29	28
1984	40	37	28	31

Source: Center for the American Woman and Politics (CAWP), National Information Bank on Women in Public Office, Eagleton Institute of Politics, Rutgers University, drawn from CBS News/*New York Times* polls. Reprinted by permission.

Women do not fit their image of a winner; not only do women look like outsiders to the existing political organization but they often, in fact, are.

Traditional campaign money flows most liquidly and easily into the coffers of incumbents. This gives incumbents an advantage in campaign funding. Incumbents have an advantage, too, of name recognition with voters as well as the resources and status of incumbency. Of course, the advantage of incumbency is available to women as well as men. But because nearly 89 percent of incumbent legislators at the national level are male—78 percent are male at the state level—the reality is that only a minority of women are in a position to take advantage of incumbency status. Most women coming into the political world find themselves facing an incumbent male opponent. Financing their campaigns becomes more difficult because contributors know the incumbent has the edge in winning votes.

In the early 1970s, women began their own network of funding and of backing candidates. EMILY (Early Money Is Like Yeast) was one of the first. Following in EMILY's footsteps have come other women's political action committees, until today, several women's organizations have set out specifically to fund feminist and women's campaigns. Some have the goal of supporting liberal women candidates, some support pro-choice candidates, some support conservative women. As part of their mandate, the PACs often hold workshops to encourage women to become candidates. These PACs, though nowhere near the size or number of traditional business and political PACs, have been instrumental in the campaigns of many of today's women in office. (For a listing of these PACs, see Chapter 6.)

Global Political Power

The twentieth century has been the century of women's suffrage. Beginning actually before the turn of the century in 1893, when women in New Zealand won the right to vote (restricted to women of European descent), women across the globe have achieved what was a radical idea at the 1848 Seneca Falls Convention. In many cases, such as in the United States, Switzerland, Spain, and France, women won the right to vote more than a century after men began voting. In other cases, their suffrage was initially restricted either by class or heritage or to local or regional elections only. In some countries, women could vote but not hold office or, as in the United States, hold office but not vote. In others, women gained voting rights when men did. As of 1997, women's suffrage was almost global. (See Table 5.12.)

The twenty-first century is being named by feminist leaders as the century that women's suffrage will take the next step to women's equality. Work in the coming decades will focus on

Table 5.12

Countries Attaining Women's Right to Vote and Hold Office, by Time Period

Before 1900
United States (elig), New Zealand (vote)

1900–1919
Canada (vote), Australia[a], Austria, Belgium (vote), Denmark, Finland, Germany, Iceland, Ireland, Luxembourg, Netherlands, New Zealand (elig), Norway, Poland, Soviet Union, Sweden[a], United Kingdom[a]

1920–1939
Belgium (elig), Bolivia[a], Brazil, Canada (elig), Chile[a], Cuba, Czechoslovakia, Maldives, Mongolia, Pakistan, Philippines, Portugal[a], Romania[a], South Africa[a], Spain, Sri Lanka, Sweden[b], Thailand, Turkey, United Kingdom[b], United States (vote), Uruguay

1940–1949
Albania, Argentina, Bangladesh, Belgium[b], Belize, Bulgaria, Cameroon, Chile[b], China, Costa Rica, Djibouti (vote), Dominican Republic, Ecuador, France, Guatemala, Guyana (elig), Hungary, Indonesia, Israel, Italy, Jamaica, Japan, Lao P.D.R., Liberia, Malta, Mexico (vote), Niger, North Korea, Panama, Romania[b], Senegal, Seychelles, Singapore, Solomon Islands, South Korea, Syria (vote), Trinidad and Tobago, Venezuela, Vietnam, Yugoslavia

1950–1959
Antigua and Barbuda, Barbados, Benin, Bhutan, Bolivia[b], Canada (vote), Colombia, Comoros, Côte d'Ivoire, Dominica, Egypt, Ethiopia, Gabon, Greece, Grenada, Guyana[b], Haiti, Honduras, India, Madagascar, Malaysia, Mauritius, Mexico (elig), Nepal, Nicaragua, Peru, St. Kitts and Nevis, St. Lucia, St. Vincent and the Grenadines, Sierra Leone, Suriname, Syria (elig), Tanzania, Togo, Tunisia, Zimbabwe (vote)

1960–1975
Afghanistan, Algeria, Angola, Australia[b], Bahamas, Botswana, Canada (elig), Cape Verde, Congo, Cyprus, El Salvador, Equatorial Guinea, Gambia, Iran, Jordan, Kenya, Kiribati, Libya, Malawi, Monaco, Morocco, Mozambique, Nauru, Papua New Guinea, Paraguay, Rwanda, São Tomé and Principe, St. Marino, Swaziland, Switzerland, Tonga, Uganda, Yemen, Zaire, Zambia

1976–1997
Central African Republic, Djibouti (elig), Guinea-Bissau, Iraq, Leichtenstein, Namibia, Portugal[b], South Africa, Vanuatu, Western Samoa, Zimbabwe (elig)

Note: "elig" refers to when women were granted eligibility to run for office; "vote" refers to the right to vote. Often these two rights were granted at separate times.
[a]When limited rights were granted to all women or when full rights were granted to certain categories of women.
[b]When full rights were granted to all women.
Source: Inter-Parliamentary Union, *Women and Political Power,* Series "Reports and Documents," 19, Geneva, 1992.

attaining actual political power and political representation for women. Thus, the call to hear the voice of women in decision-making halls across the world has been made. So far, a few voices have actually been heard. But just a few. Globally, women hold just 11.7 percent of parliamentary seats. The Inter-Parliamentary Union, an international organization of parliaments of sovereign states, concluded in its 1997 published study that "with the relative exception of Nordic countries, all countries conduct politics in a way that excludes nearly half of their human resources and talents." And, they added, "It is democracy that suffers and development that is slowed as a result of this state of affairs" (1997, 5).

The Inter-Parliamentary Union presented its idea for a new global social agreement, calling for parity and partnership. These two concepts embody its philosophy and the philosophy of many (but not all) global feminists. The concept of parity "reflects the fact that persons of one or the other sex are different but nonetheless equal"; the concept of partnership "shows that a creative synergy can be created between men and women so as to tackle the community's problems effectively" (Inter-Parliamentary Union 1997, 5). A plan of action was urgently needed, its 1994 survey concluded, not to promote one sex over the other but to correct a "major discrepancy between the two sexes" (p. 5).

Over the years it has been discovered that women's participation in government depends not only on suffrage but on many cultural, social, and political realities of their lives. Therefore, suffrage has not automatically brought women into the decision-making arena of politics. The Inter-Parliamentary Union, in a 1997 world comparative study entitled *Men and Women in Politics: Democracy Still in the Making*, analyzed the significant forces that affect women's political participation and power around the globe. In brief, they found that women's participation is affected by:

The prevailing culture. A culture that has the collective will to achieve gender equality will take steps to achieve it. Without a collective will, gender equality languishes. And in cultures that resist any changes in the roles of women and men, an equal resistance to women's participation in government can be expected.

Social movements coupled with the political opportunity structure. The women's movement, when strong, works to force open doors, but the political structure, including parties and electoral processes, must be receptive to change in order for change to happen. It has always been a fact of feminism that the power to change old systems into women-friendly systems at first lies in the hands of the *men* in power. Those men must allow the door to open. In many countries, the Nordic countries most notably, those in power have worked to bring women into the system. In others, they have not.

Women's position in political party hierarchy. Political parties support candidates for elected office and as such are the first line of change for women. Women are, globally, numerous at the grassroots level of political parties, but their numbers thin as they go up the ranks. Once again, in many cases, they are applying to men for inclusion into inner party circles. The number of women in top party positions has a direct influence on their numbers in parliaments. According to a 1997 survey, just 10.8 percent of top party hierarchies was reported to be female; 11.7 percent of parliaments was female (Inter-Parliamentary Union 1997, 16).

Gender quotas. Political parties and national parliaments have tried to remedy inequality through quotas. These quotas are considered to be a temporary measure to facilitate a change toward equality; some specify that neither gender should hold more than 60 percent of the parliamentary seats. In other cases, a certain number of seats are reserved for women. Quotas have been a successful way to get more female representation into some governments. With a quota that 30 percent of candidates put forth by political parties be women, Argentina ranks first in the Americas in representation. It reported 25.3 percent women in its Chamber of Deputies in 1995. In Norway, all political parties have, either formally or as an adopted tradition, agreed to attempt a 50 percent representation of women candidates. And Norway's parliament was 39.4 percent women in 1993. But quotas do carry with them a negative image: Quotas sometimes are seen as paternalistic, inappropriately promoting incompetent people to positions of power, or simply an unnatural boost to women's own pace in political and cultural development. They sometimes are blamed for setting up a two-tiered layer of women legislators—those elected on their own merits and those "quota-ed" in.

Women's branches. Many political parties, especially in Africa, have set up women's branches. The danger inherent in such systems is that women's issues and concerns can be marginalized. Women's branches can work against the very women they are trying to help, keeping them out of the real political arena. In

Cameroon, for example, women's branches come under party control and the oversight of men, who are acknowledged as the only political party leaders. Women in the branches are undergoing training in politics, economics, and women's policy. Yet, the Cameroon government reported "a great deal of reluctance" in 1997 "about accepting the idea of parity and partnership between men and women in politics" and admitted that the parties were strongly male dominated (Inter-Parliamentary Union 1997, 21). Women's branches can also be seen as provisional measures—as places for women to learn politics in preparation for entering the greater arena. That is the case reported in Costa Rica, where women's branches promote participation in party activities. Women's branches have also served as forums for promoting issues of special concern to women. In Germany, the Women's Union speaks for women in the Christian Democratic Union (CDU) and ensures that their interests are included in party platforms.

Female-friendly attitudes. Politics has been a male domain for centuries and as such has developed male-friendly attitudes. Such things as child care and family responsibilities have not previously been a politician's personal concern. Now they are, as women, some of them mothers, many of them wives, enter the legislatures and political party meetings in greater numbers. Their needs for child care, parental leave, and less rigid time schedules are being considered. In a few instances, as men and women move toward a more equal share in household tasks, men are benefiting alongside women when family-friendly attitudes permeate the political arena.

Women in Seats of Power

Representation in government for women worldwide has been as difficult to achieve—often more difficult—as it has been for American women. A goal of 50 percent representation in governmental bodies worldwide is still just a shimmer on the horizon in much of the world; in fact, it has yet to be reached anywhere in the world! At present, representation ranges from zero to 40.4 percent, with just 13 countries at 25 percent or above, and 67 countries at over 10 percent (Inter-Parliamentary Union 1997, 90–93). (See Table 5.13.) Progress in representation has been slow and unsteady and, in many countries, is nonlinear. That is, though women are present in parliaments, no truly secure footing has been established.

Table 5.13
Percentage of Women Occupying Seats in the Lower and
Upper Houses of Congresses and Parliaments, January 1997

Ranking	Country	Women in Lower or Single House (percentage)	Women in Upper House or Senate (percentage)
1	Sweden	40.4	
2	Norway	39.4	
3	Finland	33.5	
4	Denmark	33.0	
5	Netherlands	31.3	22.7
6	New Zealand	29.2	
7	Seychelles	27.3	
8	Austria	26.8	20.3
9	Germany	26.2	19.1
10	Iceland	25.4	
11	Argentina	25.3	2.8
12	Mozambique	25.2	
13	South Africa	25.0	17.8
14	Spain	24.6	13.3
15	Cuba	22.8	
16	China	21.0	
	Eritrea	21.0	
	Switzerland	21.0	17.4
17	South Korea	20.1	
18	Grenada	20.0	n/a
	Guyana	20.0	
	Luxembourg	20.0	
19	Vietnam	18.5	
20	Namibia	18.1	n/a
	Uganda	18.1	
21	Canada	18.0	23.1
	Turkmenistan	18.0	
22	Lithuania	17.5	
	Tanzania	17.5	
23	Chad	17.3	
24	Rwanda	17.1	
25	Costa Rica	15.8	
26	Suriname	15.7	
27	Australia	15.5	
28	Czechoslovakia	15.0	

Note: Countries are listed in descending rank according to representation in the lower or single house. The United States, not shown, is in forty-first place. Countries that show more than 15 percent representation in the upper house but not in the lower are Belgium, Trinidad and Tobago, the Bahamas, Malaysia, Antigua and Barbuda, Lesotho, Belize, Swaziland, and Saint Lucia.

Source: Inter-Parliamentary Union, *Democracy Still in the Making: A World Comparative Study,* "Reports and Documents," 28, Geneva, 1997.

Yet women's voices are being heard in more places today than ever before. Women in parliaments where women are well-represented provide role models and how-to guidelines for women in countries with weaker representation. And they form networks of governmental officials that finally do create a world-wide web of women ready to help other women.

Global Feminist Meetings

Though feminists in the United States have not yet been as successful as feminists in some other countries when it comes to female representation in the legislature, they do play a leading role in global feminism and are perceived as leaders in effecting social change. Bella Abzug, an untiring American feminist, took a leading role in conferences and conventions dedicated to furthering women's position in the world. She was joined by other American leaders, including Betty Friedan, and backed by the comparatively enormous resources of the United States. The sheer mass of the United States compared to many of the other countries where women have begun to speak out places it in a leadership position. The country's superpower status also moves with the feminists in their travels. And the power of the second-wave feminists, with their mass demonstrations, their outspoken demands, and the legal and social changes they wrought in this country, carry weight.

But hopes for real change for women globally rests not just with feminist leaders in the developed world but with the efforts of thousands of feminists working together as an ongoing force across both cultural and national borders. This comprehensive effort is now underway. It began in earnest when feminists met for the 1975 first World Conference on Women in Mexico City. The conference took women's ideas seriously, focusing on women's equality; it set off a wave of governmental consciousness raising and sparked the declaration of the International Decade of Women (1975–1985). Nongovernmental organizations (NGOs) met in their own forum alongside the conference, establishing a tradition that would grow to become as important as the official conference. Local and regional women's leaders meet in workshops, seminars, panel discussions, and informal settings at the conferences and the NGO forums; out of these meetings has grown a new communication among women of the world. And communication, feminists have found, is the foundation for change.

One of the early successes of the growing global women's movement was the United Nations General Assembly's 1979 adoption of the Convention on the Elimination of All Forms of Discrimination Against Women (CEDAW). CEDAW is a comprehensive code of women's rights in international law. It requires that women's legal protections be identical to men's; guarantees women the freedom to choose where they live, whether to marry, and whether to have children; and guarantees their continuing right to those children. As an international convention, CEDAW is both a politically and legally binding treaty. More than 150 nations have ratified the convention, though many have added "reservations." The United States was the only industrialized nation not to have ratified CEDAW by 1997. (It was submitted for Senate approval in November 1980, after Jimmy Carter had lost to Ronald Reagan. Neither President Reagan nor his successor, President Bush, sought ratification. In 1997, President Clinton and Secretary of State Madeleine Albright pledged to seek ratification.)

Further World Conferences on Women were held in 1980 in Copenhagen, Denmark; in 1985 in Nairobi, Kenya; and in 1995 in Beijing, China. With each conference, the numbers attending grew, and the goals developed and grew, too, from early requests for consideration to strong statements and demands for women's rights in all phases of life.

The fourth World Conference on Women, held in 1995 in Beijing, drew 30,000 participants. It produced a dynamic, exciting flow of ideas among women leaders from all over the world. American feminist leader Charlotte Bunch in her speech at the conference called the 1990s "a critical juncture in time throughout the world . . . a time of transition—a time when the ways of governing, the ways of living and of doing business, the ways of interacting amongst people and nations are in flux" (Bunch 1995). She reminded the delegates of the reactionary forces, both nationalist and religious, in the world that seek to control women's lives. And she reminded women of their position, fundamentally unaltered since Simone de Beauvoir's words decades earlier: "We live in a male-defined world where we are still the original 'other,' and most of the definitions of issues and approaches in this world do not fit our experience" (Bunch 1995). With this, she called women to action, urging them to take their place in the policymaking bodies of their countries, to speak in their own, woman-defined voices, and "to become a global force that must be reckoned with."

A coalition of Christian, Islamic, and Catholic fundamentalists spoke out strongly against many of the ideas that feminists wanted inserted into the final Beijing documents. They succeeded in inserting some compromises in the conference's outcome; nevertheless, feminists took their global agenda farther at the Beijing conference than in any previous worldwide meetings.

The Beijing Platform for Action, a lengthy document that calls for government response at the end of the conference, reflected a new global commitment to equality, development, and peace for women everywhere. It established the principle of shared power and responsibility between women and men at home, in the workplace, and in the wider national and international communities. Countries agreed that the advancement of women and gender equality were matters of human rights and that without sharing power with women at all levels of decision making, no real equality between women and men will ever exist. Though the conference's Platform for Action is not a legally binding document, the international delegates in Beijing all signed their commitment to it. They also committed their governments to plan strategies to implement the Platform for Action within a year.

In addition to fostering real change at national levels, the Beijing conference brought a new world image of women into the spotlight. Though the women at the conference came from many different religious and cultural backgrounds, they all came with a desire for equality in their homelands. The myth that women—any women, no matter where they are in the world—are content to be second-class citizens was dealt what feminists hoped would be a final death blow.

Other global summits and conferences have occurred in between, as well as following, the United Nations World Conferences on Women. In 1993, women were part of the United Nations World Conference on Human Rights in Vienna, Austria, that affirmed women's human rights as an "inalienable, integral, and indivisible part of universal human rights" (Sivard 1996, 7). In 1994, women attended the International Conference on Population and Development in Cairo, Egypt, to discuss the interdependence between human rights and women's reproductive rights. In 1997, American feminists Betty Friedan and Bella Abzug spoke to the 1997 Global Summit of Women in Miami, Florida, where women gathered from all over the world to discuss women's economic power and their roles as workers and leaders. Women are finding entry into world conferences that are not focused directly on women's issues, too, taking part also in environmental and economic development conferences.

With its commitment to becoming part of international decision-making bodies and building a network of women seeking change, the global women's movement is already part of the official international political community. It is becoming part of the leadership of that community, too. Following is a chronology of world conferences and events in support of women's rights.

1945   Charter of the United Nations, Article 55(c), states that the United Nations shall promote "universal respect for, and observance of, human rights and fundamental freedoms for all without distinction as to . . . sex" (Sivard 1996, 36).

1948   Universal Declaration of Human Rights prohibits discrimination based on sex.

1954   UN General Assembly urges governments to eliminate laws and customs specific to women that violate the Universal Declaration of Human Rights.

1975   First World Conference on Women is held in Mexico City. The principle themes of the conference are equality, development, and peace. The year is declared International Women's Year, and the UN later declares 1975–1985 to be the United Nations Decade of Women.

1976   International Tribunal on Crimes Against Women is held in Brussels, Belgium. The tribunal examines the crime of woman battering. Women survivors testify about violence they have endured in their homes at the hands of husbands, acquaintances, strangers, employers, and others. The crimes have been openly or tacitly sanctioned by their societies. The participants call for urgent governmental action. Out of this conference is established the International Feminist Network, a communication channel for women to help women in other countries through actions of solidarity and support, such as letter campaigns and appeals to governments.

1979   Convention on the Elimination of All Forms of Discrimination Against Women (CEDAW) obtains approval. UN member countries that agree to CEDAW, a legally binding international treaty, assume the legal duty to eliminate discrimination against women in all civil, political, economic, social, and cultural areas, including health care and family planning. Countries can agree with reservations; more reservations have been attached to this treaty than to any other human rights treaty. (As of 1995, 139 of the 185 members of the United Nations had ratified the treaty; the United States is not among them. However, in 1997, U.S. Secretary of State Madeleine Albright takes a stand for CEDAW, saying "it is long past time for Americans to become party to the Convention on Elimination of Discrimination Against Women." She also pledges "that the Clinton administration's overseas aid programs would emphasize projects that expand women's ability to obtain reproductive health care, protect themselves from violence and participate in their nations' economic and political systems" [Ross 1997].)

1980   Second World Conference on Women is held in Copenhagen and is attended by 1,326 official delegates from 145 countries. Approximately 8,000 people participate in NGO parallel forums. The theme is again development, equality, and peace.

1985   Third World Conference on Women is held in Nairobi: 1,400 delegates from 157 nations adopt the "Forward-Looking Strategies for the Advancement of Women to the Year 2000." Continuing the theme of equality, development, and peace from the previous two conferences, the third conference recommends actions to eliminate a wide range of discriminatory practices that maintain the subordination of women worldwide (Schuler 1995). The idea of regional networks to promote rights of women is pursued. Participants look at the systematic way in which laws hold women in subordinate status, and they begin to devise strategies to overcome and change those laws

for Third World women. Goals are equal rights for women, abolition of slavery and prostitution, establishment of a legal minimum age for marriage, and punishment for female infanticide. Delegates also call for women's access to maternity leave, maternal health care, family planning, nutrition, and education. An increase in national health budgets, shared parenting responsibilities, recognition of women's unpaid work, wage equity, participation by women in business and politics, and an end to abuse of women and children are other official goals of the conference (Fisher and MacKay 1996; Schuler 1995).

1992   The United Nations Conference on Environment and Development is held in Rio de Janeiro, Brazil. Known as the Earth Summit, the conference officially recognizes that women play an essential role in environmental management and sustainable development.

1993   The World Conference on Human Rights meets in Vienna. Often referred to as simply the Vienna Conference, it is a pivotal event that produces a declaration condemning all forms of violence against women, and it affirms that "the human rights of women and of the girl-child are an inalienable part of universal human rights" (Fisher and MacKay 1996, 40).

The Declaration on the Elimination of Violence Against Women, a landmark resolution, is adopted by the United Nations General Assembly. It defines acts of violence against women and calls on governments to take specific measures to prevent the violence. Its definition includes public and private violence, coercive threat of violence, and any act of violence that is likely to result in physical, sexual, or psychological harm or suffering to women. This includes battering, sexual abuse, female genital mutilation, marital rape, dowry-related violence, sexual harassment, forced prostitution, and violence condoned by the state.

1994   The Convention on the Prevention, Punishment and Eradication of Violence Against Women is adopted

1994
(cont.)
by the Organization of American States (OAS); it is the first formal treaty on the subject of violence against women. The International Conference on Population and Development is held; it recognizes the significance of women's health and rights for effective population and development policies, and it calls for shared family responsibilities and for education, empowerment, and health and reproductive health programs for women and girls.

1995
The World Summit on Social Development confirms commitment to equality and declares that women's political and economic empowerment is essential to combat poverty and social disintegration. The fourth World Conference on Women, held in Beijing, attracts 4,995 delegates from 181 countries. An estimated 30,000 participate in the NGO forum, and 16,921 are registered for the official UN conference, which concludes that the situation of women worldwide has deteriorated significantly since the first conference in 1975. Its Platform of Action points to twelve Critical Areas of Concern, including violence and discrimination against women and girls, reproductive and sexual rights, economic empowerment, equal access to education and health facilities, inclusion in the decision making of governments, and the need for family supports.

1997
The Global Summit of Women focuses on women's economic power, from their roles as workers and leaders to consumers.

1998
This is the year of the five-year review of the Vienna Declaration and Program of Action of the World Conference on Human Rights, as well as the review at the Commission on the Status of Women of sections of the Beijing Platform for Action. Also, a campaign is planned by the Center for Women's Global Leadership for the fiftieth anniversary of the UN's adoption of the Universal Declaration of Human Rights. The theme is that where the human rights of women are not respected, all human rights are undermined.

Choice Words

Feminist leaders today speak out with ever greater directness and demand as well as hope for a transformation of society. The leaders cross cultural and political boundaries with their words and create a web of communication that supports a growing feminism throughout the world. The bons mots of feminist leaders are many, and every day brings a new expression of feminist aims. Listed here are a highly selective, limited few examples.

Women united in common tasks for the welfare of others, build a bridge over which all humanity can pass.
>Dr. Mary McLeod Bethune (National
>Council of Negro Women brochure)

No change in society has ever been seen or envisioned as deep as the prospect of equality of the sexes.
>Eleanor Holmes Norton, while serving as
>chair of the New York City Commission on
>Human Rights, 1970

We are the women that men have warned us about.
>Robin Morgan (Morgan 1977, 126)

The future depends entirely on what each of us does every day.
>Gloria Steinem (Gibbs and McDowell
>1992:57)

The concept of democracy will only assume true and dynamic significance when political policies and national legislation are decided upon jointly by men and women with equitable regard for the interests and aptitudes of both halves of the population.
>Inter-Parliamentary Council, April 1992

What is really ludicrous is a political structure that denies representation to a majority of its population and then winds up fingering the victims of this situation as somehow responsible for it because of their personal inadequacies.
>Bella Abzug (Schneir 1994, 398)

For me, to be a feminist is to answer the question "Are women human?" with a yes. It is not about whether women are better than, worse than or identical with men. . . . It's about women having intrinsic value as persons rather than contingent value as a means to an end for others: fetuses, children, "the family," men.

      Katha Pollitt (Pollitt 1994, xxi)

Is athletics an important feminist issue? Yes. Participation in sports benefits women just as it does men, helping to develop leadership skills, boosting self-esteem and grades, and promoting physical fitness and health.

      Feminist Majority (Feminist Majority
      Foundation 1995)

This global force of women around the world has many different names, call it feminist, call it womanist, call it women in development, call it women's rights or women's human rights. Call it many different things because each of us has found different terms that describe best for us that reality of domination and change. Women are the most important new global force on the horizon in the world today with the potential to create a more humane future and a humane global governance.

      Charlotte Bunch, August 31, 1995, at the
      World Conference in Beijing

We can't stop with changing laws—that's just a first step. We have to change the entire culture that supports and legitimates discrimination and violence against women. And change doesn't happen just because laws are passed or because time passes; it happens because we make it happen.

      Patricia Ireland, president of the National
      Organization for Women (Ireland 1996, 293)

Look at the World through Women's Eyes

Theme of the NGO Forum on Women held in China, September 1995:
      Visualize a world where all conflicts—domestic violence, gun fights on the streets and civil wars—are solved through negotiation. When women and families feel safe in their homes, on the street and in their communities.

Visualize a society where clean water, food and housing are priorities for each citizen in every village, town and city. Where women can get credit and access to other resources they need to be fully economically productive.

Visualize nations where girls are educated and valued as much as boys, and all people are free to develop their full potential. Where men, too, are responsible for their fertility and sexuality, and family planning is transformed into comprehensive reproductive health care. Where women's knowledge and experience are integrated into every day decisions. And legislation is passed through Parliaments with a critical mass of women representatives.

Visualize the globe where the massive amounts of money spent on guns and weapons is used instead to end poverty, preserve health and well-being and create sustainable human development.

This is the kind of world women organizing for the NGO Forum on Women in Beijing want to build.

Look at the world through women's eyes.

Statement presented by the NGO Forum on Women (Fisher and MacKay 1996)

Remarks for the Fourth World Conference on Women

First Lady Hillary Rodham Clinton erases the old idea of women's rights being separate from human rights in her speech to the United Nations fourth World Conference on Women in Beijing, September 5, 1995. The shift to women's rights as human rights signifies a major step for women in international politics, human rights having long been legitimate concerns of the international community, and women's human rights having long been ignored.

Our goals for this conference, to strengthen families and societies by empowering women to take greater control over their own destinies, cannot be fully achieved unless all governments—here and around the world—accept their responsibility to protect and promote internationally recognized human rights. . . .

I believe that, on the eve of a new millennium, it is time . . . for us to say here in Beijing, and the world to hear, that it is no longer acceptable to discuss women's rights as separate from human rights.

These abuses [listed by Clinton earlier] have continued because, for too long, the history of women has been a history of silence. Even today, there are those who are trying to silence our words. The voices of this conference and of the women at Huairou [the site of the NGO Forum] must be heard loud and clear.

It is a violation of HUMAN rights when babies are denied food, or drowned, or suffocated, or their spines broken, simply because they are girls.

It is a violation of HUMAN rights when women and girls are sold into the slavery of prostitution.

It is a violation of HUMAN rights when women are doused with gasoline, set on fire and burned to death because their marriage dowries are deemed too small.

It is a violation of HUMAN rights when individual women are raped in their own communities and when thousands of women are subjected to rape as a tactic or prize of war.

It is a violation of HUMAN rights when a leading cause of death worldwide among women ages 14 to 44 is the violence they are subjected to in their own homes.

It is a violation of HUMAN rights when young girls are brutalized by the painful and degrading practice of genital mutilation.

It is a violation of HUMAN rights when women are denied the right to plan their own families, and that includes being forced to have abortions or being sterilized against their will.

If there is one message that echoes forth from this conference, it is that human rights are women's rights . . . and women's rights are human rights.

Let us not forget that among those rights are the right to speak freely.

And the right to be heard.

Women must enjoy the right to participate fully in the social and political lives of their countries if we want freedom and democracy to thrive and endure.

Hillary Rodham Clinton, September 5, 1995

References

Bunch, Charlotte. 1995. "Through Women's Eyes: Global Forces Facing Women in the 21st Century." Speech to the NGO Forum '95 on Women, Opening Plenary. August 31.

Catalyst. 1996. "Top Corporate Leadership Still Eludes Women: Catalyst Benchmark Provides Measure of Women's Advancement in Fortune 500 Companies." News release. October 17.

———. 1996. "Women Directors Open Avenues for Advancement." *Catalyst Perspective* 2.

Center for the American Woman and Politics (CAWP). 1997. "Statewide Elective Executive Women 1997." Fact sheet. National Information Bank on Women in Public Office, Eagleton Institute of Politics, Rutgers University.

Clinton, Hillary Rodham. 1995. Remarks for the United Nations fourth World Conference on Women. September 5. As available on http://www.feminist.org/other/beij905h.html.

Costello, Cynthia, and Barbara Kivimae Krimgold, eds., for the Women's Research and Education Institute. 1996. *The American Woman, 1996–97: Women and Work.* New York: W. W. Norton.

Faludi, Susan, 1991. *Backlash: The Undeclared War against American Women.* New York: Crown.

Feminist Majority Foundation. 1995. *Empowering Women in Sports.* Arlington, Va.: Feminist Majority Foundation.

Fisher, Elizabeth, and Linda Gray MacKay. 1996. *Gender Justice: Women's Rights Are Human Rights.* Cambridge, Mass.: Unitarian Universalist Service Committee.

Freeman, Jo. 1995. "The Revolution for Women in Law and Public Policy." In Jo Freeman, ed., *Women: A Feminist Perspective, Fifth Edition.* Mountain View, Calif.: Mayfield Publishing.

———, ed. 1995. *Women: A Feminist Perspective, Fifth Edition.* Mountain View, Calif.: Mayfield Publishing.

Gibbs, Nancy, and Jeanne McDowell. 1992. "How to Revive a Revolution." *Time.* March 9: 57.

Hook, Janet. 1996. "A Changing of the Guard." *Los Angeles Times.* December 3: A5.

Inter-Parliamentary Union. 1997. *Men and Women in Politics: Democracy Still in the Making* (Series "Reports and Documents" No. 28). Geneva, Switzerland: IPU.

Ireland, Patricia. 1996. *What Women Want.* New York: Dutton.

Mandel, Ruth B. 1995. "A Generation of Change for Women in Politics." In Jo Freeman, ed., *Women: A Feminist Perspective, Fifth Edition.* Mountain View, Calif.: Mayfield Publishing.

Mofford, Juliet H. 1996 (Spring/Summer). "Women in the Workplace." *Women's History* 2, 1: 14.

Morgan, Robin. 1970. "Goodbye to All That." In Robin Morgan, *Going Too Far: The Personal Chronicle of a Feminist.* New York: Random House, 1977.

National Committee on Pay Equity. 1997. Press kit.

Pollitt, Katha. 1994, 1995. *Reasonable Creatures: Essays on Women and Feminism.* New York: Random House.

Ross, Sonya. 1997. "Albright Will Press for Signing of U.N. Equal Rights Treaty." Associated Press (NewsHound). March 12.

Rossi, Alice, ed. 1973. *The Feminist Papers: From Adams to de Beauvoir.* New York: Columbia University Press.

Schneir, Miriam, ed. 1994. *Feminism in Our Time: The Essential Writings, World War II to the Present.* New York: Random House.

Schuler, Margaret A., ed. 1995. *From Basic Needs to Basic Rights: Women's Claim to Human Rights.* Washington, D.C.: Women, Law & Development International.

Sewall, Rebecca P. 1995. "Reconstructing Social and Economic Rights in Transitional Economies." In Margaret A. Schuler, ed., *From Basic Needs to Basic Rights: Women's Claim to Human Rights.* Washington, D.C.: Women, Law & Development International.

Sivard, Ruth Leger, with Arlette Brauer and Rebecca Cook. 1995. *Women—A World Survey.* Washington, D.C.: World Priorities, Inc.

Stahura, Barbara. 1996 (Fall). "Hazel Henderson's Better Bottom Line: A Feminist Futurist Redefines What Counts." *On the Issues,* pp. 34–35.

United Nations. 1995. *The World's Women 1995: Trends and Statistics.* New York: United Nations.

Wolf, Naomi. 1991. *The Beauty Myth: How Images of Beauty Are Used against Women.* New York: William Morrow and Company.

Woloch, Nancy. 1994. *Women and the American Experience, Second Edition.* New York: McGraw-Hill.

Directory of Organizations

**American Association of
University Women (AAUW)**

1111 16th Street NW
Washington, DC 20036
202-785-7700
Fax: 202-872-1425
E-mail: info@mail.aauw.org
Web site: http://www.aauw.org

One of the oldest women's organizations in the
United States, the AAUW was founded in 1881.
From the beginning, the organization's literature states, members have seen education as
"the key to achieving equity for women of all
ages, races, and creeds." In recent years, the organization has sponsored and supported studies on gender equity in classrooms. Its study *The
AAUW Report: How Schools Shortchange Girls* is
credited with opening the 1990s debate on subtle discrimination still faced by girls in American classrooms, from elementary through college years. Its local chapters organize and
support math and science days for girls, encouraging them to channel their studies into these
disciplines. The AAUW has also lent support to
studies of the problem of sexual harassment in
schools, and its educational foundation provides a wide range of fellowships and grants.

Business and Professional Women/USA (BPW/USA)

2012 Massachusetts Avenue NW
Washington, DC 20036
202-293-1100
Fax: 202-861-0298

BPW is a large organization with a long history. Founded in 1919, it was one of the original supporters of child labor laws and among the first (in 1937) to endorse the Equal Rights Amendment. In the 1970s, the BPW was an early supporter of the effort for ratification of the ERA. It continues to support equity for women in the workplace through advocacy, education, and information. It conducts conventions, sponsors scholarships, and provides its members with a quarterly magazine and information on achieving workplace equity.

Catalyst

120 Wall Street, 5th Floor
New York, NY 10005
212-514-8470
Fax: 212-477-4252
E-mail: info@catalystwomen.org

Catalyst focuses on breaking the glass ceiling and advancing women in leadership and policymaking positions. It professes a dual mission: to enable women in business and the professions to achieve their maximum potential, and to help employers capitalize on the talents of women. It conducts research and works with corporations to provide advancement strategies, identifies qualified women for board directorships, maintains a speaker's bureau, and publishes research papers and books. Its studies on women in executive and top management positions have become a standard resource of information on executive women's status for journalists in the United States.

Center for the American Woman and Politics (CAWP)

Eagleton Institute of Politics
Rutgers University
New Brunswick, NJ 08901
908-828-2210

Fax: 908-932-6778
Web site: http://www.rci.rutgers.edu/~cawp

Founded in 1971, CAWP is a think tank, education, and resource center specializing in women in politics and government. A unit of the Eagleton Institute of Politics at Rutgers, CAWP compiles data and serves as a clearinghouse for in-depth information on women's roles and impact in the political arena, including those at the national and state levels. It provides research on individual women in leadership roles and surveys of elected and appointed women. It also provides programs for college and high school students. CAWP offers numerous books, reports, and fact sheets on current political campaigns, elected officials, and issues.

Center for Women Policy Studies (CWPS)

1211 Connecticut Avenue NW, Suite 312
Washington, DC 20036
202-872-1770
Fax: 202-296-8962

An independent feminist policy research and advocacy institution, CWPS holds that all issues affecting women are interrelated; that sex, race, and class bias must be addressed simultaneously; and that analyses of the status and needs of women must reflect their diversity of race, economic status, sexual orientation, age, and disability. Founded in 1972, the CWPS publishes a newsletter and various papers.

Center for Women's Global Leadership (CWGL)

27 Clifton Avenue
New Brunswick, NJ 08903
732-932-8782
Fax: 732-932-1180
E-mail: cwgl@igc.apc.org
Web site:
http://www.igc.apc.org/womensnet/beijing/ngo/cwgl.html

An activist group, CWGL focuses on women's human rights on a global scale. It seeks to increase women's leadership and bring women's voices and feminist perspectives into global policymaking arenas. The center sees women's leadership and transformative visions as crucial in every policy area from democratization and human rights to global security and economic restructuring. It coordinated the Global Campaign for Women's Human Rights at the Vienna World Conference on Human Rights in 1993, provides resources on global efforts to end violence against women, and supplies information on organizing regional campaigns in support of women's rights. CWGL has a long publications list, including *Testimonies of the Global Tribunal on Violations of Women's Human Rights* (1993), *Gender Violence: A Development and Human Rights Issue* (1991), pamphlets on women and human rights, Women's Global Leadership Institute Reports, and videos.

Coordinating Council for Women in History (CCWH)

1500 North Verdugo Road
Glendale, CA 91208
818-240-1000, ext. 5461
Fax: 818-549-9436

The official name of this group is the Coordinating Council for Women in History: Advocates for Women in the Profession of History. It is a networking group of professional women historians coming together to promote women as historians and women in history. The group publishes a newsletter and is an advocacy group for historians.

Equal Rights Advocate (ERA)

1663 Mission Street, Suite 550
San Francisco, CA 94103
415-621-0672
ERA Hotline: 800-839-4ERA
Fax: 415-621-6744
E-mail: eradvocates@earthlink.net
Web site: http://www.equalrights.org

Founded in 1974, ERA is a legal organization dedicated to achieving equality for women. Its attorneys challenge unfair laws and practices; they have won equal pay and access for women in the U.S. Forest Service as well as in individual corporations. ERA attorneys have also been "friends of the court" in numerous cases protecting Title IX rights, fighting sexual harassment, advocating for women's work health benefits, and other related issues. ERA sponsors a free (bilingual, English and Spanish) Advice and Counseling Hotline that provides women with information on their civil rights and the avenues open to them if they find themselves the victims of sex discrimination. They also publish a newsletter and have available a video, *Keeping the Door Open: Women and Affirmative Action.*

Equality Now

250 W. 57th Street, Suite 826
New York, NY 10019
212-586-0906
Fax: 212-586-1611
E-mail: equalitynow@igc.apc.org

An international humanist group, Equality Now reports a membership of 3,000, including groups and individuals, in 100 countries around the world. The organization researches and documents violations of women's rights, publicizes them to the general media, and advocates at the governmental level (national and international) for women. It publishes "Actions" on specific issues or cases, asking members and the public to write and lobby appropriate officials. The group's strategy for change is, thus, two-pronged: applying direct pressure to governments and also increasing public awareness of violations to women. Some of the violence Equality Now has addressed: bride burning, domestic violence, female genital mutilation, forced prostitution, rape and mass rape, and the Taliban's restrictions on and punishments of women in Afghanistan.

The Feminist Majority

1600 Wilson Boulevard, Suite 801
Arlington, VA 22209
703-522-2214
Fax: 703-522-2219
E-mail: femmaj@feminist.org
Web site: http://www.feminist.org

Cofounded by Eleanor Smeal and Peg Yorkin in 1987, the Feminist Majority defines itself as a research and advocacy organization dedicated to promoting equality for women. It "seeks to transform the public debate on issues of importance to women's lives." And its name is its premise—the majority of the population supports the feminist issues of equality for women, reproductive freedom, and increased human services,

the organization's statistics reveal. The Feminist Majority
tracks legislative issues, speaks out to the government on behalf of women, and leads campaigns to help women take their
fair share of power in all sectors of society. Through its Feminist Majority Foundation, a feminist think tank, it develops
long-term strategies for feminists and supports educational
and research projects. It sponsors an intern program for college
students, holds feminist forums and conventions, and publishes fact sheets, newsletters, and a quarterly report.

Feminists for Life of America

733 15th Street NW, Suite 1100
Washington, DC 20005
202-737-3352
Fax: 202-737-0414
Web site: http://www.serve.com/fem4life

Founded in 1972, Feminists for Life is a national organization
with the beginnings of an international base. Its members identify themselves as feminists but seek an end to legal abortion.
The organization also lobbies for changes so that abortion will
not be necessary for women. It seeks aid for mothers, stiffer
penalties for fathers who fail to pay child support, federal assistance incentives for single mothers to identify fathers at birth,
and child care for women. It is also opposed to capital punishment and euthanasia, seeing these, as well as abortion, as forms
of violence in contradiction to feminist principles of justice,
nonviolence, and nondiscrimination. The organization publishes a quarterly newsletter, *The American Feminist,* and occasional pamphlets.

Institute for Women's Policy Research (IWPR)

1400 20th Street NW, Suite 104
Washington, DC 20036
202-785-5100
Fax: 202-833-4362
Web site: http://www.iwpr.org

Established in 1987, IWPR is a research institute that focuses on
policies that affect women's lives most directly, with research
projects devoted to health care, pay equity, affirmative action,
and family policies. It works with policy makers and scholars to

both execute and publicize its research. IWPR leaders have testified before Congress on behalf of women. The institute publishes
papers, fact sheets, and a newsletter.

International Black Women's Congress (IBWC)

1081 Bergen Street
Newark, NJ 07112
973-926-0570
Fax: 973-926-0818

Founded in 1983, the IBWC is a global community of women of
African descent. Concerned about the negative images of black
women, members of the International Black Women's Congress
seek to define themselves from their own perspectives. The organization provides educational, research, and charitable programs.
It holds conferences, sponsors a scholarship, and bestows the annual Oni Award to an individual of African ancestry who works
on behalf of African people or those of African ancestry. It publishes papers and a newsletter.

International Center for Research on Women (ICRW)

1717 Massachusetts Avenue NW, Suite 302
Washington, DC 20036
202-797-0007
Fax: 202-797-0020
E-mail: icrw@igc.apc.org
Web site: http://www.icrw.org

The ICRW focuses primarily on women in developing and transitional countries. It promotes women's full participation in both
social and economic life and generates information on women's
status around the globe. It also provides technical assistance on
women's productive and reproductive roles, their status in the
family, their leadership in society, and the management of environmental resources. The ICRW is an advocate for women at the
international level and with national governments. It holds forums and publishes research data and papers on women.

International Women's Tribune Center (IWTC)

777 United Nations Plaza, 3rd Floor
New York, NY 10017

212-687-8633
Fax: 212-661-2704
E-mail: iwtc@igc.apc.org
Web site: http://www.iwtc.org/

An international nongovernmental organization founded in 1975, the IWTC is an information exchange center. It produces education and information materials for an international readership. In doing so, it tries to translate research findings and policy mandates into information materials that bridge the gap between policy and action. It gets technical and political information into the hands of women, and it works with organizations to develop strategies that allow women worldwide to be part of policy shaping and agenda setting at national, regional, and international levels. It publishes numerous materials, including *Women, Ink*, a valuable catalog of current books and papers on women and development.

League of Women Voters of the United States

1730 M Street NW
Washington, DC 20036
202-429-1965
Fax: 202-429-0854
E-mail: 75352.2617@compuserve.com
Web site: http://www.lwv.org/~lwvus/

Founded in 1920 as an outgrowth of the women's suffrage movement, the League of Women Voters is a nonpartisan political organization that encourages citizens to participate in local and national government. It sponsors campaigns to register voters, and it influences public policy through education and advocacy. Though it is not a feminist organization in the strictest sense, the league brings women into the political arena through its membership and its grassroots activism.

MANA, A National Latina Organization

1725 K Street NW, Suite 501
Washington, DC 20006
202-833-0060
Fax: 202-496-0588

MANA was founded in 1974 as the Mexican American Women's National Association. Its members today include Puerto Rican women as well as women of Mexican, Cuban, Central American, and South American descent; hence, it has gone through a name adjustment. MANA promotes equal participation of Latinas in the social, educational, economic, and political arenas. Its leaders serve as the voice for Latinas in congressional arenas. The organization sponsors college scholarships and mentoring programs for girls. It promotes citizen participation and publishes a quarterly newsletter and periodic news bulletins.

Ms. Foundation for Women

120 Wall Street, 33rd Floor
New York, NY 10005
212-742-2300
Fax: 212-742-1653
E-mail: msfdn@interport.net
Web site: http://www.ms.foundation.org

The Ms. Foundation is best known for organizing Take Our Daughters to Work Day, a popular national campaign that sets aside the fourth Thursday in April each year for girls to accompany mothers and mentors into the workplace. The foundation also sponsors school scholarships for girls and grants to girls' organizations. Founded in 1972, it supports various efforts of women and girls to govern their own lives and influence the world around them. Its publications include *Body Politic: Transforming Adolescent Girls' Health* (1996), which reports the findings of a roundtable of professionals; and *Programmed Neglect: Not Seen, Not Heard* (1993), which reveals that less than 8 percent of all programs nationwide provide services to girls from age 9 to 15 and outlines the kinds of programs girls need.

National Abortion and Reproductive Rights Action League (NARAL)

1156 15th Street NW, Suite 700
Washington, DC 20005
202-973-3000
Fax: 202-973-3099
Web site: http://www.naral.org

Founded in 1969 and claiming more than 500,000 members, NARAL is the political arm of the pro-choice movement. While safeguarding the right to legal abortions, it also develops and promotes policies that make abortion less necessary. The NARAL

Foundation conducts legal and policy research, public education campaigns, and leadership training for NARAL's grassroots network of 36 state affiliates. It is one of the most consistently active advocates for reproductive rights in the United States. Its publications include *Who Decides? A State-by-State Review of Abortion and Reproductive Rights* (1997).

National Abortion Federation (NAF)

1755 Massachusetts Avenue NW, Suite 600
Washington, DC 20036
202-667-5881
FAX: 202-667-5890
E-mail: naf@prochoice.org
Web site: http://www.prochoice.org

A professional association of experts—physicians, nurses, counselors, administrators, and medical people—the NAF has a single mission: to ensure that women have access to safe, high-quality abortion services. It provides an accredited educational program of training in abortion procedures for medical personnel, testifies before legislatures considering abortion questions, supplies factual and medical background information to the media, and provides patient-oriented information for use in clinics. It is a clearinghouse and communication network for people within the medical field as well as for those outside of it. It publishes and distributes publications for patient education and for professionals. The NAF also maintains an abortion hotline: 800-772-9100.

**National Association for Girls
and Women in Sport (NAGWS)**

1900 Association Drive
Reston, VA 22091
703-476-3452
Fax: 703-476-9527
E-mail: nagws@aahperd.org
Web site: http://www.aahperd.org/nagws.html

Since 1899, the NAGWS has championed equal funding, equality, and respect for women's sports programs. It is the only professional organization devoted exclusively to providing opportunities for girls and women in sports-related disciplines and careers.

It keeps its members informed of threats to Title IX and to gender-related news in sports through its newsletter, and it publishes educational materials.

National Coalition of 100 Black Women, Inc.

38 West 32nd Street, Suite 1610
New York, NY 10001
212-947-2196
Fax: 212-947-2477

The Coalition of 100 is an advocacy organization composed chiefly of professional women who are active in their communities. It provides networking links between the organization and the corporate and political sectors, makes black women a visible force in all arenas, supports mentoring, and seeks recognition of the achievements of African American women.

National Committee on Pay Equity (NCPE)

1126 16th Street NW, Suite 411
Washington, DC 20036
202-331-7343
Fax: 202-331-7406

A membership coalition of over 170 organizations, including labor unions, private groups, and state and local pay equity networks, the NCPE acts as a central clearinghouse and information source on pay equity activities throughout the United States. It also advocates for pay equity and for fairness toward women in the workplace. It publishes pay equity fact sheets, papers, and a newsletter, *National Committee on Pay Equity NewsNotes.*

National Council for Research on Women (NCRW)

530 Broadway, 10th Floor
New York, NY 10012-3920
212-274-0730
Fax: 212-274-0821

Founded in 1981, the NCRW is a nonprofit coalition of centers and organizations. It provides resources for feminist research, policy, and educational programs for women and girls. The council links several thousand U.S. and international organizations and networks that serve the academic community, policy makers, the media, the nonprofit sector, and the public at large. The NCRW publishes *Issues Quarterly*, in which it presents overviews of current information on women's issues, and its own reports, including *Sexual Harassment: Research and Resources*. It also provides listings of research publications from selected other organizations.

National Council of Negro Women (NCNW)

633 Pennsylvania Avenue NW
Washington, DC 20004
202-737-0120
Fax: 202-737-0476

Founded in 1935 by educator Mary McLeod Bethune and representatives of African American women's organizations, the NCNW unites African American women in social planning and action on national and international levels. It is the coordinating body of 34 national women's organizations and 250 community-based sections for a combined outreach of four million women. Its programs and projects are focused on issues such as child care, economic opportunity, education, career advancement, health, housing, and hunger and malnutrition. Almost from its beginning, the NCNW has included an international division. In the 1970s, after its involvement in the International Women's Year Tribune in Mexico City, the NCNW set up programs in Africa and became a link between African and African American organizations. In 1995 it led a delegation of 112 women to the UN fourth World Conference on Women in Beijing, China. In addition to its numerous programs, the organization publishes a newsletter and has published a series of cookbooks that celebrate the heritage and history of African Americans through recipes and recollections of family reunion meals.

National Council of Women of the United States (NCW/USA)

777 United Nations Plaza
New York, NY 10017
212-697-1278
Fax: 212-972-0164

Founded in 1888 by American suffragists, the NCW/USA is a coalition of 35 women's voluntary organizations and individual members of all races, religions, and national origins. It provides a forum for addressing issues of mutual concern from a united position. Its current focus is on workplace issues of pay equity and family support policies.

National Organization for Women (NOW)

1000 16th Street NW
Washington, DC 20036
202-331-0066
Fax: 202-785-8576
E-mail: now@now.org
Web site: http://www.now.org

Formed in 1966 and considered the first political activist group of second-wave feminism, the National Organization for Women today is still the largest feminist organization in the United States. It advocates and speaks out for women's equality on all fronts. NOW was a leader in the unsuccessful struggle for passage of the Equal Rights Amendment; has worked to win and then to maintain abortion rights for women; and has lobbied, led marches, and mobilized activists to fight for equity on the job, in the courts, and in the home. It holds conferences and annual conventions, supports a forum for young feminists, and organizes demonstrations and marches in support of feminist issues. Five times a year it publishes the *National NOW Times.*

National Organization for Women Legal Defense and Education Fund (NOW LDEF)

99 Hudson Street, 12th Floor
New York, NY 10013-2871
212-925-6635
Fax: 212-226-1066

NOW LDEF is a litigating sister group to the National Organization for Women. It pursues equality for women and girls in the workplace, the schools, the family, and the courts through legal, educational, and public information programs. It is not a legal services organization for individuals but instead works on precedent-setting cases affecting issues such as abortion, violence against women, economic rights and needs of low-income women, and sexual harassment and discrimination. It publishes an informative quarterly newsletter and legal resource kits.

National Women's Health Network (NWHN)

514 10th Street NW, Suite 400
Washington, DC 20004
202-347-1140 (business)
202-628-7814 (information clearinghouse)
Fax: 202-347-1168

An advocacy group devoted to women's health, the NWHN is a group of both individuals and organizations. It lobbies Washington and provides information on a wide range of women's health issues.

National Women's History Project (NWHP)

7738 Bell Road
Windsor, CA 95492-8518
707-838-6000
Fax: 707-838-0478
E-mail: nwhp@aol.com
Web site: http://www.nwhp.org

Established in 1980, the NWHP is an educational organization that promotes multicultural women's history in schools, workplaces, and communities. It develops curriculum materials, conducts teacher training workshops, and serves as a clearinghouse for women's history information and programming ideas. It publishes a well-stocked catalog of books, posters, videos, and K–12 curriculum materials.

National Women's Law Center

11 Dupont Circle NW, Suite 800
Washington, DC 20036
202-588-5180
Fax: 202-588-5185

Founded in 1972, the National Women's Law Center protects and advances the rights of women and girls in virtually every aspect of their lives, with a particular focus on low-income women and women of color. It works to secure workplace equity through laws and enforcement of government regulations and to ensure reproductive rights, education, and family support for women. It publishes *Goals 2000 and Pregnant and Parenting Teens: Making Education Reform Attainable for Everyone; A Vision Beyond Survival: A*

Resource Guide for Women Prisoners; and *Breaking Down Barriers: A Legal Guide to Title IX in Athletics* as well as a newsletter, reports, papers, and fact sheets.

Native American Women's Health Education Resource Center

P.O. Box 572
Lake Andes, SD 57356
605-487-7072
Fax: 605-487-7964
E-mail: nativewoman@igc.apc.org
Web Site: www.nativeshop.org

This is both an advocacy center and a center for women's health.

9 to 5 National Association of Working Women

238 West Wisconsin Avenue, Suite 700
Milwaukee, WI 53203-2308
414-274-0925
Fax: 414-272-2870

9 to 5 bills itself as the "voice for working women." It works to improve pay status and respect for working women, especially low-income office workers. It combines education, advocacy, and activism to promote fair pay, an end to discrimination, safe working conditions, and access to training and promotions for all working women. It offers members a newsletter and guides to improving working conditions.

Older Women's League (OWL)

666 11th Street NW, Suite 700
Washington, DC 20001
202-783-6686
Fax: 202-638-2356

OWL focuses exclusively on women as they age, advocating for legislature for elderly women, health care, Social Security, pensions, housing, and lobbying for legislature on violence against women and the elderly. It publishes a newsletter, educational material, and occasional papers.

**Research, Action and Information Network
for Bodily Integrity of Women (RAINBO)**

915 Broadway, Suite 1109
New York, NY 10010-7108
212-477-3318
Fax: 212-477-4154
E-mail: NT61@columbia.edu
Web site: http://www.rainbo.org

RAINBO (in its official logo, the "O" is the symbol for woman) works globally and locally to pursue integrated action against female genital mutilation (FGM). RAINBO works at the international level as a nongovernmental organization to mobilize and inform the global feminist movement, and at the grassroots level to help communities organize an effective end to FGM. RAINBO sees outside efforts to impose laws and regulations against FGM as ineffective. Those efforts fail to grasp the cultural sensitivity of the issue of FGM and its interlaced connection to women's overall standing in communities that practice it, say RAINBO spokespeople. Therefore, RAINBO provides monetary and technical support to grassroots initiatives. It also advances collaborative, concerted action against FGM by international agencies, national governments, and advocacy groups in Africa, Europe, and the United States. RAINBO publishes fact sheets and maintains a resource center of printed material, videotapes, and training kits for health professionals and educators.

Third Wave

116 East 16th Street, 7th Floor
New York, NY 10003
212-388-1898
Fax: 212-982-3321
E-mail: Thirdwavef@aol.com
Web site: 3wave@nyo.com

Founded in 1992, Third Wave is devoted to young feminist activism for social change. Its leaders explain the nonprofit organization's roots: "An entire generation of women is coming of age to find that all is not okay in America. *Roe v. Wade,* a decision our mothers thought ensured us reproductive freedom, has been all but overturned for most women." Other stated concerns include domestic violence, sexual abuse and harassment, workplace and economic equality, and racist or homophobic hate crimes directed at women—a full feminist agenda. Third Wave recently inaugurated the Third Wave Fund to provide financial help for young women needing assistance for abortions, to support microenterprises of young women, to provide scholarships for college, and for general, related projects. The fund targets, but is not limited to, women who face additional prejudice, including women of color, lesbians, low-income women, and differently abled women. The Third Wave organized Freedom Summer '92 and '96, cross-country voter registration drives focusing on inner cities. It holds Third Wave Multi-Media Festivals biannually and provides a network for young feminists. It publishes a newsletter, *See It? Tell It. Change It.*

United Nations Development Fund for Women (UNIFEM)

304 East 45th Street, 6th Floor
New York, NY 10017
212-906-6400
Fax: 212-906-6705
Web site: http://www.unifem.undp.org

Created in 1976 to work inside the United Nations system, UNIFEM is an advocate for women of developing countries. It works toward women's full participation at all levels of regional and global development planning and practice. It links grassroots women to national and international policymaking bodies and into global debates. Its goals are to ensure that women have control over their lives both inside and outside the household and to counteract the disempowerment of women that often accompanies development and structural changes. UNIFEM publishes a newsletter, papers, and books on its various interests, including *Putting Gender on the Agenda: A Guide to Participating in U.N. World Conferences* (1995). It also produces videos on international women's subjects.

Women and Philanthropy

322 8th Avenue, Room 702
New York, NY 10001
212-463-9934
Fax: 212-463-9417
E-mail: womenphil@igc.apc.org

Women and Philanthropy is an association of grant makers committed to mobilizing the resources of the philanthropic community to achieve equity for women and girls. It seeks to increase funding for programs serving women and girls and to increase the number of women, especially women of color, in grantmaking leadership positions. Through conferences and workshops, internships, and research projects, the group advances its agenda of social equity. It publishes occasional papers and a newsletter.

Women Employed Institute and Women Employed

22 West Monroe Street, Suite 1400
Chicago, IL 60603
312-782-3902
Fax: 312-782-5249

The Women Employed Institute and Women Employed, a membership organization founded in 1973, focus their efforts on achieving equity for women in the workplace. Women Employed provides career and professional development services for its members and involves them in advocacy efforts. The Women Employed Institute advocates for women's access to vocational training for higher-paying jobs, and it works to improve and strengthen equal opportunity laws. It also develops model programs to enable disadvantaged women and girls to achieve self-sufficiency. The organization publishes fact sheets on topics such as the glass ceiling, affirmative action, pregnancy rights on the job, and sexual harassment.

Women in Law and Development in Africa (WiLDAF)

P.O. Box 4622
Harare, Zimbabwe
263-4-752-105
FAX: 263-4-781-886
E-mail: wildaf@mango.zw

A regional network of women's rights leaders and groups in 22 African countries, WiLDAF was formed from leaders attending the Third World Forum on Women in 1985. The organization promotes strategies that link law and development to empower women. Important issues addressed so far have been women's role in the family, custody of children, divorce rights, property ownership rights, and violence against women.

Women in Municipal Government (WIMG)

c/o National League of Cities
1301 Pennsylvania Avenue NW, Suite 550
Washington, DC 20004
202-626-3169
Fax: 202-626-3103
E-mail: gordon@nlc.org
Web site: http://www.cais.com/nlc/

Women in Municipal Government is a caucus group within the National League of Cities. Its members are local elected and appointed officials, and its purpose is to provide networking opportunities and address significant public policy issues. It holds meetings and workshops and publishes a newsletter for its members.

Women, Law and Development International (WLD)

1350 Connecticut Avenue NW, Suite 407
Washington, DC 20036-1701
202-463-7477
Fax: 202-463-7480
E-mail: wld@wld.org

WLD is a nongovernmental organization in consultative status with the Economic and Social Council of the United Nations (Category II). With a board of directors that includes leading women from all parts of the world, WLD researches and publishes information on the global status of women. It also advocates for women and promotes a global women's rights network. Its published books include the 597-page *From Basic Needs to Basic Rights: Women's Claim to Human Rights* (1995), a compilation of essays by women's rights activists and thinkers in the international women's rights community. WLD also publishes manuals and bulletins.

Women Make Movies, Inc. (WMM)

462 Broadway, Suite 500E
New York, NY 10013
212-925-0606
Fax: 212-925-2052
E-mail: info@wmm.com

Women Make Movies is a media arts organization established in 1972 to increase the number of women making movies and to improve the image of women in movies. It is a multicultural, multiracial organization that provides services to all women film and video makers. It is also a distributor and clearinghouse for women's media, providing a rich source of videos by women and about women. WMM's catalog of videos includes many on health issues, violence against women, the feminist movement both in the United States and globally, lesbian issues, and multicultural American issues. It includes both award-winning documentaries by well-known directors such as Jane Campion and Pratibha Parmar and little-known documentaries on women and women's issues. The organization rents and sells the videos on its list. Women Make Movies also holds workshops and seminars and publishes an annual catalog of its available films.

Women Work!

National Network for Women's Employment
1625 K Street NW, Suite 300
Washington, DC 20006
202-467-6346
Fax: 202-467-5366
E-mail: womenwork@worldnet.att.net

An organization dedicated to improving working opportunities and conditions for women, Women Work! advocates and acts as a network for programs to empower all women, with special attention given to displaced homemakers, single mothers, and all women seeking self-sufficiency. It focuses on education, training, improving gender equity on the job, and building an infrastructure of health and child care to support women workers. It publishes a newsletter and various guides on how to improve the workplace for girls and women.

**Women's Environment and
Development Organization (WEDO)**

845 3rd Avenue, 15th Floor
New York, NY 10022
212-759-7982
Fax: 212-759-8647
E-mail: wedo@igc.apc.org
Web site:
http://www.igc.apc.org/womensnet/beijing/ngo/wedo.html

Founded in 1990, WEDO advocates on an international level for women's equality in decision making on environment, development, population, reproductive rights, technology, political participation, and other issues affecting women's lives, their families, and the future of the planet. WEDO attempts to increase women's visibility, roles, and leadership in public policymaking through advocacy campaigns on gender, environment, and development issues, and it lobbies international networks for implementation of government agreements. It also sees itself as a communication web for women around the world and provides access through its Web site to WEDO, Women's Caucus & Women's Linkage Caucus documents, statements, speeches, and other materials.

Women's International Network (WIN)

187 Grant Street
Lexington, MA 02173
617-862-9431
Fax: 617-862-1734

WIN seeks to alert the world about female genital mutilation (FGM) and to end the mutilation. Its founder, Fran Hosken, has often been credited with sounding the first loud (and hence noticed) alarm on FGM and with opening an international debate on the subject. WIN also disseminates reports from and to women around the world on health and human rights. Publications include *WIN News* and *The Hosken Report: Genital/Sexual Mutilation of Females.*

Women's Policy, Inc.

409 12th Street SW, Suite 705
Washington, DC 20024
202-554-2323
Fax: 202-554-2346
E-mail: wompolinc@aol.com

Formed in 1995 to fill the gap left when the Congressional Caucus for Women's Issues lost its funding (along with other legislative service organizations), Women's Policy, Inc., provides information and research on legislative and executive branch actions affecting women. It produces an in-depth weekly newsletter and special reports that cover the issues.

Women's Research and Education Institute (WREI)

1750 New York Avenue NW, Suite 350
Washington, DC 20006
202-628-0444
Fax: 202-628-0458
E-mail: wrei@ix.netcom.com

WREI is a source of nonpartisan information and policy analysis on women's equity issues for federal, state, and local government officials, women's advocates, corporations, journalists, and educators. It publishes various fact sheets and status reports as well as a biannual in-depth statistical portrait of women, most recently titled *The American Woman, 1996–97: Where We Stand.*

Political Action Committees (PACs)

Some of the PACs that either donate money predominately to women candidates or have a predominately female donor base are:

Ain't I a Woman Network/PAC

P.O. Box 34484
Philadelphia, PA 19101

Alabama Solution

P.O. Box 370821
Birmingham, AL 35237
202-250-0205
Fax: 205-995-1990

American Nurses Association, Inc. (ANA-PAC)

600 Maryland Avenue SW, Suite 100W
Washington, DC 20024-2571
202-651-7095
Fax: 202-554-0189

Arkansas Women's Action Fund

1100 North University, Suite 109
Little Rock, AR 72707

501-663-1202
Fax: 501-663-1218

Committee of 21

P.O. Box 19287
New Orleans, LA 70179
504-827-0112

Democratic Activists for Women Now (DAWN)

P.O. Box 6614
San Jose, CA 95150

DAWN helps to elect progressive women to office.

Eleanor Roosevelt Fund of California

1001-158 Evelyn Terrace East
Sunnyvale, CA 94086
408-773-9791

EMILY's List

805 15th Street NW, Suite 400
Washington, DC 20005
202-326-1400
Fax: 202-326-1415
Web site: http://www.emilyslist.org

EMILY stands for Early Money Is Like Yeast—it makes the dough rise. Or, in this case, when the early money is funneled to pro-choice, Democratic women running for national and state offices, it makes it possible for women to rise to the top of the political system. In 1996, 45,000 EMILY's List members contributed $6.6 million to candidates. The group's activities also include candidate recruitment, technical assistance, and campaign staff training. EMILY's List was the first major PAC organized to support women candidates; many others followed its lead.

EMMA's List

P.O. Box 64
Louisville, KY 40201-0646

First Ladies of Oklahoma

8364 South Urbana Avenue
Tulsa, OK 74137

The fundraising arm of the Oklahoma Federated Republic Women, the First Ladies of Oklahoma supports female members of the organization, and then males, who are running for state legislative offices. Donor network.

Focus 2020

P.O. Box 660
Huntsville, AL 35804-0660

GWEN's List

4410 Flagier Street
Miami Beach, FL 33130
305-374-0521

GWEN, for Get Women Elected Now, supports Democratic women candidates in Florida state, local, and judicial races. Donor network.

Harriet's List

P.O. Box 16361
Baltimore, MD 21210
410-377-5709
Fax: 410-377-2842

Supports pro-choice, nonincumbent, Democratic women in Maryland's statewide and legislative races. Donor network and PAC.

The Hope Chest

4921 Dierker Road
Columbus, OH 43220
614-236-4268
Fax: 614-236-2449

Raises funds for pro-choice Democratic women running for Ohio state office.

HOPE-PAC

3220 East 26th Street
Los Angeles, CA 90023

213-267-5845
Fax: 213-262-1348

Independent Women's Organization

13834 Octvia Street
New Orleans, LA 70125
504-525-2256

Indiana Women's Network for Political Action

P.O. Box 88271
Indianapolis, IN 46208-0271
317-283-2066

Bipartisan, supporting pro-choice candidates in state legislative races.

Latina PAC

915 L Street, Suite C, #222
Sacramento, CA 95814
916-395-7915

The Leader PAC

P.O. Box 7001
Fairfax Station, VA 22039-7001

Los Angeles African American Women's PAC

4102 Olympiad Drive
Los Angeles, CA 90043
213-295-2382

Los Angeles Women's Campaign Fund

1410 Ventura Boulevard, Suite 402
Sherman Oaks, CA 91423
818-990-7377
Fax: 818-990-1840

Make Women Count

P.O. Box 677
Richmond, VA 23218-0677

804-644-7450
Fax: 804-643-1466

Make Women Count is a bipartisan political action committee founded in 1992. It advocates the Virginia Women's Agenda, a broad-based statement of issues important to Virginia women, and supports women candidates who are committed to the agenda.

Marin County Women's PAC

3310 Paradise Drive
Tiburon, CA 94920
415-435-2504

Michigan Women's Campaign Fund

P.O. Box 71626
Madison Heights, MI 48071
810-932-3540
Fax: 810-932-1734

Minnesota Women's Campaign Fund

550 Rice Street, Suite 106
St. Paul, MN 55103
612-904-6723
Fax: 612-292-9417

Missouri Women's Action Fund

1108 Hillside Drive
St. Louis, MO 63117
314-516-6622

National Abortion and Reproductive Rights Action League (NARAL)

1156 15th Street NW, Suite 700
Washington, DC 20005
202-973-3000
Web site: http://www.naral.org

National Federation of Business and Professional Women's Clubs (BPW/PAC)

2012 Massachusetts Avenue NW
Washington, DC 20036
202-293-1100 ext. Gov't Relations

National Organization for Women PAC (NOW)

1000 16th Street NW, Suite 700
Washington, DC 20036-5705
202-331-0066
Fax: 202-785-8573

National Women's Political Caucus

1211 Connecticut Avenue NW, Suite 425
Washington, DC 20036
202-785-1100
Fax: 202-785-3605

PAC of the Woman's Democratic Club of Delaware

1222 Arundel Drive
Wilmington, DE 19808
302-998-5038

Supports pro-choice Democratic women candidates in Delaware local and state races. Will support male candidates whose politics are in agreement.

PAM's List

P.O. Box 3311
Cherry Hill, NJ 09034

PAM's List—Power and Money for Choice and Change—supports pro-choice, viable Democratic women candidates for the New Jersey legislature. Founded in 1993.

Pennsylvania Women's Campaign Fund

P.O. Box 767
Hazleton, PA 18201

RENEW

P.O. Box 507
Alexandria, VA 22313-0507
703-836-2255

Founded in 1993, RENEW (Republican Network to Elect Women) identifies, recruits, trains, and raises funds for Republican women running at the federal, state, and local levels, with an emphasis on state and local races.

Republican Women's PAC of Illinois

223 West Jackson Boulevard, Suite 100
Chicago, IL 60606
312-939-7300
Fax: 312-939-7220

Sacramento Women's Campaign Fund

P.O. Box 162212
Sacramento, CA 95816
916-443-8421
Fax: 916-443-8440

Santa Barbara Women's Political Committee

P.O. Box 90618
Santa Barbara, CA 93190-0618
805-682-6769

Seneca Network

2035 Rough Gold Court
Gold River, CA 95670
916-638-8995
Fax: 916-638-8996

The Seneca Network is a contributor network for Republican women candidates in California but is currently inactive.

The Susan B. Anthony List

228 S. Washington Street, Suite 105
Alexandria, VA 22314

703-683-5558
Fax: 703-549-5588

The Susan B. Anthony List is a pro-life women's PAC designed to provide early money to women running for high national office.

Task Force 2000 PAC

P.O. Box 36183
Houston, TX 77236
713-495-7539
Fax: 281-495-0594

Task Force 2000 is a consortium of Houston business leaders working to get more women involved in public office and public and private boards. The PAC provides financial support and counsel to viable women candidates for the Houston city council, county commission races in the Houston area, local school board races, and key Texas legislative races.

Voters for Choice

P.O. Box 53301
Washington, DC 20009-9301
202-588-5200
Fax: 202-588-0600
E-mail: VFC@igc.apc.org
Web Site: http://www.igc.org

Founded by Gloria Steinem and other feminist activists, Voters for Choice supports pro-choice candidates. The organization has branched out to include the Voters for Choice Educational Fund, too, which focuses on voter registration, voter education, and leadership training.

VOW

6002 South Atlanta Court
Tulsa, OK 74105
405-749-5629

VOW (Voices of Oklahoma Women) is a bipartisan donor network formed in 1991 to support Oklahoma women running in local, state, and federal races.

Wednesday Committee

1531 Purdue
Los Angeles, CA 90025
310-477-8081

The Wednesday Committee is a network of PACs in the Los Angeles area.

WISH List

3205 North Street NW
Washington, DC 20007
202-342-9111
Fax: 202-342-9190

Contributes to pro-choice Republican women candidates at local, state, and federal levels.

Women For:

8913 West Olympic Boulevard, Suite 103
Beverly Hills, CA 90211-3552
310-657-7411
Fax: 310-289-0719

Women For: Orange County

P.O. Box 5402
Irvine, CA 92716
714-854-8024

Women in Psychology for Legislative Action

13 Ashfield Street
Roslindale, MA 02131
617-327-8015

Women in the Nineties (WIN)

P.O. Box 50452
Nashville, TN 37208
615-298-1250
Fax: 615-298-9858

Women of Delaware

302-798-2028
Fax: 302-798-3153
E-mail: wdcofde@aol.com

Women Organizing Women PAC (WOW PAC)

233 Everit
New Haven, CT 06511

Women's Campaign Fund

734 15th Street NW, Suite 500
Washington, DC 20002
202-393-8164
Fax: 202-544-4517

The Women's Campaign Fund is a bipartisan PAC dedicated to supporting pro-choice women candidates at all levels of government. The organization typically invests in candidates early in—as well as throughout—campaigns. One-half of its financial assistance goes to local and state candidates. It also provides technical support and leadership training.

Print Resources

Only a few books or periodicals were available on feminism prior to the rise of the second wave in the 1970s. Publishers in general were not interested in feminist works; few saw a market for the books. Feminist presses arose in the 1970s to address this lack in the industry, including Auntie Lute Books, Daughters, Inc. (which first published novelist Rita Mae Brown), Kitchen Table: Women of Color Press, Persephone Press (now defunct), and the Shameless Hussy Press. Feminist books today continue to be published by feminist presses (some of which are major houses now), but feminist books are being picked up, too, by major mainstream publishers: Many feminist books have been best-sellers. The market for these resources continues to expand. In fact, in the last few years, the growth of feminist and women's studies books has been "astonishing," reports the *Women's Review of Books,* adding, "Those of us who once lamented the scarcity of writing about women are beginning to feel overwhelmed by its volume"—a cause for celebration among feminists.

Books

Anderson, Bonnie S., and Judith P. Zinsser. *A History of Their Own: Women in Europe from Prehistory to the Present, Volumes I and II.* New York: Harper, 1988.

Authors Anderson and Zinsser have reconceptualized European history from the ninth century A.D. to the present to place women and women's experiences at the center. The events of the traditional view of history—the wars, the politicians, the Industrial Revolution—are not used as the organizing force of history. Instead, the authors, discovering that women's lives, experiences, and opportunities were based on "place" and "function," created new categories for their history—for example, Women of the Fields, Women of the Walled Towns, and Women of the Courts. The authors researched less traditional historical sources such as poems, plays, wills, diaries, and letters. They have created a rich history, one that shows women not to be simply the victims of sociopolitical and religious limitations but as dignified survivors. It draws a picture of women's true position in the various eras and places, showing their influence on events, their participation, and the power they wielded as individuals and as a group. It is a history that deepens the study of the past for both women and men—a valuable reference and resource.

Beauvoir, Simone de. *The Second Sex.* New York: Knopf, 1953.

Controversial in France when first published in 1949, *The Second Sex* was translated into English and distributed in the United States in 1953. It soon became regarded as the bible of the feminist movement. De Beauvoir described woman as "the other" and man as the norm. Woman, she wrote, is bound in by society's guidelines, which are learned and incorporated into her every action from an early age. As an adult, woman relates to the world from an inferior political/social position. Women have occupied second place in relation to men since patriarchal times began; this position is not a biological imperative, says de Beauvoir, but a culturally concocted one that is enforced and reinforced through education, society, and by the control of men. Also, because woman is brought up without the necessity of taking charge of her own existence, she grows to search for and to accept someone else's protection and guidance; therefore, she reinforces her own second-class position. Feminists have pointed out that *The Second Sex* contains the seeds of all of modern feminism.

Belenky, Mary Field, Blythe McVicker Clinchy, Nancy Rule Goldberger, and Jill Mattuck Tarule. *Women's Ways of Knowing: The Development of Self, Voice, and Mind*. New York: HarperCollins Basic Books, 1986.

An influential book in teaching circles that has led to changes in the way math, science, and all courses are taught, *Women's Ways of Knowing* studies "perspectives from which women view reality and draw conclusions about truth, knowledge, and authority." Classroom techniques, the authors explain, have been "designed by men, and most continue to be run by men." It's been assumed that these would be suitable for women, too, or that women would adapt. The authors studied mental processes and the labeling of them as male or female, and they describe the underlying, old biases in favor of abstract, impersonal, authority-oriented classrooms—a "banking" concept of teaching. Women learn better in classrooms with more interaction, say the authors, and with more connection of classroom lessons to real-world situations. And rote memorization is not as effective a learning tool as are process-oriented methods—thinking things through. *Women's Ways of Knowing* has helped professors reorganize their classes to better serve women; at the same time, it has shown them an approach that deepens men's education.

The Boston Women's Health Book Collective. *The New Our Bodies, Ourselves: A Book by and for Women*. New York: Simon & Schuster Touchstone, 1992.

Now in a revised and updated (twenty-fifth anniversary) edition, *Our Bodies, Ourselves* was originally compiled by a group of women, most of them medical professionals, whose goal was to demystify medicine and empower women. Women were beginning to question the medical establishment of godlike doctors and minimal information-sharing. They wanted to take charge of their own reproductive and overall health, and they wanted the natural processes of menstruation, pregnancy, and menopause taken out of the disease category. The impact of *Our Bodies, Ourselves* was profound as a part of the women's movement. The book did, indeed, empower women and inspire them to become bolder and more independent in their health care. It also brought a woman's voice into the previously old-boys-club atmosphere of the medical profession. Once women began to ask questions, they demanded changes—and changes were made. The new edition continues to be an empowering compendium of straightforward women's health information and holistic, healthy attitudes. In addition to health information, it includes bibliographies of feminist writings on health and of books on specific health issues, lists of publications, articles and videos on health issues, and lists of organizations in several health categories.

Brownmiller, Susan. *Against Our Will: Men, Women, and Rape.* New York: Ballantine Books Edition, 1993 (originally published by Simon & Schuster, 1975).

Susan Brownmiller, the organizer of the 1970 sit-in of the *Ladies Home Journal,* raised the consciousness of the nation in 1975 with the publication of *Against Our Will.* Reviewers called it a "landmark," "a thoroughly chilling eye opener," and "an overwhelming indictment." It is all of these things even today, when many (but not all) of the laws and traditions that govern and inform rape have altered. Her study includes a history of rape from its Biblical and Greek mythological heritage through its part in the lives of European and British knights, royalty, and their subjects as well as its use in war. She reveals the relatively unknown prevalence of rape of Native Americans by European Americans, of African American slaves by white slaveholders, of African Americans by the Ku Klux Klan, and by soldiers in wars from World War I to Vietnam. She points out that underlying the history of rape is the concept of women as property; the way to seek revenge from a man is through destruction or theft of property, thus the rape of "his" women. Based on this concept, men have defined rape and made laws governing it throughout history. Brownmiller defines rape as "a sexual invasion of the body by force." It is a simple definition, one that does not exclude or excuse husbands, friends, or acquaintances—a radical notion in the 1970s. Brownmiller countered the beliefs of the day that rapists were the product of domineering wives and mothers or the results of pent-up lust triggered by a scantily dressed women. Using police reports and statistics, she shows that the rapist is "an unextraordinary, violence-prone fellow." His goal is to intimidate, control, humiliate, and hurt or kill women. Brownmiller considers rape as not just an individual act but as a functioning part of the system of patriarchy under which women live. Rape, she writes, "is nothing more or less than a conscious process of intimidation by which *all men* keep *all women* in a state of fear," perpetuating male domination of women. She adds that "men who commit rape have served in effect as front-line masculine shock troops, terrorist guerrillas in the longest sustained battle the world has ever known." She proposes some early avenues of change to end the crime of rape, including that half of the country's police officers be women, that laws change to end the revictimization of rape victims in police headquarters and courts, that the public be educated on the reality of rape, and that women learn to fight back through self-defense and early athletic training. These changes have begun over the past twenty years but have not ended rape; it is still a terrorizing part of modern society. Nevertheless, Brownmiller's feminist vision is an enduring one: "A world without rapists would be a world in which women moved freely without fear of men." *Against Our Will* is still informative and chilling today, especially in its historical and cultural perspectives and in its examinations of the glamorization of the historical and modern rapist.

———. *Femininity.* New York: Simon & Schuster, 1984.

Brownmiller explains early in *Femininity* that "biological femaleness is not enough" to guarantee femininity in Western women. Femininity "is a romantic sentiment, a nostalgic tradition of imposed limitations," she writes. Brownmiller explores these limitations and conflicting regulations that prescribe a woman's femininity. From hair—and the outcry across the nation when women began cutting their long hair in the 1920s—to clothes—and the rocks thrown at women when they wore "bloomers" in the 1850s—to women's voice inflections and feminine movements, Brownmiller reveals the underside of what is usually accepted as natural to the female—not so natural at all and clearly imposed by outside forces, she asserts. An interesting and often wryly amusing study, *Femininity* provides a look at accepted conventions (a man's guiding hand in the small of a woman's back, a woman's high-heeled wobble) and at their historical, cultural, and religious roots. Her feminist perspective provides an insight into the everyday antifeminist events incorporated into a woman's life.

Davis, Flora. *Moving the Mountain: The Women's Movement in America since 1960.* New York: Simon & Schuster, 1991.

A definitive and in-depth look at the politics of feminism from 1960 through 1990, this book is the story of the building of the second wave of feminism, the founding of modern feminist organizations, and the issues that inspired the women of the times to take action. Davis covers the Equal Rights Amendment's emergence and defeat, the fight for reproductive rights and the diminishing of those rights, the radical women's liberation movement, changes in women's health rights and beliefs, changes in rape laws, and attitudes about violence against women. Davis's book is replete with examples of the times, from the airline attendants who filed a complaint in 1964 over airlines' policy of firing women when they either got married or reached their thirty-second birthday to the clever methods feminists used to insert Title IX into the law.

Denfeld, Rene. *The New Victorians: A Young Woman's Challenge to the Old Feminist Order.* New York: Warner Books, 1995.

Denfeld, who identifies herself as an equality feminist, takes the feminist movement to task for its adoption of difference feminism theory. (See Chapter 4 for an explanation of these two views of feminism.) She disagrees with modern feminism's inclusion of many diverse subgroups, such as spiritual feminists and ecofeminists, under the broad heading of feminism itself. Denfeld vents her frustrations with the movement, drawing a picture of feminists as fearful perpetrators of a "victim mythology." She writes, "From rape redefinitions to feminist theory on the 'patriarchy,' victimization has become the subtext of the movement." She also expresses frustration with the inclusion of lesbian rights as an important feminist issue and reports that "they [feminists] are telling young women they must be lesbians *in order* to be feminists." She also questions the existence of a backlash and in a chapter entitled "Dirty Pictures" paints almost all feminists as antipornography activists. Difference feminists responded to what they believe are Denfeld's distortions and exaggerations by labeling her an antifeminist. Despite or because of the controversy, Denfeld's book became an international best-seller.

Dworkin, Andrea. *Pornography: Men Possessing Women.* New York: E. P. Dutton, 1989 (paperback edition of 1979 original).

Dworkin's exploration of pornography and its connections to misogyny and violence against women opened debate for feminists on what should or could be done about the images of women in pornographic publications and films. Dworkin presents pornography as exploitative of women and, what's more, as an agent in the oppression of women. Pornography is not about sex or women's sexuality, she asserts, but about domination of men over women and violence of men against women. She writes, "Male power is the raison d'être of pornography; the degradation of the female is the means of achieving this power." She addresses the role that pornography plays in shaping boys' and men's ideas of women's place in their lives and discusses the negative effects that has on women. She explores images of rape and violence in pornography and connects those images to the limitations on women's status in society.

Ehrenreich, Barbara, and Deirdre English. *For Her Own Good: 150 Years of the Experts' Advice to Women*. New York: Doubleday, 1978.

The title *For Her Own Good* refers to all the advice medical professionals and experts have given women over the past 150 years, much of it bizarre by today's standards and torturous by any, but all of it given to a woman "for her own good." Ehrenreich, a columnist and journalist with a background in biology, traces the history of modern medicine's treatment of women. The history has included women healers burned as witches (touched on briefly in this book), an early confrontation between women healers and the profession of medicine, the end of midwifery, and twentieth-century medical misunderstandings and mistreatment of women. Ehrenreich provides the links through history necessary to make sense of the medical community's relation to women. The nineteenth-century medical opinion of the uterus and ovaries as the cause of all of women's problems—emotional as well as physical—became the twentieth-century orientation of the reproductive organs as a problem easily removed. The image of the pregnant woman as a mere vessel and the placenta and fetus as a separate implantation is an outgrowth of these early medical opinions. (Feminists are leading the medical community now to a more integrated, holistic view of pregnant and unpregnant women.) Ehrenreich's work is fascinating as a study of the sociopolitical agendas that silently rule, even in the science of medicine.

Eisler, Riane. *The Chalice and the Blade: Our History, Our Future.* San Francisco: Harper, 1987.

The Chalice and the Blade is a book that reignited the flame of debate over woman's role in prehistory. One of the premises of Eisler's book, that all prehistory is interpretation and up until recently virtually all has shown a male bias, is backed by her analysis of prehistoric European cultures. Eisler expresses a belief in the possibilities for a nonpatriarchal society, one that she calls a *gylany*—a *"linking* of both halves of humanity" rather than a ranking or hierarchical system. She also examines the stories of ancient man, and man's invention of tools and support of the community. She agrees with recent studies by scientist Nancy Tanner (and others) that show women, the gatherers, not men, the hunters, to have played the more critical role in evolution. Women, feeding babies, were most likely to have developed tools for their survival and most likely to have walked on two feet to free their hands for gathering food. Eisler and "most scholars today," she writes, agree, too, that it would "have been more likely that it was women who first dropped seeds on the ground" for farming, and who first tamed and cared for animals. From prehistory, Eisler moves through the civilizations of Crete and the ancient world, through Biblical times, and into an interpretation incorporating her ideas into a theory of the possibilities of a partnership between women and men today.

Epstein, Cynthia Fuchs. *Deceptive Distinctions: Sex, Gender, and the Social Order.* New Haven, Conn.: Yale University Press (and New York: Russell Sage Foundation), 1988.

In a well-documented argument, Epstein presents evidence that females and males are more similar than different. She challenges many of the assumptions that support a rigid dichotomy of roles and expectations of behavior between females and males. She presents evidence of restrictions on women's roles that range from the simple self-fulfilling prophesy of stereotypes to legal restrictions and even to physical force used as a weapon to keep women in their place. She refutes arguments of gender differences that have been based on psychology, sociology, biology, or a combination of all, many of which have been accepted as truisms in modern society. "Dichotomous systems of thought serve the existing power structures and organization of society by reinforcing the notion of the 'we' and the 'not-we,' the deserving and the undeserving," she writes. Epstein comes in firmly on the side of nondichotomous thinking and equality feminism.

Estés, Clarissa Pinkola. *Women Who Run with the Wolves: Myths and Stories of the Wild Woman Archetype.* New York: Ballantine Books, 1992.

A Jungian analyst and storyteller, Estés has inspired women of the 1990s to get in touch with their wild woman archetype. That archetype is a healthy animal with "keen sensing, playful spirit, and a heightened capacity for devotion," she says. It also has great endurance and strength, along with intuition and a natural curiosity. The author turns to myths and stories to lead women to self-awareness and individuation. She includes familiar stories such as the "Ugly Duckling" and less familiar tales such as "Vasalisa the Wise." Her analysis of the stories has made this book required reading among feminists. The "wild" elemental feminine spirit has been tamed in most women in most societies, says Estés, and retrieval of that wild spirit is what breaks women free from the patriarchal trappings of their cultures. *Women Who Run with the Wolves* added to the dialogue on what makes women strong; it also brought the dialogue into the homes of many women who had been silently howling in the night.

Faludi, Susan. *Backlash: The Undeclared War against American Women.* New York: Crown, 1991.

The author, a Pulitzer Prize–winning journalist, delineates a backlash against feminists that gained strength in the 1980s. Media stories of the decade declared that professional women were depressed, that they were desperate to marry and were finding no men to marry, and that women were simply miserable. The backlash laid the blame for that misery at the doorstep of feminists and especially at the changes feminists had achieved in jobs, careers, and social equality. The backlash, says Faludi, showed up in movies, in magazine cover stories, in fashion, and in beauty industries. Feminists lost ground to the New Right Conservatives in Washington, D.C., and women's rights and control over their bodies during pregnancy were curtailed. *Backlash* is one of the defining books of the feminist movement. It outlines the myriad forces intent on slowing down or stopping the feminist movement. It has been criticized as depicting a "conspiracy" of antifeminist activity, but Faludi does not describe a conspiracy; instead, she points to the many separate attacks on women's rights that have come from many directions, often forcing feminists into a fragmented defensive posture.

French, Marilyn. *The War against Women.* New York: Ballantine Books, 1992.

French's book describes a pervasive, worldwide repression of women not as a historical event but as it is happening today. It outlines the international and religious systems that place women in an inferior class, reveals institutional discrimination in the medical and legal arenas, and illuminates the woman-hatred embedded in cultures through language, arts, and the military. And it compiles personal assaults on women. The sum of it all is a chilling global tapestry of repression.

Friedan, Betty. *The Feminine Mystique.* New York: W. W. Norton, 1963.

Friedan's book is based on an intensive questionnaire sent to her Smith College classmates on their fifteenth anniversary of graduation. Initially Friedan was surprised by the results of her survey. She had simply been seeking to show that education did not preclude women from finding happiness in home and marriage. But she found instead "a strange stirring" and a "problem that has no name." Women thought they were alone in their quiet desperation, Friedan reported, but they were not: Desperation permeated the supposedly serene suburbs of America. There, the women who had gone home to a life of domestic bliss following World War II were stifled and dissatisfied. *The Feminine Mystique* came as a revelation to women across America who read it, identified with it, and declared themselves ready to do something about this "problem with no name." *The Feminine Mystique* is often credited with setting off the second wave of feminism.

Gilligan, Carol. *In a Different Voice: Psychological Theory and Women's Development.* Cambridge, Mass.: Harvard University Press, 1982.

A landmark study, Gilligan's work came at a time when difference feminism was again gaining ground. *In a Different Voice* refers to the differences between how females and males speak.

Gilligan discerns "different modes of thinking about relationships" and writes that the women's modes have been misunderstood as problems or deficiencies by male-defined theories of psychology. She concludes from her studies that women generally seek closeness in their relationships, that they define themselves based on these relationships, that they judge others by the quality of their relationships, and that they make their own judgments based more on care and responsibility than on abstract rights. Whereas men live for a hierarchical valuation of achievement, women look for a web of successful relationships. Gilligan cautions that her studies are "a work in progress" and should not be used to make generalizations about either sex. However, they were quickly put to use, boosting the growth of cultural (difference) feminism.

Gimbutas, Marija. *The Goddesses and Gods of Old Europe 7000–3500 BC.* Berkeley: University of California Press, 1974. (Reprinted as *The Goddesses and Gods of Old Europe: Myths and Cult Images.* Berkeley: University of California Press, 1982, 1992.)

Gimbutas, a Lithuanian American archeologist and professor, documented her theories about Old Europe through explication of archaeological relics—sculpture, vases, and cult objects from sites in southeastern Europe. Old Europe, she concluded from her archaeological examinations, "was characterized by a dominance of woman in society and worship of a Goddess incarnating the creative principle as Source and Giver of All." The culture was matrifocal, she writes, "and probably matrilineal, agricultural and sedentary, egalitarian and peaceful." But it was not polarized into female and male, and it was not a mirror image of patriarchal domination. Female and male complemented each other, Gimbutas concludes, and "all resources of human nature, feminine and masculine, were utilized to the full as a creative force." Waves of infiltrating, warlike, and patriarchal groups from the Russian steppe between 4500 and 2500 B.C. conquered these civilizations, thus imposing their myths and sociopolitical systems over the existing ones. The impact of Gimbutas's work on feminists was a clarification and reiteration of the idea that patriarchy is a sociopolitical system, not a biologically determined destiny. Her work has inspired spiritual feminism in its search for religious metaphors to replace the male and patriarchal metaphors of established religions.

Greer, Germaine. *The Female Eunuch.* New York: McGraw-Hill, 1970.

A best-seller in Great Britain in 1970, then released in the United States, *The Female Eunuch* guaranteed Germaine Greer a place in feminist history. Her message in *The Female Eunuch* is based on Simone de Beauvoir's idea of woman as a social construct devised by males. Men and women are not much different, but society shapes them and forces women to behave in ways that emphasize and exaggerate the differences. Greer saw society's ideal woman as a castrated creature, one devoid of true womanly strength and confidence. She would be young and hairless, with buoyant flesh, no sexual organs, no libido, no intelligence or humor, but with a continuous ingratiating smile on her face. Society's ideal of a sexless woman holds women captive as they contort themselves to attain the ideal. Greer would replace this eunuch-creature with a fully realized, sexual woman. *The Female Eunuch* sought to empower women by freeing them from society's sexual repression and also to encourage them to experience their own physical joys and strengths.

Millett, Kate. *Sexual Politics.* New York: Avon, 1971. (Hardcover published by Doubleday, New York, 1969.)

Sexual Politics is a doctoral dissertation that became a best-seller. It also became a standard on every feminist bookshelf. Millett delineates the "political aspect" of sex through literary and cultural criticism. Sex, she writes, does not exist in a vacuum and cannot be separated from the political system in which women live. In sex, men dominate women just as they do through politics. She supports her theory with historical and political documentation, but primarily with analyses of major literary works by D. H. Lawrence, Henry Miller, Norman Mailer, and Jean Genet. In Lawrence's *Lady Chatterly's Lover,* for example, she finds the author purporting a doctrine of masculine as aggressive/dominant and feminine as passive/submissive—a doctrine that presents the phallus as a revered political weapon. The purpose of much of the sex in the book is to put the women in a subservient position and, on occasion, to humiliate them. The effect of such a literarily acclaimed and accepted work on the psyches of generations of women is devastating. Millett also presents an overview of the history of women's movements and of women's political and social rights. Throughout, her focus is on patriarchy, its methods of containment, and the constantly fortified sexual politics upon which it rests. A sexual revolution that truly undoes double standards toward male and female sexuality and ends traditional sexual taboos, she writes, "would bring the institution of patriarchy to an end, abolishing both the ideology of male supremacy and the traditional socialization by which it is upheld in matters of status, role, and temperament."

Nelson, Mariah Burton. *Are We Winning Yet? How Women Are Changing Sports and Sports Are Changing Women.* New York: Random House, 1991.

Sports are important to feminists, and Nelson explains why. She points to positive, confidence-enhancing values of sports on an individual level as well as societal benefits. As she looks at women who have broken ground in sports—the first woman on a college baseball team, record-making triathletes, and Iditarod sled-dog racers as a few examples—she also examines the impact women can have on the violent, dominator theme of many sports. She proposes a "partnership" model of sports that echoes Riane Eisler's partnership societies.

Pollitt, Katha. *Reasonable Creatures: Feminism and Society in American Culture at the End of the Twentieth Century.* New York: Knopf, 1994.

Pollitt's compilation of her essays, taken largely from her contributions to the *Nation* and the *New York Times,* covers a range of feminist issues from affirmative action to abortion, rape, and difference versus equality feminism. As one of the many varied voices of third-wave feminism, Pollitt espouses equality feminism. Her essays, which combine journalism, scholarship, and wit, have won admiration from feminist academics and sister writers. She points to flaws in commonly accepted arguments and views—for example, a common argument against affirmative action, she says, is that "advancing women and minorities on the basis of sex and race damages their self-esteem." In response, Pollitt offers up the commonly accepted "affirmative action" of preference for children of alumni at prestigious universities and wonders if their self-esteem is suffering because they got into their schools on their parents' coattails, not on their own merit? She also takes on Katie Roiphe's accusations of feminists portraying women as victims (see next entry), especially as victims of men in sexual relations. Pollitt points out that sex according to Katie Roiphe is still seen as a "boys' game," and women are told to adjust to the boys' rules. Pollitt adds that the problem with this view is "that the discourse about sexuality says so little about female pleasure." Pollitt's insights add new energy to feminist discussions; her essays are written for a wide, general audience as well as for feminists.

Roiphe, Katie. *The Morning After: Sex, Fear, and Feminism.* Boston: Little, Brown, 1993.

Roiphe expresses concern that the ideology of the feminist movement has become too monolithic and that its leaders are intolerant. She speaks from her experience as a Harvard undergraduate and Princeton graduate student observing the feminist discussions among students. She paints a picture of herself as a strong, confident woman able to defend herself against any assault and able to get into any position or to take part in any discussion she pleases. She is not dominated by men, and she is derisive of those who can be. She belittles men who question their own sexist thoughts and women who demand extra street lights on college campuses. She fears that campus feminists paint a picture of women as victims and as too weak to defend themselves against harassment or to hold their own in debates with men. Feminist leaders have responded to her book with anger at its accusations, possibly a reaction to Roiphe's sarcasm more than to her points. Her book is important not because of its scholarship (most of it is based on her casual observation of friends and family, and she presents Catharine MacKinnon as a representative of all feminists) but because it was picked up by the media as an expression of new, third-wave feminism. Roiphe's book does not reflect the global attitudes or awareness of the third wave but does express Roiphe's own frustrations with the rhetoric that surrounds women's studies at Harvard and, by extension, at other university campuses.

Sommers, Christina Hoff. *Who Stole Feminism? How Women Have Betrayed Women.* New York: Touchstone/Simon & Schuster, 1994.

A critic of feminism, Sommers, an associate professor of philosophy at Clark University, joins Camille Paglia and Katie Roiphe in questioning the ideology of today's feminist leaders. Sommers takes a victim-of-feminists stance: Acknowledging her research support from conservative foundations (Bradley, Carthage, and

Olin), Sommers responds: "It is easy enough to get grants for feminist research aimed at showing how women are being short-changed and 'silenced' by the male establishment. It is not so easy to receive grants for a study that criticizes the feminist establishment for its errors and excesses." Sommers accuses feminists of seeing themselves as victims. She renames today's feminists "gender feminists," a term she defines to imply angry, male-bashing victimization. She writes in a breezy style and attempts to poke holes in feminist statements and studies. She disdains the idea that domestic violence increases on Super Bowl Sunday; questions the American Association of University Women's interpretation of its study on the loss of self-esteem among adolescent girls; paints a picture of hysterical, omnipresent feminists "colonizing" college departments; and describes feminists themselves as privileged, self-absorbed, and resentful. Since the book's publication, feminist leaders and organizations have refuted the points in it one by one. The impact of the book, however, goes beyond its scholarship. Like Camille Paglia, Sommers calls herself a feminist and is picked up by the media as a representative of feminism and conflict within the feminist movement. Certainly, there is conflict and a variety of ideas within the movement, and Sommers, though misidentified as a feminist, is a vocal critic.

Stone, Merlin. *When God Was a Woman.* San Diego: Harvest/Harcourt, 1976. (Hardcover published by Dial Press, New York, 1976; originally published in Great Britain under the title *The Paradise Papers,* Virago Limited in association with Quartet Books Limited, 1976.)

Stone's study of the religions that predated Judaism, Christianity, and Islam presents a picture of ancient societies. She delves into ancient goddess religions and into the ways and means that they were subsumed or annihilated. She juxtaposes biblical references to ancient religions with archaeological evidence of those religions. She explores the "political origins" of Judeo-Christian theology and describes the war that this new theology wrought on the societies of the day. Her goal is not a revival of the ancient female-oriented religions but an understanding of religion's role in the political and social status of women in today's world. Stone believes that many of the double standards of today are the direct result of male-defined religions. Her hope is that once people know that patriarchy has not always been the sole system of societies, they will be "opening the way for a more realistic recognition of the capabilities and potential of children and adults, whether female or male, as individual human beings."

Wallace, Michelle. *Black Macho and the Myth of the Superwoman.* New York: Dial, 1978.

Wallace's book, written when she was just 26 years old, explores male chauvinism in the Black Power movement of the 1960s. Wallace argues that there was a deep chauvinism surfacing in the movement, with newly empowered African American men wanting women of color to cater to their whims in the same way that they saw white women catering to white men. Wallace perceived a growing resentment between African American men and women, and she presents an emotional and angry critique of the civil rights movement. Black women, she writes, had supported their men in the 1960s and had lost their own power and seen themselves redefined as a hurdle in the way of men, their strength and resilience redefined as matriarchal and castrating faults. Wallace's book was greeted with both great enthusiasm and great criticism—as important in perspective and flawed in reasoning and content.

Wolf, Naomi. *The Beauty Myth: How Images of Beauty Are Used against Women.* New York: William Morrow, 1991.

Wolf argues that one of the feminist movement's irritations—that men gain stature as they age and women lose it at the first signs of wrinkles—should evoke more than irritation. It should bring women to the edge of fury. Wolf's premise is partly that a double standard has invaded the workplace as well as the culture. Professional men must be well groomed, but successful women must be that and also attractive and youthful. The modern woman's quest for this required youthful beauty has kept her hungry and under the cosmetic surgeon's knife. The beauty requirement helps to keep women underconfident and "in their place." Wolf makes a strong argument in this best-selling, controversial book, and she adds another piece to the puzzle of how a culture controls its population.

Woloch, Nancy. *Women and the American Experience.* New York: McGraw-Hill, 1984, 1994.

In an authoritative and well-documented textbook on women in the United States—beginning with women in the Jamestown and

Plymouth colonies—Woloch focuses on everyday women's experiences and what life has truly offered American females. She highlights women who stood out or made significant contributions in politics and social struggles, and she traces changing cultural biases and limitations placed on women's lives. Native American, African American, and other minority women as well as women of European ancestry are considered. This is a solid foundation for further women's studies.

Anthologies

Diamond, Irene, and Gloria Feman Orenstein, eds. *Reweaving the World: The Emergence of Ecofeminism.* San Francisco: Sierra Club Books, 1990.

The essays gathered in this anthology combine to explain and explore ecofeminism. The new culture, or transformation, sought by ecofeminism is more than a simple dichotomy of nature over culture, or women versus men. It is, the editors assert, "the embeddedness of all the Earth's peoples in the multiple webs and cycles of life." The contributors are established experts and authors such as Riane Eisler, Charlene Spretnak, and Starhawk. The essays cover spiritual connections between feminism and ecology, with analysis of the origins of established religion and of feminist spirituality. Most of the essays, however, cover politics and related feminist theory, along with prospects for transformation through ecofeminism.

Freeman, Jo, ed. *Women: A Feminist Perspective, Fifth Edition.* Mountain View, Calif.: Mayfield Publishing, 1995.

Freeman, a feminist author whose essays have appeared in numerous national magazines, has brought together original essays by professors and professionals in feminism-related fields. Some of the essays focus on women's status and the progress that has been made in economic and political arenas; others are feminist analyses of issues and society. Freeman herself outlines twentieth-century feminism, and a few of the authors explore the issues of feminist women of color, while others look into violence against women. *Women* is a rich source of current, original feminist essays and thinking.

Moraga, Cherrie, and Gloria Anzaldúa, eds. *This Bridge Called My Back: Writings by Radical Women of Color, Second Edition.* New York: Kitchen Table: Women of Color Press, 1983. (First edition published by Persephone Press, Watertown, Mass., 1981.)

A book that became a mainstay in women's studies when it was first published in 1981, *This Bridge Called My Back* is an anthology of essays and poems on feminism by women of color. Writers represented are, in addition to the editors, Barbara Cameron, Jo Carrillo, the Combahee River Collective, Audre Lorde, Rosario Morales, Mitsuye Yamada, and others. The contributors examine racism in the women's movement, evaluate their self-images and sexism, examine American stereotypes of minority cultures, and analyze lesbianism and the women's movement. The works chosen for the anthology, says Moraga in her foreword to the second edition, are "concentrated on relationships *between women*" rather than on the usual relations between the sexes. *This Bridge Called My Back* provided new voices and insights to all feminist thinking and helped to broaden feminist theory from a theory of simple sexism to one that includes racism and classism in its analysis.

Morgan, Robin, ed. *Sisterhood Is Powerful: An Anthology of Writings from the Women's Liberation Movement.* New York: Random House, 1970.

As the second wave of the women's movement was just gaining momentum in the late 1960s, Robin Morgan gathered together the writings of radical feminists. Some of the collected essays, poems, personal testimonies, and manifestos were already known in inner circles of radical feminism. Others were original, and they ranged from humorous jabs at patriarchy to politically savvy explanations of the positions of women of color. The writers ranged from high school girls to professional women, all focusing on sexism in their lives and society. The book includes the Redstockings Manifesto, statements by the New York Radical Women, the National Organization for Women Bill of Rights, and other documents.

Rossi, Alice, ed. *The Feminist Papers: From Adams to de Beauvoir.* New York: Columbia University Press, 1973.

This is an anthology of original writings of the feminist movement. Rossi includes an introduction to each section of the book, illuminating the era of the writing and the impact of it. In addition to the expected—excerpts from Mary Wollstonecraft, John Stuart Mill, Charlotte Perkins Gilman, and Virginia Woolf—are some gems of the feminist movement. Included, for example, are letters of Angelina and Sarah Grimké, a firsthand description of Sojournor Truth's speech at the Akron Convention in 1879, Elizabeth Cady Stanton's introduction to *The Women's Bible,* an excerpt of writing by Emma Goldman, Suzanne LaFollette's *Concerning Women,* and an essay by Jane Addams.

Schneir, Miriam, ed. *Feminism in Our Time: The Essential Writings, World War II to the Present.* New York: Random House, 1994.

In excerpts of writings from Simone de Beauvoir's *The Second Sex* to Ruth Bader Ginsburg's response to her U.S. Supreme Court nomination, Schneir covers the second wave of feminism. This book includes works of the major authors of the era, such as Germaine Greer, Kate Millett, and Robin Morgan, but also offers the Redstocking Manifesto, the statement of purpose of the National Black Feminist Organization, and writings of the Radicalesbians. Schneir provides an introductory note to each excerpt, placing it in context and time.

Spretnak, Charlene, ed. *The Politics of Women's Spirituality: Essays on the Rise of Spiritual Power within the Feminist Movement.* New York: Doubleday Anchor Books, 1982.

In this anthology Spretnak gathers the writings of feminists exploring women's image, their strength, and their wisdom. Included are excerpts from the writings of Gloria Steinem, Mary Daly, and Judy Chicago. The focus is on postpatriarchal spirituality, on the essays and poetry of the women exploring this end of feminism. Represented also are Ntozake Shange, June Jordan, and Adrienne Rich; Starhawk's thoughts on current Goddess religions and Merlin Stone's on ancient Goddess religions and societies round out the anthology. The essays discuss feminist spirituality, the hierarchy of patriarchal religions, and the burgeoning women's spirituality that is empowering women to question the assumptions of established religion.

Magazines, Journals, and Periodical Publications

Most feminist groups issue periodical newsletters and reports; see Chapter 6 of this book for a listing of organizations and their publications. In addition, following is a selected, short list of feminist publications.

The Feminist Bookstore News

2180 Bryant Street #207
P.O. Box 882554
San Francisco, CA 94188
415-626-1556
Fax: 415-626-8970
E-mail: FBN@FemBkNews.com

A bimonthly, *The Feminist Bookstore News* began publishing in 1977 and describes itself as "the communications vehicle for the informal network of feminist bookstores." It covers trade news of interest in feminist, lesbian, and gay bookselling and publishing, with short book reviews and articles on the feminist end of the bookstore business.

Feminist Issues

Transactions Periodicals Consortium
Rutgers University
New Brunswick, NJ 08903
908-445-2280
Fax: 908-445-3138
E-mail: trans@transactionpub.com
Web site: http://www.transactionpub.com

Founded in 1980, *Feminist Issues* is a forum of open debate on feminism and women's issues. It is a semiannual journal.

Ms. Magazine

135 West 50th Street
New York, NY 10020
212-445-6100

E-mail: ms@echonyc.com
Web site: http://www.womweb.com

One of the largest feminist publications, with an estimated circulation of 150,000, *Ms.* was first published in 1972, edited by Gloria Steinem. Through the years, it has gone through growing pains and ownership changes, but it has remained the flagship magazine for feminism. Today its editor, Marcia Ann Gillespie, maintains the magazine's focus on political and social issues and feminist advances, both global and national. Articles by major feminist authors have been continually featured in *Ms.*

Off Our Backs: A Women's Newsjournal

2337B 18th Street NW
Washington, DC 20009
202-234-8072
Fax: 202-234-8092
E-mail: offourbacks@compuserve.com

Published since 1970, *Off Our Backs* describes itself as "a collective where decisions are made by consensus." A tabloid monthly, it has an in-the-trenches look and attitude, with articles that take unblinking looks at issues affecting women.

On the Issues: The Progressive Woman's Quarterly

97-77 Queens Boulevard
Forest Hills, NY 11374
718-459-1888
Fax: 718-997-1206
E-mail: onissues@echonyc.com
Web site: http://www.echonyc.com/~onissues or
http://www.igc.apc.org/onissues

A quarterly magazine, *On the Issues* describes itself as "a feminist, humanist magazine of critical thinking, dedicated to fostering collective responsibility for positive social change." It tackles feminist issues with verve, reporting on both positive and negative national and global events and changes.

Signs: Journal of Women in Culture and Society

University of Chicago Press
5801 Ellis Avenue

Chicago, IL 60637
773-702-7700
Web site: http://www.journals.uchicago.edu

A quarterly journal founded in 1975, *Signs* publishes peer-reviewed essays on feminist issues from a variety of feminist perspectives. Its coverage is both national and international.

Sojourner: The Women's Forum

42 Seaverns Avenue
Jamaica Plain, MA 02130
617-524-0415
E-mail: sojourn@tiac.net
Web site: http://www.tiac.net/users/sojourn/

Sojourner is a tabloid-format feminist publication. Its articles explore sexism, racism, and homophobia along with other issues relevant to feminism. Published out of Massachusetts, it has a distinctly East Coast, specifically Boston, orientation, but most of its features and reviews are national in scope.

W.I.G. Magazine

P.O. Box 158
Heber City, UT 84032
801-654-5398
Fax: 801-654-5881
E-mail: WigMag@aol.com

W.I.G.—for Women in General—is a young feminist quarterly magazine launched in 1995. It speaks for "Generation F," which roughly translates to the Title IX generation of feminist-inspired women. Covering young voices in music, the arts, and especially sports, *W.I.G.* presents a modern, new vision of womanhood. Its founder, Kathleen Gasperini, explains why she started the magazine: Even in 1995, she could find no magazine that "reflected my culture or made me stoked on life & sports &, well, being female." *W.I.G.* expresses the profound joy of living a strong, female life and is a source for information on young feminists and on the ideas and women who shape them.

The Women's Review of Books

Wellesley College
Center for Research on Women

Wellesley, MA 02181
617-283-2555
Fax: 617-283-3645

Published since 1983, the *Women's Review of Books* is a monthly periodical that covers writing by and about women. It includes author interviews, articles on feminist issues, and full book reviews. An excellent source for intelligent and in-depth reviews, the *Women's Review of Books* is written chiefly by feminists who hold impressive credentials as authors and professors. The editors see themselves as fulfilling a continuing need to cover books, authors, and ideas ignored by mainstream publications. In recent years, a great number of books have been published annually on feminist and women's issues; reading the *Review* is one way to keep up with new feminist print resources and issues.

Nonprint Resources

8

Internet/Web Sources

The Web grows exponentially with each passing day, so it is impossible to list all of its reliable and informative feminist sites. What is attempted here, instead, is a list of entry sites on the Web that cover issues of concern to feminists. These sites offer links to other related resources. Also listed are representative feminist search gateways on the Web; these are excellent points of entry to information on women's issues. In addition, government resources provide updated statistics and reports on women's status and issues; some of these are included. Most feminist organizations today maintain Web sites, and these, too, are rich sources of information. Web sites for many of today's major feminist organizations are indicated in Chapter 6.

African and African American Women Resources

http://www.lawrence.edu/
~bradleyc/war.html
Titled Women of Africa Resources, this site provides bibliographies, some on-line articles, and links, chiefly African women's sites but some from African American women, too, and also a few other related sources. One of the links is to

269

Africa Online, which features access to chat rooms and more links (site address is http://www.AfricaOnline.com/AfricaOnline/women.html). A related site is Online Resources for African American Women and Womanist Studies, which provides resources, periodicals, biographies, and links (site address is http://www.uic.edu/~vjpitch/).

Body Politic Home Page

http://www.bodypolitic.org
A pro-choice site, Body Politic is the Web site of the *Body Politic* magazine. It provides full-length articles from issues of its Monthly Pro-Choice Report, dating from 1991 to the present. Under News Flashes it includes updated information on abortion clinic arsons, bombings, and violence as well as on legislative activities. It also maintains links to other reproductive freedom sites and to abortion information sites, with lists of clinics.

Chicana Studies Home Page

http://Latino.sscnet.ucla.edu/women/womenHP.html
Officially titled CLNET's Chicana Studies Home Page, this site is building links to gophers and Web pages on Chicana feminism and should prove to be an excellent entry point.

Feminist Internet Gateway

http://www.feminist.org
A search engine as well as a gateway maintained by the Feminist Majority Foundation Online, this site is a mediated listing of Web sites. It is a valuable, clean gateway (click on Feminist Internet Gateway) with links to sites on health, sports, politics, reproductive rights, lesbian sites, the arts, and other issues and topics. Their "violence against women" link provides U.S. Department of Justice statistics on violence against women. The Feminist Internet Gateway also maintains links to list servers and news groups.

FGM Research Home Page

http://www.hollyfeld.org/fgm/
A networking page for organizations working against female genital mutilation, this site includes information, statistics, and links to other related sites.

Gender Equity in Sports

http://www.arcade.uiowa.edu/proj/ge/
As evidenced by the site address, this Web site is maintained as a project through the University of Iowa. Its subject is Title IX and intercollegiate sports. It contains information on the law, its history, and its application.

Guerilla Girls

http://www.guerrillagirls.com
The Guerilla Girls is a group of artists and art professionals who challenge sexism and racism in the art world. They usually appear when an exhibition or museum neglects female artists or is discriminating against woman-created art. They are easily identified by the gorilla masks they wear when they appear at a site or event. They challenge through humor (hence the gorilla masks); they remain anonymous; and they create artistic protest posters. This site gives a peek into the group's various activities.

Institute for Global Communications (IGC)

http://www.igc.org
The IGC describes itself as "the nation's only unionized Internet service provider"; it is a community of activists and organizations, including a "womensnet" gateway that focuses on women's issues. Womensnet takes a progressive viewpoint and includes recent articles and features as well as links to related organizations and resources.

Inter-Parliamentary Union (IPU)

http://www.ipu.org
An international organization of parliaments, the IPU conducts surveys and advocates for peace and cooperation among peoples and for representative democracies worldwide. Its work includes statistical reports and analyses of women's presence in politics. IPU's maps and data are accessible through its Web site, either directly or through E-mail order. The site also includes links to all parliaments with Internet presence.

Lesbian Links

http://www.lesbian.org
This site, established in 1995, promotes lesbian visibility on the Internet. It maintains links to national and local organizations as well as to more informal sites—a good starting point to Web sites on lesbian issues.

Middle East Studies

http://www.columbia.edu/cu/libraries/indiv/area/Middle East/women.html
Columbia University maintains these links to Web sites and resources on women in the Middle East. The site covers Afghani, Arab, Armenian, Iranian, Israeli/Jewish, Kurdish, Maltese, and Turkish women and issues.

Resources on Women and Gender

http://www.libraries.rutgers.edu/rulib/artshum/womstd/index.html#menu5.4
Though this source begins with a description of the Rutgers University library, scrolling down puts users in front of a list of links for academic studies.

Russian Feminism Resources

http://www.geocities.com/Athens/2533/russfem1.html
Chiefly in English, but some of it bilingual Russian and English, the categories at this source include the arts, lifestyles, health, politics, activism, lesbian issues, and academics. Also, a few individual women have home pages here. The site maintains articles, some full text, and links, including links to women in other post-communist countries.

South Asian Women's Network

http://www.umiacs.umd.edu/users/sawweb/sawnet
This network is an excellent gateway to sites and pages on women in Bangladesh, Bhutan, Burma, India, Nepal, Pakistan, and Sri Lanka. It includes the text of articles; lists of organizations, with mailing lists; discussion groups; and links to related resources.

United Nations

http://www.un.org
The UN home page provides access to databases and documents, including some from the fourth World Conference on Women in Beijing. The site also provides access to the full texts of some international treaties on women.

Women in Development Network

http://www.focusintl.com/widnet.htm
A site with an international focus, the WIDNET site maintains links to international women's organizations as well as to related women's resources on the Web. It also provides information on women's conferences and has uploaded representative documents from international meetings, including the Beijing Platform of 1995.

Women's Studies on the Internet

http://dizzy.library.arizona.edu/users/dickstei/homepg.htm
A research-oriented site, Women's Studies on the Internet maintains links to a variety of sites, including those that originate from women's studies programs in universities. It also maintains links to sites with an international focus or ethnic and heritage focus, and to national organizations.

Women's Studies Resources

http://www.inform.umd.edu/EdRes/Topic/WomensStudies/
A site reached through the University of Maryland, Women's Studies Resources is a valuable listing of links to women's issues sites. It also has the entire texts of a few books, including *A Vindication of the Rights of Woman* by Mary Wollstonecraft. In addition, it maintains a bank of academic papers on feminist issues.

WWWomen

http://www.wwwomen.com
This site calls itself "The Premier Search Directory for Women Online," and possibly it is. It provides links to sites relating to women's issues, with categories that include arts and enter-

tainment, business, community, government, education, culture, computers, feminism, lesbian issues, history, health, and sports.

Documentaries Available on Videotape

A selective list, the documentary videos here were chosen for their value as history for feminists or as exposition of the feminist consciousness and viewpoint. More and more films are being made every year, and more women than ever today are directing and producing major feature films as well as independent documentary films.

A Century of Women

Type: VHS videocassette
Length: A 3-tape series, 95 minutes each
Date: 1994
Cost: Rental
Distributor: Available at many video rental stores or through
              Turner Home Entertainment
                One CNN Center
                Atlanta, GA 30303

An entertaining way to learn some of women's history, achievements, and feminist concerns, *A Century of Women* is the story of twentieth-century American women, with emphasis on the second half of the century. Jane Fonda narrates, and a cast of women actors, including Olympia Dukakis and Talia Shire, forms a discussion framework for the newsclips, interviews, and narration in the film. Each tape in the series focuses on certain aspects of life; they are subtitled *Work and Family, Sexuality and Social Justice,* and *Image and Popular Culture.*

    Work and Family focuses on women's balancing act between job and family responsibilities, showing that this is not a new problem but one that has challenged women throughout the century. Early factory strikes, the thoughts of feminist economist Charlotte Perkins Gilman, Depression workers, World War II workers, and the effects of politics on women's opportunities and domestic roles are shown. Women who effected changes in labor laws speak through interviews, news clips, and photos, revealing the legal discrimination in hiring and pay policies that continued until second-wave feminists came forward. The tape covers the groundbreaking case of Ida May Phillips, who was refused employment because she had young children—though men with small children were hired—along with the impact of her case. Interviews include farmworker activist Dolores Huerta, former U.S. Representative Patricia Schroeder, Supreme Court Justice Ruth Bader Ginsburg, and feminist Betty Friedan.

Sexuality and Social Justice focuses on women who have publicly crusaded for the vote and for women's control over their own destinies through birth control and the women's liberation movement. The issue of birth control, Margaret Sanger's work on family planning, the impact of the birth control pill on women's lives, and the "sexual revolution" of the 1960s are explored. Women's political equality is looked at through the work of suffragist Alice Paul and a narration of the women fighting for the vote before 1920. Also explored is the work of the women fighting for the Equal Rights Amendment in the 1970s, along with responses from those who fought against it. Interviews include feminist Gloria Steinem, Senator Barbara Boxer, author Shere Hite, and singer Joan Baez.

Image and Popular Culture focuses on the ideal of beauty and the effect of its idealization on women. The video touches on the Miss America pageant, with Robin Morgan recapping the 1968 pageant protest. It profiles women cosmetics moguls such as Madame C. J. Walker and Elizabeth Arden and explores the emphasis on beauty and femininity that female athletes face. Comedians Carol Burnett and Roseanne Barr discuss the impact of the *I Love Lucy* television show—feminist for its time. The video gives a sampling of women in the arts and the barriers they overcame, from blues singer Bessie Smith to writer Willa Cather, dance choreographer Martha Graham, and artists Georgia O'Keefe and Judy Chicago. Chicago points out the value of such documentaries and of a knowledge of women's history, explaining that O'Keefe provided shoulders for subsequent female artists to climb up on, and Chicago's work, if seen by women, would in turn provide young artists with another shoulder. Also interviewed are television producer Linda Bloodworth Thomason and author/poet Maya Angelou.

From Danger to Dignity: The Fight for Safe Abortion

Type:	VHS videocassette or 16 mm
Length:	57 minutes
Date:	1995
Cost:	Purchase $175; rental $150 for 16 mm, $90 for video
Source:	Women Make Movies, Inc.
	462 Broadway, Suite 500 E
	New York, NY 10013
	(212) 925-0606

This award-winning documentary weaves together parallel stories in the years leading up to *Roe v. Wade:* the grassroots network of activists that helped women find safe abortions outside the law, and the political network of legislators and activists that worked to change the laws. The film presents current interviews of the activists, including members of the Jane Collective, clergy activists, legislators who spoke out for abortion law reform, and founder of the Society for Humane Abortions, Patricia Maginnis. Their comments and recollections are intercut with photographs and newsclips of women and men demonstrating, passing out pamphlets, exploring abortion clinics in Mexico, speaking before legislative bodies, and attending their own court cases after arrests for their activities. One highlight of *From Danger to Dignity* is a Jane Collective member recalling the group's demystification of the abortion process and their counseling and guides to self-induced abortion. Women can seize control, she discovers, when they know their bodies and learn that abortion is an "ordinary," understandable procedure. *From Danger to Dignity* also honors the men and women in power who spoke up for women's reproductive freedom in state legislatures, in some cases putting their political careers at risk. It traces the history and dedicated efforts of reformists from the first whispers of activism to *Roe v. Wade.*

It's Up to Us

Type:	VHS videocassette
Length:	58 minutes
Date:	1986
Cost:	Purchase $195; rental $75
Source:	Women Make Movies, Inc.
	462 Broadway, Suite 500 E

New York, NY 10013
(212) 925-0606

This subtly inspiring documentary follows the National Black Women's Health Project delegation at the 1985 United Nations End of the Decade for Women Conference in Nairobi, Kenya. It provides a historical view of women in the developing region and touches on strategies for global feminism. As the American women meet with and share ideas with women of Sudan, South Africa, Ghana, and other parts of the world, a consciousness of all that women have in common, despite differing levels of cultural limitations, arises. A few minutes of speeches given by Bella Abzug and Betty Friedan are included, but the highlights of *It's Up to Us* are the unknown women who reach out to each other in small groups, realizing the breadth of their experiences and the commonality as well. Activist Angela Davis is impressive as she explains that because some women can rise above society's limitations, leaving others behind, does not mean that women have won equality. That will only be assured when those women on the bottom rise up; they will push everyone above them up with them. Then, and only then, can women begin to feel secure in their equal status. Global feminism is, therefore, a necessity for developed countries as well as developing ones. *It's Up to Us* provides a view of global feminism as of 1985 and personalizes the movement for viewers.

A Place of Rage

Type: VHS videocassette or 16 mm
Length: 52 minutes
Date: 1991
Cost: Purchase $295; rental $175 for 16 mm, $90 for video
Source: Women Make Movies, Inc.
             462 Broadway, Suite 500 E
             New York, NY 10013
             (212) 925-0606

This film by award-winning director Pratibha Parmar celebrates African American women's contributions to the civil rights and feminism movements. Included are interviews of poet June Jordan, writer Alice Walker, and activist and educator Angela Davis. The women contemplate the impact of women such as Fannie Lou Hamer and Rosa Parks as well as the unnamed masses of women who served as the backbone of the civil rights movement. They look at the inequities women faced in the civil rights and leftist movements of the 1960s and assess the role of women of color today as they assert both gender and racial pride. June Jordan's poetry, highlighted in a few segments, reveals and explains the web of racism and sexism that traps women. She joins Angela Davis in addressing the need to educate the public about the shared source of racism, sexism, and homophobia in American society. *A Place of Rage* is a window to the historical activities of women of color and a thoughtful look at the feminist and womanist ideals of today.

Some American Feminists

Type:	VHS videocassette
Length:	56 minutes
Date:	1980
Cost:	Purchase $225; rental $90
Source:	Women Make Movies, Inc.
	462 Broadway, Suite 500 E
	New York, NY 10013
	(212) 925-0606

This documentary is a fascinating look into the roots of the second wave of feminism through the words of some of its major leaders. Betty Freidan, Rita Mae Brown, Ti-Grace Atkinson, and Kate Millett describe their experiences in the feminist movement, focusing especially on their 1960s involvement. Kate Millett describes the influence that Simone de Beauvoir's work had on her life. She tells of her resentment at patriarchal culture's theft of a woman's soul and explains the feminist goal to reveal and overcome women's self-defeating internalization of this culture's sexism. Margo Jefferson describes her early work in the civil rights movement and brings her insight to the complexity of African American feminist needs and white feminists' early failure to deal with it. Rita Mae Brown describes feminists' attempts to first distance themselves from lesbian issues and then, in the early 1970s, to join forces with lesbian feminists and work together for common cause. Intercut with interviews of the women are newsreel clips that add a dimension of understanding to what made women speak out in the 1960s. They also provide visual clues for women today who were not alive then or do not remember the realities of women's lives prior to the second wave: Men boo and catcall as women demonstrate for equal pay; a young woman speaks of the "click," the moment of truth, that brought her into the movement; women picket to end gender-separate want ads in newspapers. *Some American Feminists* makes a good addition to a political documentary of the movement, providing an in-depth look at the ideas of the 1960s and 1970s.

Something Like a War

Type:	VHS videocassette
Length:	52 minutes
Date:	1991
Cost:	Purchase $295; rental $90
Source:	Women Make Movies, Inc.
	462 Broadway, Suite 500 E
	New York, NY 10013
	(212) 925-0606

A provocative film, *Something Like a War* goes behind the political curtain to talk to those most affected by the politics of population control—the women. It examines India's family planning program. In India between 1985 and 1990, 31 million women were sterilized, 25 million had intrauterine devices (IUDs) inserted, and 14.5 million received other methods of birth control. The brutality and questionable hygienics of a doctor who is lamenting that he is allowed to do only 100 sterilizations a day are juxtaposed with the conversation of Indian women questioning the motive behind the government's aggressive pursuit of sterilization, especially among the poor. The film looks into both the makeshift surgery rooms where doctors do the sterilizations and the faces of the young women waiting in line to have them done. It reveals the corruption of the system and the women's position in it. Women talk of side effects from the Norplant implants and IUDs and of their marathon efforts to get the devices removed when they wanted them out. Women in line for abortion or birth control listen to the repeated suggestions of medical workers that they get sterilized. A thread running through the film is the discussion of a group of women. Their savvy assessment of their own status as women and of the government's family planning program includes the final comment by one, Gyarsi Bal, that "they're killing the poor, not poverty."

The Veiled Hope

Type:	VHS videocassette
Length:	55 minutes
Date:	1994
Cost:	Purchase $250; rental $75
Source:	Women Make Movies, Inc.
	462 Broadway, Suite 500 E
	New York, NY 10013
	(212) 925-0606

There are feminists in Palestine. This educational film explores the women's movement there, documenting early efforts of women, their demonstrations, and positions in government. Through thoughtful interviews of women's leaders and of young women struggling with their society's limitations, *The Veiled Hope* provides a portrait of Palestinian feminists. They are alive and hopeful and are examining their cultural codes. At the time of the filming, they were also dealing with their hopes for, and position in, the Palestine liberation movement. This film provides a much-needed "behind the scenes" glimpse into the political, social, and economic lives of feminists who are usually not seen or heard in the Western press.

The Vienna Tribunal

Type:	VHS videocassette
Length:	48 minutes
Date:	1994
Cost:	Purchase $195; rental $60
Source:	Women Make Movies, Inc.
	462 Broadway, Suite 500 E
	New York, NY 10013
	(212) 925-0606

An award-winning film (including the National Educational Film and Video Festival Bronze Apple), *The Vienna Tribunal* spotlights the testimonies of women at the Global Tribunal on Violations of Women's Rights that was held in conjunction with the UN World Conference on Human Rights in Vienna, Austria, in 1993. As the women give their testimony on the abuses they have suffered, or as they speak for women who could not be there, the global nature of abuse becomes clear. The women speak out about domestic abuse and incest, about forced prostitution, wartime rape, female genital mutilation, and government-supported stoning executions of women accused of adultery. The abuses are varied but connected by a thread of women as targets. The women's goal was to define violence against women as a violation of women's human rights, and they were successful. The Vienna conference resulted in the landmark UN Declaration on the Elimination of Violence Against Women. *The Vienna Tribunal* was made in conjunction with the Center for Women's Global Leadership, Rutgers University.

Warrior Marks

Type:	VHS videocassette or 16 mm
Length:	54 minutes
Date:	1993
Cost:	Purchase $295; rental $175 for 16 mm, $85 for video
Source:	Women Make Movies, Inc.
	462 Broadway, Suite 500 E
	New York, NY 10013
	(212) 925-0606

Warrior Marks was produced through the combined talents of award-winning director Pratibha Parmar and Pulitzer Prize–winning author Alice Walker. It is a profoundly powerful analysis of female genital mutilation (FGM). A good portion of the film follows Walker as she meets women from cultures that require female genital mutilation. She interviews an ancient female "circumcisor" whose comments reveal her unquestioning belief in the procedure. She talks with a mother while awaiting the return of a young child undergoing unanesthetized FGM. A Mali woman who has escaped to France tells her story of fear and rejection because of her decision to run from FGM. Her fiancé has denounced her, and her mother has been thrown out of her house because of the escape. Interviews include women from Senegal, Gambia, Burkina Faso, England, and the United States. *Warrior Marks* explores the political and cultural complexities of female genital mutilation and is remarkable in its embracing of the pain of the women living with the reality of FGM as well as of the courage of the women who are leading movements to end FGM. A dancer whose movements are intercut with the film embodies the psychic and physical pain of FGM; film footage also covers some of the rituals that accompany FGM for some girls. (For some girls, there is no ritual; they are simply grabbed one day, and FGM is done to them.) Walker and Parmar also collaborated on a book about the making of the film, titled *Warrior Marks: Female Genital Mutilation and the Sexual Blinding of Women.*

With a Vengeance: The Fight for Reproductive Freedom

Type:	VHS videocassette or 16 mm
Length:	40 minutes
Date:	1989
Cost:	Purchase $225; rental $90 for 16 mm, $75 for video
Source:	Women Make Movies, Inc.
	462 Broadway, Suite 500 E
	New York, NY 10013
	(212) 925-0606

This engrossing film succeeds as a history of the struggle for women's reproductive freedom since the 1960s. But it also succeeds as a connection between the ideology of second-wave feminism and the politics of women's struggle for abortion rights. The history covers how abortion became illegal in the United States and how women in the 1950s and 1960s attained abortions, with a compelling account of women waiting on street corners to be taken blindfolded in hearses to illegal clinics. In rare footage, a member of the Jane Collective describes her workshops on menstrual extraction, and film footage shows part of the procedure. In additional footage, clips of the twentieth reunion of the 1969 Redstockings speakout on abortion are intercut with a member's description of the excitement of the time. Also, Flo Kennedy and Byllye Avery comment on African American women, connecting the early reluctance of African American women to speak out for abortion rights to racism and health care for the poor that provides sterilization but not abortion. Young feminists of 1989 comment on the growth of their awareness of the connections among reproductive freedom, feminism, and racism. The interviews, news footage, and narrative combine to make *With a Vengeance* a thoughtful view of the feminist perspective on reproductive freedom.

A Woman's Place: An Inspiring Documentary of Achievement

Type:	VHS videocassette
Length:	25 minutes

Date: 1987
Cost: Rental
Distributor: Available at many video rental stores or through
VIEW Video
34 East 23rd Street
New York, NY 10010
(212) 674-5550

Narrated by Julie Harris, this is a short documentary based in part on the material gathered for *Life* magazine's special issue titled Remarkable American Women. A combination of still photos and live motion footage, it is a sweeping overview of women who have had an impact on, or broken barriers to, women in the arts, sciences, business, and politics. *A Woman's Place* would serve as a good primer for young feminists wanting to learn some of the fundamentals of their own women's history.

Feature Films Available on Videotape

A selective list, these major motion pictures have been chosen for how they illustrate feminist concerns at the time of their filming, how they portray women of strength and courage, or how they illustrate women's position in society. Many great films with strong women characters are not listed here; many more are being added to the roster every year.

Alice Doesn't Live Here Anymore

Type: VHS videocassette
Length: 112 minutes
Date: 1974
Cost: Rental
Distributor: Available at many video rental stores

Ellen Burstyn won an Oscar for her performance as Alice, a 35-year-old woman suddenly alone, penniless, and with a young son to raise. The story follows Alice's escape from an oppressive married life and her journey out of a small town (also oppressive) and into a life of her own making. In her marriage, Alice had been afraid and desperate to please an irritable, unappreciative, and overbearing husband. She is portrayed as Everywoman, who in her case is an ordinary woman with a modicum of musical talent. She remembers a life before marriage, when she was an independent singer and piano player, and her journey is to recapture that independent, prehusband woman. While working as a waitress in Tucson, Arizona, she stands up to a man who loves her but is on the path to dominating her and her son, just as her husband had dominated them in her marriage. That action—standing up for herself—is what feminists of the time embraced. *Alice Doesn't Live Here Anymore* became a symbol for women who finally had had enough and were leaving the limiting roles that society was allowing them. Alice was a woman who in the context of her own time took control of her life and stopped identifying herself only in relation to men. In 1975, the National Organization for Women held a women's strike, calling it Alice Doesn't Day. And "Alice Doesn't Live Here Anymore" became a catchphrase meaning that a woman was no longer accepting male domination and was making her own decisions. Knowing the feminist symbol that Alice became, watching this film today can be a jolting experience. It shows the banal acceptance throughout society in the 1970s of the supposed rights of male dominance. It illustrates the great distance women had to come in the second wave of feminism and how difficult a personal struggle it was for each woman who attempted it. It also celebrates the individual woman's struggle.

Nine to Five

Type:	VHS videocassette
Length:	110 minutes
Date:	1980
Cost:	Rental
Distributor:	Available at many video rental stores

Though this movie is a farce about women office workers who take revenge on a sexist male boss, its message was one that rang true across the country. Even by 1980, the year *Nine to Five* was produced, women were reporting that they were being passed over for promotions in favor of male colleagues, that they were still seen as "girls" in the office, and that the corporate world made no allowances for women's domestic responsibilities. The corporate world was still male-run, male-oriented, and male-friendly. Females, who still shouldered more responsibility for child-rearing and family duties, had to adapt, double up their schedules, or fail. Comedian Lily Tomlin teamed with Dolly Parton and Jane Fonda as the "girls" who had finally had enough. Through a series of sometimes slapstick, sometimes farcical events, they kidnap their male boss, make female-friendly changes in the office (child care, flexible time schedules, and individualized office cubicles), and end with an office of their own making—a female-friendly office. The movie, according to feminist author Marilyn French, inspired women to form groups to fight sex discrimination and poor treatment in offices.

Roe vs. Wade

Type:	VHS videocassette
Length:	92 minutes
Date:	1989
Cost:	Rental
Distributor:	Available at many video rental stores

Roe vs. Wade chronicles the story behind the U.S. Supreme Court battle for abortion rights for women. Holly Hunter stars as the Jane Roe of the case, and Amy Madigan plays Sarah Weddington, the young Texas attorney who surprises everyone by taking the case all the way to the Supreme Court. Produced as a television docudrama, *Roe vs. Wade* is a valuable insight for today's young feminists, who were not of age at a time when abortions were illegal. The plight of Jane Roe, who seeks a back-alley abortion only to be repelled by the filth of the room, and who is too poor to travel to a location with legal abortions, is viewed as the plight of thousands of American women of the time. But this woman, an uneducated drifter, ill-equipped to raise a child, is in the right place at the right time for attorney Weddington's needs. She becomes the test case to bring before the courts.

Thelma and Louise

Type:	VHS videocassette
Length:	124 minutes
Date:	1991
Cost:	Rental
Distributor:	Available at many video rental stores

A female buddy/chase movie, and one of the first of its kind, *Thelma and Louise* presents women as doing something that previously only men did in major motion pictures. They bond together and run free, throwing caution to the wind and allowing themselves the luxury of responding viscerally to the world around them. The story gets its first boost into the genre of buddy/chase movies when Louise (Susan Sarandon) shoots and kills a man who has just attempted to rape Thelma (Geena Davis). Later in the film Thelma recalls the astonished look on the man's face, a look that registered surprise at being shot and surprise that women would fight back with such deadly, fierce force. *Thelma and Louise,* said feminist Marilyn French, focuses on women as oppressed human beings who liberate themselves joyously. In taking violent revenge on predatory men, the film breaks two major taboos: It shows men at war against women, and women retaliating against men. *Thelma and Louise* was a major hit, and women responded to the film with elation. It seemed to suggest a feeling of the times—that women had had enough of male dominance and were taking their destinies into their own hands, come what may. To "do a Thelma and Louise" became a slang term for a short time, meaning to go on a freedom-seeking road trip with a female buddy.

Glossary

antifeminist   One who is against granting equality to women in political, social, and/or economic arenas.

CEDAW   Convention on the Elimination of All Forms of Discrimination Against Women. (See also United Nations convention, below.)

chauvinist   Used in the early women's liberation circles to mean a male who clung to male supremacist beliefs and actions. Also used pejoratively, as in "male chauvinist pig."

"click"   In the 1970s, used by feminists to express the moment of clarity and understanding that accompanied women's recognition of gender discrimination and/or bias in society, usually followed by their own feminist awakening and raised consciousness.

consciousness raising   Improving the self-awareness of individuals. Consciousness raising became popular with individual feminists and groups in the 1960s; for feminists, the improved awareness centered on acknowledging and recognizing cultural discrimination against women.

EEOC   Equal Employment Opportunity Commission, the agency formed in 1965 and charged with enforcing Title VII provisions of the Civil Rights Act of 1964.

empower A term that surfaced with renewed meaning in the 1980s. To empower is to enable a person to believe in her own personal abilities and resources, to give a person back her own "power" that has been reduced by her culture's low expectations of her.

ERA Equal Rights Amendment.

feminism A system of beliefs that advocates equality for women and men in political, economic, and social arenas. For categories of feminism, see Chapter 4, "Defining Feminism."

feminist One who seeks political, economic, and social equality for women. The term first appeared in the literary journal *Athenaeum* in 1895 and described a woman who could and would fight her way to independence.

feminist movement The organized actions of people working toward the goals of feminism.

FGM Female genital mutilation.

gender gap Differences in voting patterns between women and men. The term is also often applied to differences in party identification, judgments about presidential performance, and public policy opinions.

glass ceiling First coined by the *Wall Street Journal* in 1986, the glass ceiling describes the invisible barriers that stand between women and their rise to corporate executive positions and to the top levels of other business and political structures.

glass wall Invisible wall between students in many university departments, with the majority of male students on one side in the "hard" sciences such as mathematics and engineering, while women are on the other side in the "soft" studies such as education, humanities, and psychology.

International Monetary Fund (IMF) Founded in 1944 by Western industrial powers, the IMF oversees currency exchange rate policies and provides financing to member states. In the 1980s, the IMF conditioned many of these loans on the recipient country's adoption of structural adjustment policies.

Ms. A 1930s secretarial handbook listed Ms. as the proper address if a woman's marriage status is unknown. Gloria Steinem and her staff at *Ms.* magazine found the word while searching for a name for the magazine. It has since become the accepted manner to address any woman, unless she requests her marriage status be included in her name.

nongovernmental organizations (NGOs) Organizations involved in service provision and/or advocacy, such as the Women's Environment and Development Organization (WEDO). Often these organizations work with their own nations and in conjunction with other organizations internationally.

sati (from suttee) (India) Dowry death. The murder of a wife, usually by setting her on fire, with the motivation being anger over inadequate dowry or nonpayment of dowry.

suffragette Diminutive term for a suffragist.

suffragist One who sought enfranchisement for women.

suttee Illegal since 1829, the immolation of a Hindu widow on the funeral pyre of her husband. Though it has been customary to believe that widows would throw themselves willingly onto the funeral pyre, Mary Daly in *GynEcology* points out that widows had little choice in the matter. Many were pushed in by their relatives; many others simply realized that their fate as a widow (they could not remarry) was lifelong harassment by their relatives and possibly prostitution.

United Nations convention A legally binding treaty or agreement among the nations that sign it. Usually nations require ratification of conventions through their parliaments and signature by the head of state.

womanist Coined by Alice Walker to define a person committed to the survival and wholeness of both males and females, used most often to refer to African American feminists. Also, *womanism* stands for the movement in support of womanist aims.

women's liberation From the liberation political movements of the 1960s, early radical feminists called themselves, and were called by the media, "women's liberationists." The radical arm of the movement was called Women's Liberation. The term is also often used to refer to the feminist movement of the 1960s in general.

World Bank Established in 1944, the World Bank provides long-term loans to developing nations in an effort to promote free market policies. In the 1980s, the World Bank conditioned many of these loans on the recipient country's adoption of structural adjustment policies.

Index

Judith Harlan is a journalist and educational author of books for young adults. She focuses on feminism and feminist-inspired empowerment for girls and boys. Harlan is the author of five educational titles, including *Girl Talk* (1997, Walker and Co.).